CHILTON'S Repair and Tune-Up Guide

Firebird

ILLUSTRATED

Prepared by the

Automotive Editorial Department

Chilton Book Company
Chilton Way
Radnor, Pa. 19089
215—687-8200

president and chief executive officer **WILLIAM A. BARBOUR;** executive vice president **K. ROBERT BRINK;** vice president and general manager **WILLIAM D. BYRNE;** editor-in-chief **JOHN D. KELLY;** managing editor **JOHN H. WEISE, S.A.E.;** assistant managing editor **PETER J. MEYER;** senior editor **STEPHEN J. DAVIS;** technical editors **Ronald L. Sessions, N Banks Spence Jr**

CHILTON BOOK COMPANY   RADNOR, PENNSYLVANIA

Manufactured in the United States of America

Library of Congress Cataloging in Publication Data

Chilton Book Company. Automotive Editorial Dept.
    Chilton's repair and tune-up guide: Firebird.
    1. Firebird automobile.   I. Title.   II. Title:
Repair and tune-up guide: Firebird.
TL215.F57C45   1974   629.29'7'22   74-16191
ISBN 0-8019-5995-0
ISBN 0-8019-5996-9 (pbk.)

ACKNOWLEDGMENT

Chilton Book Company wishes to express its appreciation to

Pontiac Motor Division
General Motors Corporation
Pontiac, Michigan 48053

for assistance in the preparation of this book.

Contents

1 · General Information and Maintenance

Introduction

After the introduction of the Ford Mustang and its immediate rise to popularity, Pontiac was quick to introduce its own "pony" or personal sports car, the Firebird, in 1967. Along with its sister car, the Camaro, the Firebird was General Motors' entry into a burgeoning market. Customers could literally order blank "build" their Firebird from a long option list. Choices ranged from 3-speed economy models to 400 cubic inch Ram Air, 4-speed supercars. GT and luxury outfits were available for the ordering by checking off the right blocks on the order blank.

1967 through 1969 were years of detail refinement. Firebirds were available as 2-door coupes and convertibles. A long wait for the new model proved worthwhile when, in 1970, the redesigned Firebird was introduced. The new body shell, shared with the Camaro, was a departure from preceding models and had a European GT flavor. The convertible Firebird was dropped in 1970 along with the overhead cam six engine. Body styles were limited to the 2-door coupe, while the conventional OHV six replaced the

cammer. Despite rumors of its demise due to receding sales and the burden of emission and safety standards, the Firebird continues to be a stylish alternative to mundane transportation.

Year Identification

1967

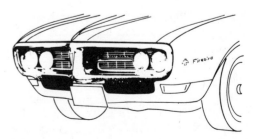

1968

1

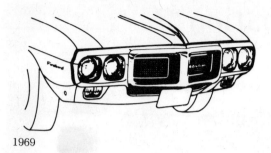

1969

1970–71

1973

1974

Serial Number Identification

VEHICLE

1967

The vehicle serial number is located on a plate attached to the left front door hinge pillar. The number is broken down below:

1968–74

The vehicle serial number is located on a plate attached to the top of the instrument panel, left-hand side, visible through the windshield. The number is interpreted as follows:

1967–71

First Digit: Car Division
Second and third digits: Series Number
Fourth and fifth digits: Body style code
Sixth digit: Year manufactured
Seventh digit: Plant
Eighth digit: Engine used
Ninth to thirteenth digits: Sequential serial number

1972–74

First digit: Car division
Second digit: Series number
Third and fourth digits: Body style code
Fifth digit: Engine used
Sixth digit: Year manufactured
Seventh digit: Plant
Eighth to thirteenth digits: Sequential serial number

ENGINE

Six-Cylinder

1967–69

The engine code is stamped on the engine block behind the oil filler tube at the point where the cylinder head mates with the block.

1967–69 OHC six-cylinder engine code

1970–74

On the OHV six, the engine code is stamped on the right-side of the engine block on the distributor mounting plate.

1970–74 OHV six-cylinder engine code

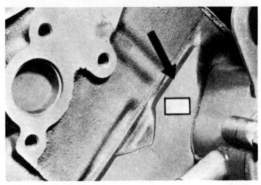

V8 engine code

Eight–Cylinder

1967–74

The engine code on V8 engines is located on a pad on the right-side of the front of the engine block directly below the production engine number.

TRANSMISSION

Two-Speed Automatic

1967–69

The identification number can be found on the right-side of the transmission on the lower servo cover.

1970–74

The identification number is located on the right-side of the transmission torque converter housing.

Turbo Hydra-Matic (M-38)

The identification number is located in the center of the right-side. The serial number begins with the letter J and is followed by another letter that shows the particular engine with which it is used. A two-digit number denoting the model year completes the identification number.

Turbo Hydra-Matic (M-40)

The identification number for this transmission is located on the right-side of the transmission case. The number begins with the letter P meaning Pontiac, followed by the engine code letter and completed with a two-digit number which signifies the model year.

1968 Engine Identification

DISPLACEMENT	HORSEPOWER	ENGINE CODE	TRANS.		CARB.			COMP. RATIO				CAMSHAFT							STANDARD DISTRIBUTOR							VALVE SPRINGS			
			MANUAL	AUTOMATIC	1-BBL	2-BBL	QUADRAJET	9.0	9.2	10.5	10.75	9777254	9779066	9779067	9779068	9785744	9790826	9792539	1110430	1110431	1111281	1111282	1111447	1111270	1111449	SINGLE	STD. TWO	H.D. TWO (SPEC.)	RAM AIR
250 Cu. In. (six)	175	ZK	X		X			X													X						X			
	175	ZN		X	X			X												X							X			
	215	ZD	X				X			X										X								X		
	215	ZE		X			X			X										X								X		
350 Cu. In. (V8)	265	WC	X			X		X				X									X							X		
	265	YJ		X		X		X				X									X							X		
	320	WK	X				X			X			X											X				X		
	320	YM		X			X			X			X										X					X		
400 Cu. In. (V8)	335	XN		X			X				X			X											•					X
	335	WQ	X				X				X			X												•			X	
	335	WI	X				X				X					X										•				X
	335	WZ	X				X				X						X									•			X	
	330	YW		X			X				X						X								•		X			
	330	YT		X			X				X							X							•		X			

• With 60 PSI Oil Pump Spring
All Cars Use CCS

1969 Engine Identification

HORSEPOWER	ENGINE CODE	250	350	400	MANUAL	AUTOMATIC	1 BBL (MV)	2 BBL (2GV)	4 BBL (4MV)	9.0:1	9.2:1	10.5:1	10.75:1	9790826	9792539	9796327	9777254	9779067	9779068	9794041	1110474	1110475	1111941 (b)	1111942	1111945	1111946 (b)	1111952 (b)	1111960	SINGLE	STD-DUAL	H.D.-DUAL	H.D. SPEC.-DUAL	RAM AIR IV-DUAL	SMALL VALVE	LARGE VALVE
175	(a)ZK ZC	X			X		X			X				X								X							X					X	
175	(a)ZN ZF	X					X	X		X				X								X							X					X	
230	(a)ZD ZH	X			X			X				X				X						X								X				X	
235	(a)ZE ZL	X				X		X				X				X						X								X				X	
265	(a)WC WM		X		X			X			X							X										X			X				X	
265	(a)XL XB		X			X		X			X							X								X					X				X	
(c) 265	(a)YJ YE		X		X			X			X							X						X							X				X	
325	(a)WT WN		X		X				X			X							X									(e)				X				X
325	(a)XC XC		X			X			X				X							X							(d)					X				X
330	WZ			X	X				X				X							X						X							X			X
330	YT			X		X			X				X							X							X					X				X
335	WQ			X	X				X				X						X									X				X				X
335	YW			X		X			X				X							X							X					X				X
345	WH			X	X				X				X								X				X									X		X
345	XN			X		X		X					X								X				X									X		X

(a) Early production (small valve) engines with 30° intake valve seat angle. Later production (small valve) engines use 45° intake valve seat. NOTE: all large valve engines use 30° intake valve seat.

(b) Uses hardened drive gear for use with 60 psi oil pump and high tension distributor points.

(c) Two speed (M31) if equipped with A/C; Turbo-Hydramatic (M38) optional without A/C.

(d) Uses distributor 1111965

(e) Uses distributor 1111966

1971 Engine Identification

ENGINE CODE	Engine No. (Last Two Digits)	HORSEPOWER	"F" SERIES	250 L-6	350 V-8	400 V-8	455 V-8	MANUAL (3-Speed)	MANUAL (4-Speed)	AUTOMATIC	MV (1 Bbl.)	2GV (2 Bbl.)	4MV (4 Bbl.)	8.5:1	8.0:1	8.2:1	8.4:1	PRESSED-IN	THREADED	SINGLE	DUAL (STD.)	DUAL (H.D.)	SMALL	LARGE	3864897	483555 (W)	9779066 (N)	9779067 (P)	9779068 (S)	HIGH-BALL (STD.)	HIGH-BALL*	LOW-BALL	1110489	1112069	1112068	1112070	1112072	1112073	1112083	1112089	1112090
CAA	51	145	X	X				X			X			X				X		X			X							X			X								
CAB	52	145	X	X						X	X			X				X		X			X							X			X								
WR	94	250	X		X			X				X			X					X		X		X			X				X							X				
WN	90	250	X		X			X				X			X					X		X		X			X				X										X
WU	92	250	X		X				X			X			X					X		X		X			X				X							X				
YP	98	250	X		X				X			X			X					X		X		X			X				X										X
YU	96	250	X		X					X		X			X					X		X		X			X				X								X		
WP	97	250	X		X					X		X			X					X		X		X			X				X										X
XR	95	250	X		X					X		X			X					X		X		X			X				X								X		
YN	99	250	X		X					X		X			X					X		X		X			X				X										X
WT	78	300	X			X		X					X		X			X		X	X		X		X					X				X						
WK	74	300	X			X				X			X		X			X		X	X		X		X					X				X						
XX%	73	265	X		X			X					X		X			X		X	X		X		X					X					X					
YX	71	265	X		X					X	X			X		X			X		X		X		X					X								X		
YS	79	300	X		X					X			X	X				X		X		X		X					X				X						
WL†	18	335	X				X		X				X				X	X			X		X		X				X		X				X				X	
WC†	15	335	X				X		X				X				X	X			X		X		X				X		X				X				X	
YC+	19	325	X				X			X			X	X		X		X			X		X		X				X			X				X				X
YE†	16	335	X				X			X			X				X	X			X		X		X				X		X				X				X	

* Lifter Body with Cast-Iron Foot

** "YU" is used with M35 transmission; "XR" is used with M38 transmission.

† 455 H.O. Engine

% Man. Trans. Models use WS engine code

+ Man. Trans. Models use WJ engine code

& Man. Trans. Models use WG engine code

1970 Engine Identification

HORSEPOWER	ENGINE CODE	DISPLACEMENT 250	350	400	TRANS. MANUAL	AUTOMATIC	CARB. 1 BBL (MV)	2 BBL (2GV)	4 BBL (4MV)	COMP. RATIO 8.5:1	8.8:1	10.0:1	10.25:1	10.5:1	CAMSHAFT 364897	9777254 (U)	9779067 (P)	9779068 (S)	9794041 (T)	DISTRIBUTOR 1110463	1110464	1111485	1111765	1112007	1112008	1112009S	1112013*	1112024S	VALVE SPRING SINGLE	STD.-DUAL	H.D.-DUAL	H.D SPEC.-DUAL	SUPER DUTY-DUAL	CYL. HEAD SMALL VALVE	LARGE VALVE
155	ZB	X			X		X			X					X					X									X					X	
155	ZG	X				X	X			X					X						X								X					X	
255	WU		X		X			X				X				X										X				X				X	
255	YU		X			X		X				X				X										X				X				X	
265	XX			X		X		X				X				X									X					X				X	
330	WT			X	X				X				X				X							X						X					X
330	YS			X		X			X					X			X							X						X					X
345	WS ¶			X	X				X	X								X				X										X			X
345	YZ ¶			X		X			X	X								X				X										X			X
370	WH §			X	X				X	X									X								X						X		X
370	XN §			X		X			X	X									X								X						X		X

¶ RAM AIR III
§ RAM AIR SUPER DUTY
* Uses cadmium gear for use with R.A. Super Duty only.
S Uses hardened drive gear.

1967 Engine Identification

No. Cyls	Cu In. Displ	Type	Code	No. Cyls	Cu In. Displ	Type	Code
6	230	AT, 1 BBL	ZG	8	326	AT, 2 BBL w/Ex. Em.	XF
6	230	3 Spd, MT, 1 BBL	ZK	8	326	AT, 4 BBL w/Ex. Em.	XG
6	230	AT, 4 BBL w/Ex. Em.	ZL	8	400	AT, 2 BBL w/Ex. Em.	XL
6	230	AT, 1 BBL	ZM	8	400	AT, 2 BBL	XM
6	250	AT, 1 BBL	ZN	8	400	AT, 4 BBL	XP
6	230	MT, 4 BBL w/Ex. Em.	ZR	8	326	MT, 4 BBL w/Ex. Em.	XR
6	230	3 Spd, MT, 1 BBL	ZS	8	400	MT, 4 BBL	XS
8	400	3 Spd, MT, 4 BBL	WT	8	400	AT, 4 BBL w/Ex. Em.	YI
8	400	4 BBL w/Ex. Em.	WV	8	400	AT, 4 BBL w/Ex. Em.	YQ
8	400	MT, 4 BBL w/Ex. Em.	WW	8	400	MT, 4 BBL w/Ex. Em.	YR
8	326	3 Spd, MT, 2 BBL w/Ex. Em.	WX	8	400	AT, 4 BBL (335 HP)	YS
8	326	3 Spd, MT, 2 BBL	WP	8	400	AT, 4 BBL (360 HP)	YZ

1967 Engine Identification (cont.)

No. Cyls	Cu In. Displ	Type	Code	No. Cyls	Cu In. Displ	Type	Code
8	326	3 Spd, MT, 4 BBL	WR	6	230	3 Spd, MT, 4 BBL	ZD
8	400	3 Spd, MT, 4 BBL	WS	6	230	AT, 4 BBL	ZE
8	400	AT, 4 BBL w/Ex. Em.	XE	6	230	3 Spd, MT, 1 BBL	ZF

1972–74 Engine Identification

The second letter in the vehicle identification number is the engine code

Type	Displacement	All Series Carburetor	Exhaust	Code
L6	250	1 BBL.	Single	D
V8	350	2 BBL.	Single	M
V8	350	2 BBL.	Dual	N
V8	400	2 BBL.	Single	R
V8	400	2 BBL.	Dual	P
V8	400	4 BBL.	Single	S
V8	400	4 BBL.	Dual	T
V8	455	2 BBL.	Single	V
V8	455	2 BBL.	Dual	U
V8	455	4 BBL.	Single	W
V8	455	4 BBL.	Dual	Y
V8	455 H.O.①	4 BBL.	Dual	X

①—SD in 1973

Borg Warner 3-Speed

The serial number is stamped on a boss located in the right rear corner of the extension housing.

Dearborn 3-Speed

The serial number is stamped on the lower left mounting flange of the case.

Muncie 3-Speed

The serial number is stamped on a boss directly above the filler plug.

Saginaw 3 and 4-Speed

The serial number is stamped on the lower left (1967–68) or lower right (1969–74) side of the case next to the rear of the cover.

Muncie 4-Speed

The Muncie serial number is stamped on the left (1967–68) or right (1969–74) of the case at the bottom of the side cover.

Routine Maintenance

AIR CLEANER

The air cleaner consists of a metal housing for a replaceable paper filter or permanent polyurethane element and the necessary hoses connecting it to the crankcase ventilation system. The air cleaner cover is held by a wing nut on all models. If your Firebird is equipped with a paper element, it should be replaced once every 12,000 miles or 12 months, whichever comes first. Inspection and replacement should come more often when the car is operated under dusty conditions. To check the effectiveness of your paper element, remove the air cleaner assembly and, if the idle speed increases noticeably, the element is restricting airflow and should be replaced. High-performance models or cars equipped with optional air cleaners use a polyurethane element that must be removed, cleaned, and reoiled at 12,000 mile or 12 month intervals. Remove the filter and clean it in kerosene. Do not use paint thinner or a similar solvent, as it will attack the foam. Soak it in the solvent and then squeeze it dry. Allow it to soak in SAE 30 oil and again squeeze it dry using a clean cloth to remove excess oil. High-performance models equipped with the cold air induction system have a dual stage air cleaner. The inner element is paper and must be replaced every 12,000 miles or 12 months, while the outer element is polyurethane and is cleaned as outlined above. Clean the inside of the air cleaner housing before reinstalling either type of filter.

POSITIVE CRANKCASE VENTILATION (PCV)

Once every 12,000 miles or 12 months, check the hoses and clean or replace them as necessary. At the same time,

Six-cylinder PCV valve location

V8 PCV valve location

clean and oil the ventilation filter located in the air cleaner, if so equipped. The PCV valve should also be replaced during this operation. The valve is located in the intake manifold of early models. PCV valves on later models are located in the valley cover (pushrod cover under the intake manifold) of V8s and in the rocker arm cover of sixes. PCV service has been lengthened to 24,000 miles or 24 months on 1972 and later models.

EVAPORATIVE EMISSIONS CONTROL SYSTEM

This system, standard since 1970, eliminates the release of unburned fuel vapors into the atmosphere. The only periodic maintenance required is an occasional check of the connecting lines of the system for kinks or other damage and deterioration. Lines should only be replaced with quality fuel line or special hose marked "evap." Every 12,000 miles or 12 months, the filter in the bottom of the carbon canister which is located in the engine compartment should be removed and replaced.

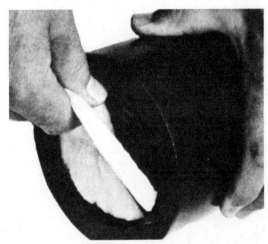

Replacing carbon canister filter

FLUID LEVEL CHECKS

Engine Oil

The engine oil level is checked with the dipstick, which is located at the left-side of the engine block on a V8 and on the right-side of the engine on a 6-cylinder.

NOTE: *The oil should be checked before the engine is started or five min-*

utes after the engine has been shut off. This gives the oil time to drain back to the oil pan and prevents an inaccurate oil level reading.

Remove the dipstick from its tube, wipe it clean, and insert it back into the tube. Remove it again and observe the oil level. It should be maintained between the "full" and "add" marks without going above "full" or below "add."

CAUTION: *Do not overfill the crankcase. It may result in oil-fouled spark plugs or oil leaks caused by oil seal failure.*

Transmission Fluid

MANUAL TRANSMISSION

Remove the filler plug from the side of the transmission. The oil should be level with the bottom edge of the filler hole. This should be checked at least once every 6,000 miles and more often if any leakage or seepage is observed. Fill with SAE 80 or 90 multipurpose gear lubricant.

AUTOMATIC TRANSMISSION

Run the engine until it reaches normal operating temperature. Park the car on a level surface. With the transmission in Park and the engine idling, the fluid level on the dipstick should be between the "full" mark and ¼ inch below "full" mark. Replace the dipstick making sure that it is pushed fully into the filler tube.

Automatic transmission fluid dipstick

CAUTION: *Do not overfill the automatic transmission. Use Dexron® automatic transmission fluid or any other equivalent fluid. One pint raises the level from "add" to "full."*

Brake Master Cylinder

Once every 6,000 miles or four months, check the brake fluid level in the master cylinder. The master cylinder is mounted on the firewall and is divided into two reservoirs and the fluid level in each reservoir must be maintained at ¼ inch below the top edge. Use only heavy-duty brake fluid which is recommended for disc brake applications.

Coolant

Check the coolant level when the engine is cold. The level of coolant should be maintained 2 in. below the bottom of the filler neck.

CAUTION: *Allow the engine to cool considerably and then add water while the engine is running.*

Rear Axle

STANDARD DIFFERENTIAL

The rear axle oil level should be checked when the chassis is lubricated. Remove the plug from the side of the housing. The lubricant level should be maintained at the bottom of the filler plug hole. When replacing oil, use SAE 80 or 90 multipurpose hypoid gear lubricant.

SAFE-T-TRACK DIFFERENTIAL

Lubricant level should be checked at each chassis lubrication and maintained at the bottom of the filler plug hole. Special Safe-T-Track oil must be used in this differential.

CAUTION: *Never use standard differential lubricant in a Safe-T-Track differential.*

Steering Gear

Check the lubricant by removing the center bolt on the side cover of the steering gear. Grease must be up to the level of this bolt hole.

Power Steering Reservoir

Maintain the proper fluid level as indicated on the cap of the reservoir. Check this level with the engine off and warm. Use GM power steering fluid or automatic transmission fluid.

Battery

The electrolyte level in the battery should be checked about once every month and more often during hot weather or long trips. If the level is below the bottom of the split ring, distilled water should be added until the level reaches the ring.

Capacities

Year	Engine No. Cyl (Cu In.) Displacement	Engine Crankcase Add 1 Qt for New Filter	TRANSMISSION Pts to Refill After Draining			Drive Axle (pts)	Gasoline Tank (gals)	COOLING SYSTEM (qts)	
			3-Speed	Manual 4-Speed	Automatic ●			With Heater	With A/C
'67	6-230 OHC	5	2.8	2.5	15	3	18.5	12.1	12.7
	8-326	5	2.8	2.5	15	3	18.5	18.6	20.2
	8-400	5	2.8	2.5	19	3	18.5	12.8	19.4
'68	6-250 OHC	5	3.5	3.5	15	3	18.5	12.1	12.7
	8-350	5	3.5	2.8	15	3	18.5	18.6	20.2
	8-400	5	3.5	2.8	19	3	18.5	17.8	19.4
'69	6-250 OHC	5	3.5	3.5	15④	3	21.5	11.9	12.3
	8-350	5	3.5①	2.5	15④	3	21.5	19.9	20.3
	8-400	5	2.8	2.5	19	3②	21.5	18.3	18.7
'70	6-250	4	3.5	——	6	3②	19.5③	13	——
	8-350	5	3.5①	2.5	6	3②	19.5③	19.9	19.9
	8-400	5	2.5	2.5	7.5	3②	19.5③	18.3	18.3
	8-455	5	2.5	2.5	7.5	3②	19.5③	17.5	17.5
'71	6-250	4	3.5	——	6	4.25	17	12	12.4
	8-350	5	3.5①	2.5	6	4.25	17	20	20.5
	8-400	5	2.8	2.5	7.5	4.25	17	18.6	18.7
	8-455	5	2.8	2.5	7.5	4.25	17	17.9	16.8
'72	6-250	4	3.5	——	6	4.25	17	12	12.4
	8-350	5	3.5	2.5	6	4.25	17	20	20.5
	8-400	5	2.8	2.5	7.5	4.25	17	18.6	18.7
	8-455	5	——	2.5	7.5	4.25	17	17.9	19
'73	6-250	4	3.5	——	7.5	4.25	18	12.5	——
	8-350	5	3.5	2.5	7.5	4.25	18	22.4	22.7

Capacities (cont.)

Year	Engine No. Cyl (Cu In.) Displacement	Engine Crankcase Add 1 Qt for New Filter	TRANSMISSION Pts to Refill After Draining			Drive Axle (pts)	Gasoline Tank (gals)	COOLING SYSTEM (qts)	
			Manual		Automatic ●			With Heater	With A/C
			3-Speed	4-Speed					
'73	8-400	5	——	2.5	7.5	4.25	18	22.4	22.7/23.5④
	8-455	5	——	2.5	7.5	4.25	18	20.9	21.8
'74	6-250	4	3.5	——	7.5	4.25	21.5	13.5	——
	8-350	5	3.5	2.5	7.5	4.25	21.5	22.1	22.7
	8-400	5	——	2.5	7.5	4.25	21.5	21.9	22.7/23.5④
	8-455	5	——	2.5	7.5	4.25	21.5	21.9	22

● '70 and later specifications do not include torque converter
① 2.8 pts with heavy duty 3-speed transmission
② 4 pts with heavy duty axle
③ California cars—18.5 gals
④ Lower figure indicates 2 bbl model; higher figure indicates 4 bbl engine
OHC Overhead camshaft
—— Not applicable

DRIVE BELTS

Check the drive belts every 6,000 miles for evidence of wear such as cracking, fraying, and incorrect tension. Determine the belt tension at a point halfway between the pulleys by pressing on the belt with moderate thumb pressure. The belt should deflect about ¼ inch at this point. If the deflection is found to be too much or too little, loosen the mounting bolts and make the adjustments.

TIRES

Check the air pressure in your tires every few weeks. Make sure that the tires are cool, as you will get a false reading when the tires are heated because air pressure increases with temperature. A decal located on your glovebox door will tell you the proper tire pressure for the standard equipment tires. Naturally, when you replace tires you will want to get the correct tire pressures for the new ones from the dealer or manufacturer. It pays to buy a tire pressure gauge to keep in the car, since those at service stations are usually inaccurate or broken.

While you are checking the tire pressure, take a look at the tread. The tread should be wearing evenly across the tire. Excessive wear in the center of the tread indicates overinflation. Excessive wear on the outer edges indicates underinflation. An irregular wear pattern is usually a sign of incorrect front wheel alignment or wheel balance. A front end that is out of alignment will usually pull the car to one side of a flat road when the steering wheel is released. Incorrect wheel balance is usually accompanied by high speed vibration. Front wheels which are out of balance will produce vibration in the steering wheel, while unbalanced rear wheels will result in floor or trunk vibration.

Rotating the tires every 6,000 miles or so will result in increased tread life. Use the correct pattern for your tire switching. Most automotive experts are in agreement that radial tires are better all around performers, giving prolonged

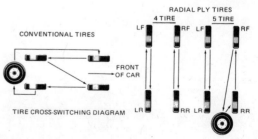

Tire rotation patterns

wear and better handling. An added benefit which you should consider when purchasing tires is that radials have less rolling resistance and can give up to a 10% increase in fuel economy over a bias-ply tire.

Tires of different construction should never be mixed. Always replace tires in sets of four or five when switching tire types and never substitute a belted tire for a bias-ply, a radial for a belted tire, etc. An occasional pressure check and periodic rotation could make your tires last much longer than a neglected set and maintain the safety margin which was designed into them.

FUEL FILTER

The filter element should be replaced every 12 months or 12,000 miles. To replace, follow these procedures:

1. Using an open-end wrench (preferably a line wrench), disconnect the fuel line connection from the larger fuel filter nut.

2. Remove the larger nut from the carburetor with a box-end wrench or a socket.

3. Remove the filter element and spring from the carburetor.

4. Check the bronze element for dirt blockage by blowing on the cone end. If the element is good, air should pass through easily.

5. If the car has a paper element instead of a bronze element, check by blowing into the fuel inlet end. If air does not pass through easily, replace the element. Do not attempt to clean these elements.

6. Install the spring and then the ele-

ment into the carburetor, making sure that the small end of the bronze cone is facing outward.

7. Install a new gasket on the large nut and tighten securely.

8. Insert the fuel line and tighten the nut with a line wrench.

BATTERY

In addition to routinely checking the electrolyte level of the battery, some other minor maintenance will keep your battery in peak starting condition. Two inexpensive battery tools, a hydrometer and a post and cable cleaner, are available in most auto or hardware stores for about a dollar and more than earn back that small outlay. Besides checking the level of electrolyte, you should occasionally take a specific gravity reading to see what's going on inside the battery cells. Using your hydrometer, insert the tip into each cell and withdraw enough electrolyte to make the float ride freely. While holding the hydrometer straight up, take a reading. The specific gravity of a fully charged battery (at 80° F) is 1.270. Most commercially available hydrometers also have colored sections to save you reading the scale and these will clearly tell you your battery cell is (a) charged, (b) borderline—should be recharged, or (c) dead. Repeat the specific gravity for each cell.

NOTE: *Battery electrolyte or "acid" is very caustic and will dissolve skin and paintwork with equal relish, so be careful. Readings should be taken in as normal a room temperature atmo-*

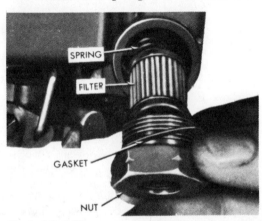

Typical fuel filter

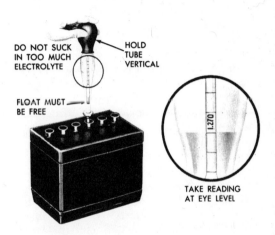

Specific gravity check

sphere as possible. If the temperature varies from the 80°F standard above, add or subtract four (0.004) points for every 10° above (+) or below (−) the standard.

The most completely charged battery will do you no good on a cold, rainy evening if the cables and posts are caked with corrosion. This is where your little wire brush cleaner comes in. Loosen and remove the cable clamps from the battery posts. Using the pointed end of the brush, give the inside surface of the clamp a good cleaning until it shines. Next, take the other end and place it over the post. Clean the post with a rotating motion until you achieve a shiny post. This done, install the clamps and re-tighten.

A slightly different procedure is used for 1972 and later Firebirds which are equipped with Delco side terminal batteries. The cable is cleaned in the same manner, but the internal threads in the battery can be cleaned with a special tool now available for that purpose. Exercise care when removing the cable retaining bolts on side terminal batteries, as it is easy to strip them.

Keep the top of the battery clean, as a film of dirt can sometimes completely discharge a battery. A solution of baking soda and water may be used to clean the top surface, but be careful to flush this off with clear water and that none of the solution enters the filler holes.

Lubrication

OIL AND FUEL

Pontiac recommends the use of a high quality, heavy-duty detergent oil having the proper viscosity for prevailing temperatures and an SE service rating. The SE rating will be printed on the top of the can. Under the classification system adopted by the American Petroleum Institute (API) in May, 1970, SE is the highest designation given for normal passenger car use. The S stands for passenger car and the second letter denotes a more specific application. SA oil, for instance,

Oil Viscosity Selection Chart

	Anticipated Temperature Range	SAE Viscosity
Multi-grade	Above 32° F	10W—40 10W—50 20W—40 20W—50 10W—30
	May be used as low as −10° F	10W—30 10W—40
	Consistently below 10° F	5W—20 5W—30
Single-grade	Above 32° F	30
	Temperature between +32° F and −10° F	10W

contains no additives and is suitable only for very light-duty. Oil designated MS may also be used, since this was the highest classification under the old API rating system. Pick your oil viscosity with regard to the anticipated temperatures during the period before your next oil change. Using the chart below, choose the oil viscosity for the lowest expected temperature. You will be assured of easy cold starting and sufficient engine protection.

Fuel should be selected for the brand and octane which performs without pinging. Find your exact engine model in the "General Engine Specifications" chart in Chapter 3. If the compression ratio is higher than 9.0:1, you will have to use a premium gasoline. If your compression ratio is lower than 9.0:1, you can safely go with regular octane. Most 1971 and later models will operate successfully on regular if the car is properly tuned, especially as to correct ignition timing

OIL CHANGES

The mileage figures given in your owner's manual are the Pontiac recommended intervals for oil and filter changes assuming average driving. If your Firebird is being used under dusty, polluted, or off-road conditions, change the oil and filter sooner than specified. The same thing goes for cars driven in stop-and-go traffic or only for short distances.

Always drain the oil after the engine has been running long enough to bring it to operating temperature. Hot oil will flow easier and more contaminants will be removed along with the oil than if it were drained cold. You will need a large capacity drain pan, which you can purchase at any store which sells automotive parts. Another necessity is containers for the used oil. You will find that plastic bottles, such as those used for bleach or fabric softener, make excellent storage jugs. One ecologically desirable solution to the used oil disposal problem is to find a cooperative gas station owner who will allow you to dump your used oil into his tank. Another is to keep the oil for use around the house as a preservative on fences, railroad tie borders, etc.

Pontiac recommends changing both the oil and filter during the first oil change and the filter every other oil change thereafter. For the small price of an oil filter, it's cheap insurance to replace the filter at every oil change. One of the larger filter manufacturers points out in its advertisements that not changing the filter leaves one quart of dirty oil in the engine. This claim is true and should be kept in mind when changing your oil.

Changing Your Oil

1. Run the engine until it reaches normal operating temperature.

2. Jack up the front of the car and support it on safety stands.

3. Slide a drain pan of at least 6 quarts capacity under the oil pan.

4. Loosen the drain plug. Turn the plug out by hand. By keeping an inward pressure on the plug as you unscrew it, oil won't escape past the threads and you can remove it without being burned by hot oil.

5. Allow the oil to drain completely and then install the drain plug. Don't overtighten the plug, or you'll be buying a new pan or a trick replacement plug for buggered threads.

6. Using a strap wrench, remove the oil filter. Keep in mind that it's holding about one quart of dirty, hot oil.

NOTE: *You can remove the oil filter on 1970 and later six cylinders from above.*

7. Empty the old filter into the drain pan and dispose of the filter.

8. Using a clean rag, wipe off the filter adapter on the engine block. Be sure that the rag doesn't leave any lint which could clog an oil passage.

9. Coat the rubber gasket on the filter with fresh oil. Spin it onto the engine *by hand;* when the gasket touches the adapter surface give it another ½–¾ turn. No more, or you'll squash the gasket and it will leak.

10. Refill the engine with the correct amount of fresh oil. See the "Capacities" chart.

11. Crank the engine over several times and then start it. If the oil pressure "idiot light" doesn't go out or the pressure gauge shows zero, shut the engine down and find out what's wrong.

12. If the oil pressure is OK and there are no leaks, shut the engine off and lower the car.

13. Wait a few minutes and check the oil level. Add oil, as necessary, to bring the level up to Full.

CHASSIS GREASING

Chassis greasing can be performed with a pressurized grease gun or it can be performed at home by using a hand-operated grease gun. Wipe the grease fittings clean before greasing in order to prevent the possibility of forcing any dirt into the component.

WHEEL BEARINGS

Once every 12 months or 12,000 miles, clean and repack wheel bearings with a wheel bearing grease. Use only enough grease to completely coat the rollers. Remove any excess grease from the exposed surface of the hub and seal.

It is important that wheel bearings be properly adjusted after installation. Improperly adjusted wheel bearings can cause steering instability, front-end shimmy and wander, and increased tire wear. For complete adjustment procedures, see the "Wheel Bearings" section in Chapter 9.

Pushing, Towing, and Jump Starting

PUSH STARTING

This is the least recommended method of starting a car and should be used only in an extreme case. Chances of body damage are high with a low automobile like the Firebird, so be sure that the pushcar's bumper does not override your bumper. If your Firebird has an automatic transmission forget any idea of push starting, modern automatics are not designed to be used in this manner. In an emergency, you can start a manual transmission car by pushing. With the bumpers evenly matched, get in your car, switch on the ignition, and place the gearshift in Second or Third gear—do not engage the clutch. Start off slowly. When the speed of the car reaches about 15–20 mph, release the clutch. If the car doesn't start on the second or third try, tow it to a warm, dry place where you can apply the troubleshooting techniques in Chapter 2.

TOWING

The car can be towed safely (with the transmission in Neutral) from the front at speeds of 35 mph or less. The car must either be towed with the rear wheels off the ground or the driveshaft disconnected if:

a. towing speeds are to be over 35 mph;

b. towing distance is over 50 miles;

c. transmission or rear axle problems exist.

When towing the car on its front wheels, the steering wheel must be secured in a straight-ahead position. Tire-to-ground clearance should not exceed 6 in. during towing.

JACKING

The standard jack utilizes slots in the bumper to raise the car. The jack supplied with the car should never be used for any service operation other than tire changing. Never get under the car while it is supported by only a jack. Always block the wheels when changing tires.

The service operations in this book often require that one end or the other, or both, of the car be raised and safely supported. The ideal method, of course, would be a hydraulic hoist. Since this is beyond both the resource and requirement of the do-it-yourselfer, a small hydraulic, screw or scissors jack will suffice for the procedures in this guide. Two sturdy jackstands should be acquired if you intend to work under the car at any time. An alternate method of raising the car would be drive-on ramps. These are available commercially or can be fabricated from heavy boards or steel. Be sure to block the wheels when using ramps. Never use concrete blocks to support the car. They may break if the load is not evenly distributed.

2 · Tune-Up and Troubleshooting

Tune-Up Procedures

SPARK PLUGS

In addition to performing their basic function of igniting the air-fuel mixture, spark plugs can also serve as very useful diagnostic tools. Once removed, compare your spark plugs with the samples in the "Troubleshooting" Section at the back of this Chapter. Typical plug conditions are illustrated along with their causes and remedies. Plugs which exhibit only normal wear and deposits can be cleaned, gapped, and reinstalled. Before removing the spark plug leads, number the towers on the distributor cap with tape. Trace the No. 1 lead and then proceed in the firing order. Use the firing order illustrations in Chapter 3 if you get lost. This prevents mix-ups when reinstalling the leads and also comes in handy when you're replacing wires or the distributor cap. Grasp each spark plug boot and pull it straight out.

Use a $^{13}/_{16}$ in. spark plug socket on all models through 1969, and all V8s through 1971. Six-cylinder models from 1970 and V8s from 1972 are equipped with tapered seat spark plugs which require a $^5/_8$ in. socket. Install the spark plug socket on the plug's hex and remove

Tapered seat plug socket (1970–74 six and 1972–74 V8)

it. If removal is difficult, loosen the plug only slightly and drip some light oil onto the threads. Allow the oil to penetrate and then unscrew the spark plug. Proceeding this way will prevent damaging the threads in the cylinder head. Be sure to keep the socket straight to avoid breaking the ceramic insulator. Inspect the plugs using the "Troubleshooting" Section illustrations and then clean or discard them according to their condition.

15

Tune-Up Specifications

When analyzing compression test results, look for uniformity among cylinders rather than specific pressures.

Year	ENGINE No. Cyl Displacement (cu in.)	hp	SPARK PLUGS Type	Gap (in.)	Distributor Point Dwell (deg)[10]	IGNITION TIMING (deg)[7] Man Trans	Auto Trans	Valves Intake Opens [9](deg)[8]	Fuel Pump Pressure (psi)	IDLE SPEED (rpm)[7] Man Trans	Auto Trans
'67	6-230 OHC	165	44N	.035	32½	5B(TDC)	5B(TDC)	7	4-5½	600(700)	500(600)
	6-230 OHC	215	44N	.035	32½	6B	6B	14	4-5½	600(700)	500(600)
	8-326	250	45S	.035	30	6B	6B	22	5-6½	600[2](700)	500[2](600)
	8-326	285	45S	.035	30	6B	6B	22	5-6½	600[2](700)	500[2](600)
	8-400	325	45S	.035	30	6B	6B	22/30	5-6½	600[2](700)	500[2](600)
	8-400 Ram Air	325	45S	.035	30	6B	6B	22/30	5-6½	600[2](700)	500[2](600)
'68	6-250 OHC	175	44N	.035	32½	TDC	TDC	14	4-5½	700[1]/500	600[1]/500
	6-250 OHC	215	44N	.035	30	5B	5B	14	4-5½	800[1]/600	600[1]/500
	8-350	265	45S	.035	30	9B	9B	22	5-6½	700[1]/500	600[1]/500
	8-350	320	45S	.035	30	9B	9B	23/30	5-6½	850[1]/650	650[1]/500
	8-400	330	44S	.035	30	9B	9B	31/23	5-6½	850[1]/650	650[1]/500
	8-400	335	44S	.035	30	9B	9B	31/23	5-6½	850[1]/650	650[1]/500
	8-400 Ram Air	335	44S	.035	30	9B	9B	38/31	5-6½	1000[1]/650	650[1]/500
'69	6-250 OHC	175	R-44NS	.035	32½	TDC	TDC	14	4-5½	700[1]/500	600[1]/500

6-250 OHC	215	R-44NS	.035	32½	5B	5B	22/14	4-5½	850①/600	600/500①
6-250 OHC	230	R-44NS	.035	32½	5B	5B	22/14	4-5½	850/600①	600/500①
8-350	265	R-46S	.035	30	9B	9B	22	5-6½	850	650
8-350	325	R-45S	.035	30	9B	9B	38/23	5-6½	1000	650
8-400	330	R-45S	.035	30	9B	9B	23	5-6½	1000	650
8-400	335	R-45S	.035	30	9B	9B	23	5-6½	1000	650
8-400 Ram Air	345	R-44S	.035	30	9B	9B	31/38	5-6½	1000/650①	650/500①
'70 6-250	155	R-46T	.035	32½	TDC	4B	16	4-5½	850/500①	650/500①
8-350	255	R-46S	.035	30	9B	9B	22	5-6½	800	650
8-400	265	R-46S③	.035	30	9B	9B	22	5-6½	800	650
8-400	330	R-45S	.035	30	9B	9B	30	5-6½	950	650
8-400 Ram Air	345	R-44S	.035	30	9B	9B	30	5-6½	950	650
8-400 Ram Air	370	R-44S	.035	30	15B	15B	30	5-6½	1000/650①	750/500①
'71 6-250	145	R-46TS	.035	32½	4B	4B	16	4-5	850/550①	650/500①
8-350	250	R-47S	.035	30	12B	12B	26/30⑤	5-6½④	800	600
8-400	265	R-47S	.035	30	8B	—	26	5-6½④	—	600
8-400	300	R-46S	.035	30	12B	12B	23	5-6½④	1000/600①	700
8-455	325	R-46S	.035	30	12B	—	23	5-6½④	—	650

Tune-Up Specifications (cont.)

When analyzing compression test results, look for uniformity among cylinders rather than specific pressures.

Year	ENGINE No. Cyl Displacement (cu in.)	hp	SPARK PLUGS Type	Gap (in.)	Distributor Point Dwell (deg)⑩	IGNITION TIMING (deg)Ⓣ Man Trans	Auto Trans	Valves Intake Opens ⑨(deg)⑧	Fuel Pump Pressure (psi)	IDLE SPEED (rpm)Ⓣ Man Trans	Auto Trans
'71	8-455	335	R-46S	.035	30	12B	12B	31	5-6½④	1000/600①	700
'72	6-250	110	R-45T	.035	32½	4B	4B	16	4-5	700①/450	600①/450
	8-350	160	R-46TS	.035	30	8B	10B	23/30⑤	5-6½	800	625
	8-400	175	R-46TS	.035	30	—	10B	23/26⑤	5-6½	—	625
	8-400	250	R-45TS	.035	30	8B	10B	23	5-6½	1000/600①	700/500①
	8-455	300	R-45TS	.035	30	8B	10B	31	5-6½	1000/600①	700/500①
'73	6-250	100	R-46TS	.035	32½	6B	6B	16	4-5	700/450①	600
	8-350 SE	150	R-46TS	.040	30	10B	12B	26/30⑤	5-6½	900/600①	650
	8-350 DE	175	R-46TS	.040	30	10B	12B	26/30⑤	5-6½	900/600①	650
	8-400 SE	170	R-46TS	.040	30	10B	12B	26	5-6½	—	650
	8-400 DE	230	R-45TS	.040	30	10B	12B	23/30⑤	5-6½	1000/600①	650
	8-455 DE	250	R-45TS	.040	30	10B	12B	23	5-6½	1000/600①	650
	8-455 SD, DE	310	R-44TS	.040	30	10B	12B	42	5-6½	1000/600①	750/500①

'74

Engine		Spark Plug	Gap							
6-250	All	R-46TS	.035	32½	6B	6B	16	4-5	700/450①	600
8-350 SE	All	R-46TS	.040	30	10B	12B⑥	26/30⑤	5-6½	900/600①	650
8-400 2 bbl	All	R-46TS	.040	30	10B	12B⑥	26	5-6½	900/600①	650
8-400 4 bbl	All	R-45TS	.040	30	10B	12B⑥	23/30⑤	5-6½	1000/600①	650
8-455	All	R-45TS	.040	30	10B	12B⑥	23	5-6½	1000/600①	650
8-455 SD	290	R-45TS	.040	30	10B	12B⑥	42	5-6½	1000/600①	750/500①

SE Single Exhaust
DE Dual Exhaust
SD Super Duty
B Before Top Dead Center
TDC Top Dead Center
— Not applicable

① Lower figure indicates idle speed with solenoid disconnected
② Adjust idle on air conditioned 100 rpm higher with A/C off, except on California vehicles
③ R-45S with automatic transmission
④ 6½-8 with A/C
⑤ Lower figure represents manual transmission models; higher figure indicates automatic transmission
⑥ 10B on California engines
⑦ See text for procedure
⑧ Figure in parentheses indicates California engine
⑨ All figures are in degrees Before Top Dead Center. Where two figures appear, the first represents timing with manual transmission, the second with automatic transmission
⑩ Point gap is .019 in. in all models except the '72/8-455, where not applicable

Checking spark plug gap

ADJUST DWELL
ANGLE SETTING OR
POINT OPENING

Adjusting six-cylinder point gap

Most new spark plugs come pre-gapped, but double check the setting or reset them if you desire a different gap. Recommended spark plug gap is given in the "Tune-Up Specifications" chart. Use a spark plug wire gauge for checking the gap. The wire should pass through the electrodes with just a slight drag. Using the electrode bending tool on the end of the gauge, bend the side electrode to adjust the gap. Never attempt to adjust the center electrode. Lightly oil the threads of the replacement plug and install it. If you have a torque wrench, tighten the plugs to 20 ft lbs on OHC 6 cylinder engines or 15 ft lbs on OHV 6 cylinders and all V8s. Be very careful not to overtighten the plug in the cylinder head.

NOTE: *Always replace the points and condenser as a unit. Uniset® points are available for V8 engines which combine the point set and condenser, greatly simplifying installation.*

BREAKER POINTS AND CONDENSER

Removal and Replacement

SIX-CYLINDER

1. Remove the distributor cap from the distributor and place it out of the way.
2. Remove the rotor.
3. Make a note of the wire connections and then remove the wires from the contact point terminal.
4. Remove the mounting screws and lift the point set condenser from the breaker plate.
5. Clean the breaker plate.
6. Install a new point set onto the breaker plate.

7. Install a new condenser and connect the primary and condenser lead wires to the contact point terminal.
8. Check the points for alignment. Contact surfaces must align with each other. If alignment is necessary, bend only the stationary contact support and not the movable one.
9. Using a flat feeler gauge, set the point opening at 0.019 in. for new points, 0.016 in. for used points. Observe the points while an assistant lightly activates the ignition switch. Turning the ignition key to the START position will rotate the distributor shaft and cause the points to open and close. When the points open completely (this occurs when the rubbing block is resting on the high point of the cam lobe), TURN THE IGNITION KEY OFF and check the space between the open points. This space or gap should be 0.019 in. for new points. If not, slightly loosen the point set mounting screw and, using a screwdriver to move the point support, adjust the gap until correct. Tighten the mounting screw.
10. Install the rotor and distributor cap.
11. Start the engine, check the dwell angle and then the ignition timing.

V8

NOTE: *The capacitive discharge and unit distributor systems require no maintenance other than checking the condition of the cap and wires. There are no points to wear out or adjust.*

Point alignment is preset at the factory and requires no adjustment. Point sets using the push-in type wiring terminal should be used on those distributors

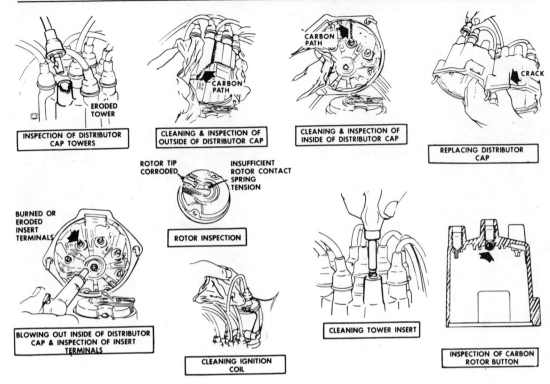

Distributor cap and rotor checkpoints

Removing R.F.I. shield

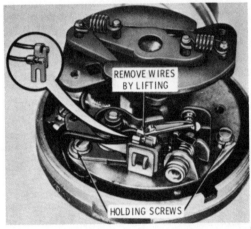

V8 point set removal

equipped with an R.F.I. (radio frequency interference) shield (1970–74). Points using a lockscrew type terminal may short out due to the shield contacting the screw.

1. Remove the distributor cap.
2. Remove the rotor.
3. If so equipped, remove the two-piece R.F.I. shield.
4. Loosen the two mounting screws and slide the contact point set from the breaker plate.
5. Remove the primary and condenser leads from the terminal.

6. Loosen the condenser bracket screw and slide the condenser from the bracket.
7. Install the new point set and condenser and then tighten the mounting screws.
8. Install the wires to the terminal so that they will not interfere with the cap, weight base, or breaker advance plate. Install the half of the R.F.I. shield which covers the points first.

9. Using a ⅛ in. allen wrench, make an initial point setting of 0.019 in.

10. The cam lubricator (if so equipped) must be replaced after 12 months or 12,000 miles. The end of the lubricator should be adjusted to just touch the cam lobes. Additional grease should not be applied to the lubricator.

11. Start the engine and check the point dwell and the ignition timing.

DWELL ANGLE

Dwell angle is the amount of time (measured in degrees of distributor cam rotation) that the contact points remain closed. Initial point gap (0.019 in.) determines dwell angle. If the points are set too wide they open gradually and dwell angle (the time they remain closed) is small. This wide gap causes excessive arcing at the points and, because of this, point burning. This small dwell doesn't give the coil sufficient time to build up maximum energy and so coil output decreases. If the points are set too close, the dwell is increased but the points may bounce at higher speeds and the idle becomes rough and starting is made harder. The wider the point opening, the smaller the dwell and the smaller the gap, the larger the dwell. Adjusting the dwell by making the initial point gap setting with a feeler gauge is sufficient to get the car started but a finer adjustment should be made. A dwell meter is needed to check the adjustment.

Six-Cylinder

1. Perform Steps 8 and 9 in the above procedure ("Breaker Points and Condenser Replacement") and then check the dwell angle with a dwell meter. Compare the reading on the meter with that listed in the "Tune-Up Specifications" chart and adjust as necessary. If the dwell angle is less than the specified minimum, check for misaligned points or worn distributor cam lobes. Accelerate the engine to 1,750 rpm and check for dwell variation. If the dwell angle changed more than three degrees from idle to 1,750 rpm, then check for a worn distributor shaft, shaft bushing, or a loose breaker plate.

IMPORTANT: *After changing the dwell angle, it will be necessary to set the ignition timing. Changing the*

dwell changes the ignition timing although changing timing does not affect the dwell angle. Therefore, when performing both settings, dwell angle adjustment must be done before timing.

V8

1. Run the engine to normal operating temperatures and then let it idle.

Adjusting V8 point gap/dwell angle

2. Raise the adjusting window on the distributor cap and insert a ⅛ in. allen wrench into the adjusting screw.

3. Turn the adjusting screw until the specified dwell angle is obtained on the dwell meter.

IGNITION TIMING

Adjustment

1. Disconnect and plug the distributor vacuum advance hose.

2. Start the engine and run it at idle speed.

3. Connect the timing light and, with the engine running at an idle, aim it at the timing tab on the front engine cover.

NOTE: *It may be necessary to clean off the tab and slash mark on the crankshaft pulley before proceeding any further. To further improve visibility, take a piece of chalk and fill in the slash mark on the crankshaft pulley. The "0" marking on the tab is TDC and all the BTDC (before top dead center) settings are on the "before" (advance) side of the "0" or, on the 1970 and later 6 cylinder, on the "A" (advance) side of the "0." On the 1968 and 1969 six-cylinder models, the BTDC settings are on the + (advance)*

OHC six-cylinder timing marks

OHV six-cylinder timing marks

Sighting line on air conditioned V8

V8 timing marks

side of the "0." On air conditioned V8s, sight on the timing marks as shown in the illustration.

4. Loosen the distributor clamp bolt and turn the distributor until the slash on the crankshaft pulley lines up with the specified timing mark on the tab. Once the timing is correct, tighten the distributor clamp bolt and recheck the timing.

5. Turn off the engine, remove the timing light, and connect the vacuum advance hose.

VALVE LASH

NOTE: *Before adjusting the valves, thoroughly warm up the engine.*

Adjustment

OVERHEAD CAM SIX-CYLINDER

The OHC six-cylinder engine is equipped with automatic valve lash adjusters. No adjustment is necessary or possible.

OVERHEAD VALVE SIX AND ALL V8S EXCEPT RAM AIR AND SUPER DUTY

No adjustment is necessary on these hydraulic lifters. If the engine has been disassembled, use the preliminary and final valve adjustment procedures in Chapter 3.

RAM AIR IV AND SUPER DUTY V8S

By their design characteristics, these engines may require an occasional adjustment. To adjust these limited travel lifters. proceed as follows. If the engine has been disassembled use the preliminary procedure in Chapter 3 first.

1. Start the engine and tighten the rocker arm on any valve that is clattering. Tighten until' the noise just disappears.

2. Allow the engine to run until normal operating temperature is reached, then loosen each rocker arm adjusting nut until the clattering begins again. Retighten the nut until the noise disappears (this brings the pushrod slightly into the top of lifter travel) and, with the adjusting nut in this position, tighten the locknut to 30–40 ft. lbs.

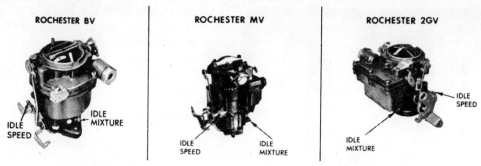

ROCHESTER BV   ROCHESTER MV   ROCHESTER 2GV

One and two-barrel idle speed and mixture screw location (1967–70)

CARBURETOR

Idle Speed and Mixture Adjustment

1967

Without Air Injection System

Adjust with air cleaner removed.

1. Remove the air cleaner.
2. Connect a tachometer to the engine, set the parking brake, and place the transmission in Neutral.
3. Turn in the idle mixture screws until they *gently* seat, then back out 1½ turns.
4. Start the engine and allow it to come to the normal operating temperature. Make sure that the choke is fully open, then adjust the idle speed screw to obtain the specified idle speed (automatic in Drive, manual in Neutral).
5. Adjust the idle mixture screw(s) to obtain the highest steady vacuum at the specified idle speed, except for the Rochester BV. For this carburetor, adjust the idle mixture screw out ¼ turn from lean "drop off," the point where a 20–30 rpm drop is achieved by leaning the mixture.

NOTE: *On carburetors having a hot idle compensator valve (A/C models), hold the brass valve down with a pencil while making the mixture adjustment.*

6. Repeat Steps 4 and 5 as necessary.
7. Turn off the engine, remove the gauge, and install the air cleaner.

With Air Injection System

Adjust with the air cleaner removed.

1. Remove the air cleaner.
2. Connect a tachometer to the engine, set the parking brake, and place the transmission in Neutral.
3. Turn in the idle mixture screw(s)

until they *gently* seat, then back them out 3 turns.

4. Start the engine and allow it to reach normal operating temperature. Make sure that the choke is fully open, then adjust the idle speed screw(s) to obtain the specified idle speed (automatic in Drive, manual in Neutral).
5. Turn the idle mixture screw(s) clockwise (in) to the point where a 20–30 rpm drop in speed is achieved—this is the lean "drop off" point. Back out the screws ¼ turn from this point.

NOTE: *During this adjustment, air conditioning should be turned off on V8 engines.*

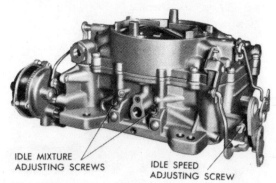

IDLE MIXTURE ADJUSTING SCREWS   IDLE SPEED ADJUSTING SCREW

Carter AFB idle speed and mixture screw locations

6. Repeat Steps 4 and 5 as necessary.
7. Turn off the engine, remove the tachometer and install the air cleaner.

1968–69

6 Cylinder

NOTE: *Make these adjustments with the air cleaner installed.*

1. Turn in the mixture screws until they lightly seat, then back them out 5 turns.

2. Start the engine, connect the tachometer, and allow the engine to warm up to normal operating temperature. On automatic tranmission cars, place the selector in Drive and turn off the A/C, if so equipped.

3. Adjust the idle stop solenoid screw to obtain 610 rpm for automatic transmission (1 bbl and 4 bbl), 730 rpm for manual transmission (4 bbl), or 880 rpm for 1969 manual transmission (4 bbl).

4. Turn the mixture screws clockwise to obtain 600 rpm for automatic transmission (1 bbl and 4 bbl), 700 rpm for manual transmission (1 bbl), 800 rpm for 1968 manual transmission (4 bbl), or 850 rpm for 1969 manual transmission (4 bbl).

5. Disconnect the idle stop solenoid and adjust the idle speed screw on the carburetor to obtain 600 rpm for manual transmission (4 bbl) and 500 rpm for all others.

NOTE: *Don't disturb the idle mixture screws or stop the solenoid after this point.*

6. Reconnect the solenoid and adjust the fast idle speed.

V8

1. Turn in the idle mixture screws until they are lightly seated, then back them out 4 turns (2 bbl) or 6 turns (4 bbl).

2. Connect a tachometer, start the engine, and allow it to warm up to normal operating temperature. On cars with automatic transmission and A/C, turn off the A/C.

3. Place the car in Drive (automatic) or Neutral (manual). With the idle stop solenoid energized, adjust the mixture screws for the best lean idle speed.

4. Adjust the idle stop solenoid screw to obtain the specified idle speed for all 1968 and only 1969 Ram Air; use the idle screw for all other 1969 cars.

5. Disconnect the idle stop solenoid, then adjust the idle speed screw on the carburetor to obtain 650 rpm idle for manual tranmission (4 bbl), 500 rpm for all others.

6. Place the fast idle lever on the top step of the cam and adjust the fast idle speed.

1970

NOTE: *Make this adjustment with the air cleaner installed.*

1. On California cars, remove the fuel filler cap.

2. Disconnect and plug the distributor vacuum advance hose.

3. Plug the hot idle compensator on all automatic transmission V8s with the Quadrajet (4MV) carburetor except the Ram Air III and IV. Also plug the compensator on all 6 cylinder and V8 2 bbl with automatic transmission and A/C.

With the car in Drive (automatic) or Neutral (manual), adjust the curb idle speed as follows:

Six-Cylinder and Ram Air IV

a. With the idle stop solenoid energized, adjust the solenoid screw to obtain 830 rpm for the 6 cylinder, 1,000 rpm for the Ram Air IV, 630 rpm for the automatic 6 cylinder, and 750 rpm for the automatic Ram Air IV.

b. Adjust the mixture screws equally to obtain lean best idle at 1000 rpm for the Ram Air IV (manual), 750 rpm for the automatic Ram Air IV, 750 rpm for the manual 6 cylinder, and 600 rpm for the automatic 6 cylinder.

c. Disconnect the solenoid wire and adjust the carburetor idle speed screw to obtain 400 rpm for the 6 cylinder, 500 rpm for the Ram Air IV (automatic) and 650 rpm for the Ram Air manual.

350, 400, 455 V8s

a. Back out the mixture screws 3–5 turns from the lightly seated positions.

b. Adjust the carburetor idle speed screw to obtain 850 rpm for the manual

ROCHESTER 4MV

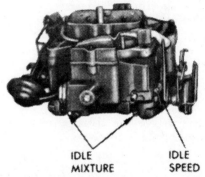

IDLE MIXTURE   IDLE SPEED

Rochester 4MV idle speed and mixture screw locations (1967–70)

350 and 400 2 bbl, 1050 rpm for the manual 400 and 455 4 bbl, or 675 rpm for all automatic 350, 400, 455 engines.

c. Lean the mixture screws equally (turn in) to obtain 800 rpm for manual 350 and 400 2 bbl, 950 rpm for manual 400 and 455 4 bbl, or 650 rpm for all automatic 350, 400, 455 engines.

1971–72

Adjust with air cleaner installed.

On some models, the idle stop solenoid is no longer used, having been replaced by the combination emission control valve. This valve is energized through the transmission to increase idle speed under conditions of High gear deceleration and to provide full vacuum spark advance during High gear operation. The valve is de-energized at curb idle and in lower gears to provide a retarded spark under these conditions, the result of which is lower hydrocarbon emission. *The valve need not be adjusted unless the solenoid or throttle body is removed, or the carburetor overhauled.*

V8 Idle Speed

1. Disconnect the carburetor "EVAP" hose from the vapor storage canister.
2. Disconnect and plug the carburetor-to-vacuum (distributor vacuum) solenoid hose at the solenoid. Disconnect the throttle solenoid wire on 4 bbl manual transmission engines.
3. Set the dwell and timing (in that order) at specified idle speed.
4. Adjust the carburetor speed screw to obtain the specified idle speed, automatic in Drive, manual in Neutral.
5. On 4 bbl manual transmission models, reconnect the throttle solenoid wire, manually extend the solenoid screw and adjust to specified idle rpm.
6. Place automatic in Park, manual in Neutral and check the fast idle speed with the screw on top step of the cam. Adjust the fast idle screw to obtain 1700 rpm.
   NOTE: *2 bbl carburetor fast idle cannot be adjusted.*
7. Reconnect the distributor vacuum and vapor storage hoses.

6 Cylinder Idle Speed

1. Disconnect the fuel tank "EVAP" hose from the vapor storage canister.

2. Disconnect and plug the distributor vacuum advance hose.
3. Set the dwell and timing (in that order) at the specified idle speed.
4. Adjust the carburetor idle speed screw to obtain 550 rpm for manual, 500 rpm for automatic (in Drive). Do not adjust the solenoid screw.
5. Place automatic in Park and manual in Neutral, then place the fast idle tang on the top step of the fast idle cam and check the fast idle speed. Adjust to obtain 2400 rpm.

V8 and 6 Cylinder Idle Mixture

If the carburetor has been overhauled, or the plastic caps removed from the mixture screws, the following procedure must be used to adjust the idle speed and mixture. It must be emphasized that the manufacturer does not recommend this procedure as a substitute for the preceding methods, in that exhaust emission quality can be adversely affected unless the proper test equipment is available.

1. Turn in the mixture screw(s) until lightly seated, then back them out 3½ turns.
2. Start the engine and adjust the carburetor idle speed screw to obtain a speed 25 rpm above the specified idle (automatic), 75 rpm higher for 6 cylinder and 2 bbl V8 (manual), or 100 rpm higher for 4 bbl V8 (manual).
3. Turn the mixture screw(s) in equally until specified idle speed is obtained. At this point, a CO meter should be employed to adjust the mixture. A reading of 1.0% or less must be maintained.
4. Shut off the engine and install new limiter caps.
5. Adjust the fast idle speed, as previously described.

1973–74

All six-cylinder engines, V8s with manual transmissions, and all 455 cu in. Super Duty carburetors are equipped with an idle stop solenoid. Idle adjustments must be made with the engine at normal operating temperature, choke open, air conditioning off, all vacuum lines disconnected and plugged, and automatic tranmissions in Drive.

CAUTION: *Ensure that the parking*

brake is set and the drive wheels blocked.

Six-Cylinder

1. Disconnect the fuel tank evaporative hose from the canister.

2. Disconnect the distributor vacuum hose and plug it.

3. Dwell and ignition timing must already be set and correct.

4. Disconnect the idle stop solenoid wire. Using a ⅛ in. allen wrench, adjust the screw in the idle stop solenoid for the lower idle speed figure in the "Tune-up Specifications" chart (solenoid is not energized).

5. Reconnect the idle stop solenoid wire. Set the idle rpm to the higher figure in the chart by rotating the body of the idle stop solenoid (solenoid energized).

6. On manual transmission models, use a pair of needlenose pliers to extend the plunger on the C.E.C. valve to the end of its travel. Use an open-end wrench to adjust the hex on the plunger until it just touches the throttle lever and idle speed is 850 rpm.

7. With automatic transmission in Park or manual in Neutral, check the fast idle speed with the fast idle tang on the top step of the cam. If the fast idle speed is not at 2400 rpm on 1973 models or 1800 rpm on 1974 models, bend the tang to correct it.

V8

1. Disconnect the carburetor hose from the vapor canister.

2. Disconnect the distributor and EGR valve vacuum hoses, plug the hoses to the carburetor, and disconnect the wire from the idle stop solenoid (if so equipped).

3. Check the dwell and ignition timing if you haven't already done so.

4. Adjust the carburetor idle speed screw to figure specified in the "Tune-up Specifications" chart (solenoid not energized).

5. Reconnect the idle stop solenoid wire, if so equipped. Extend the solenoid screw by hand and adjust the idle speed to the higher figure in the "Tune-up Specifications" chart (solenoid energized).

6. On 4 bbl carburetors, with automatic transmission in Park or manual transmission in Neutral, check the fast idle speed with fast idle speed screw on the top step of the cam. Turn the screw to adjust the fast idle to 1500 rpm (except 455 SD, which should be 2000 rpm).

NOTE: *Fast idle is not adjustable on 2 bbl carburetors.*

Engine Tune-Up

Engine tune-up is a procedure performed to restore engine performance, deteriorated due to normal wear and loss of adjustment. The three major areas considered in a routine tune-up are compression, ignition, and carburetion, although valve adjustment may be included.

A tune-up is performed in three steps: *analysis*, in which it is determined whether normal wear is responsible for performance loss, and which parts require replacement or service; *parts replacement or service*; and *adjustment*, in which engine adjustments are returned to original specifications. Since the advent of emission control equipment, precision adjustment has become increasingly critical, in order to maintain pollutant emission levels.

Analysis

The procedures below are used to indicate where adjustments, parts service or replacement are necessary within the realm of a normal tune-up. If, following these tests, all systems appear to be functioning properly, proceed to the Troubleshooting Section for further diagnosis.

—Remove all spark plugs, noting the cylinder in which they were installed. Remove the air cleaner, and position the throttle and choke in the full open position. Disconnect the coil high tension lead from the coil and the distributor cap. Insert a compression gauge into the spark plug port of each cylinder, in succession, and crank the engine with

Maxi. Press. Lbs. Sq. In.	Min. Press. Lbs. Sq. In.	Max. Press. Lbs. Sq. In.	Min. Press. Lbs. Sq. In.
134	101	188	141
136	102	190	142
138	104	192	144
140	105	194	145
142	107	196	147
146	110	198	148
148	111	200	150
150	113	202	151
152	114	204	153
154	115	206	154
156	117	208	156
158	118	210	157
160	120	212	158
162	121	214	160
164	123	216	162
166	124	218	163
168	126	220	165
170	127	222	166
172	129	224	168
174	131	226	169
176	132	228	171
178	133	230	172
180	135	232	174
182	136	234	175
184	138	236	177
186	140	238	178

Compression pressure limits
© Buick Div. G.M. Corp.)

the starter to obtain the highest possible reading. Record the readings, and compare the highest to the lowest on the compression pressure limit chart. If the difference exceeds the limits on the chart, or if all readings are excessively low, proceed to a wet compression check (see Troubleshooting Section).

—Evaluate the spark plugs according to the spark plug chart in the Troubleshooting Section, and proceed as indicated in the chart.

—Remove the distributor cap, and inspect it inside and out for cracks and/or carbon tracks, and inside for excessive wear or burning of the rotor contacts. If any of these faults are evident, the cap must be replaced.

—Check the breaker points for burning, pitting or wear, and the contact heel resting on the distributor cam for excessive wear. If defects are noted, replace the entire breaker point set.

—Remove and inspect the rotor. If the contacts are burned or worn, or if the rotor is excessively loose on the distributor shaft (where applicable), the rotor must be replaced.

—Inspect the spark plug leads and the coil high tension lead for cracks or brittleness. If any of the wires appear defective, the entire set should be replaced.

—Check the air filter to ensure that it is functioning properly.

Parts Replacement and Service

The determination of whether to replace or service parts is at the mechanic's discretion; however, it is suggested that any parts in questionable condition be replaced rather than reused.

—Clean and regap, or replace, the spark plugs as needed. Lightly coat the threads with engine oil and install the plugs. CAUTION: *Do not over-torque taper-seat spark plugs, or plugs being installed in aluminum cylinder heads.*

28

SPARK PLUG TORQUE

Thread size	Cast-Iron Heads	Aluminum Heads
10 mm.	14	11
14 mm.	30	27
18 mm.	34*	32
7/8 in.—18	37	35

* 17 ft. lbs. for tapered plugs using no gaskets.

—If the distributor cap is to be reused, clean the inside with a dry rag, and remove corrosion from the rotor contact points with fine emery cloth. Remove the spark plug wires one by one, and clean the wire ends and the inside of the towers. If the boots are loose, they should be replaced.

If the cap is to be replaced, transfer the wires one by one, cleaning the wire ends and replacing the boots if necessary.

—If the original points are to remain in service, clean them lightly with emery cloth, lubricate the contact heel with grease specifically designed for this purpose. Rotate the crankshaft until the heel rests on a high point of the distributor cam, and adjust the point gap to specifications.

When replacing the points, remove the original points and condenser, and wipe out the inside of the distributor housing with a clean, dry rag. Lightly lubricate the contact heel and pivot point, and install the points and condenser. Rotate the crankshaft until the heel rests on a high point of the distributor cam, and adjust the point gap to specifications. NOTE: *Always replace the condenser when changing the points.*

—If the rotor is to be reused, clean the contacts with solvent. Do not alter the spring tension of the rotor center contact. Install the rotor and the distributor cap.

—Replace the coil high tension lead and/or the spark plug leads as necessary.

—Clean the carburetor using a spray solvent (e.g., Gumout Spray). Remove the varnish from the throttle bores, and clean the linkage. Disconnect and plug the fuel line, and run the engine until it runs out of fuel. Partially fill the float chamber with solvent, and reconnect the fuel line. In extreme cases, the jets can be pressure flushed by inserting a rubber plug into the float vent, running the spray nozzle through it, and spraying the solvent until it squirts out of the venturi fuel dump.

—Clean and tighten all wiring connections in the primary electrical circuit.

Additional Services

The following services *should* be performed in conjunction with a routine tune-up to ensure efficient performance.

—Inspect the battery and fill to the proper level with distilled water. Remove the cable clamps, clean clamps and posts thoroughly, coat the posts lightly with petroleum jelly, reinstall and tighten.

—Inspect all belts, replace and/or adjust as necessary.

—Test the PCV valve (if so equipped), and clean or replace as indicated. Clean all crankcase ventilation hoses, or replace if cracked or hardened.

—Adjust the valves (if necessary) to manufacturer's specifications.

Adjustments

—Connect a dwell-tachometer between the distributor primary lead and ground. Remove the distributor cap and rotor (unless equipped with Delco externally adjustable distributor). With the ignition off, crank the engine with a remote starter switch and measure the point dwell angle. Adjust the dwell angle to specifications. NOTE: *Increasing the gap decreases the dwell angle and vice-versa.* Install the rotor and distributor cap.

—Connect a timing light according to the manufacturer's specifications. Identify the proper timing marks with chalk or paint. NOTE: *Luminescent (day-glo) paint is excellent for this purpose.* Start the engine, and run it until it reaches operating temperature. Disconnect and plug any distributor vacuum lines, and adjust idle to the speed required to adjust timing, according to specifications. Loosen the distributor clamp and adjust timing to specifications by rotating the distributor in the engine. NOTE: *To advance timing, rotate distributor opposite normal direction of rotor rotation, and vice-versa.*

—Synchronize the throttles and mixture of multiple carburetors (if so equipped) according to procedures given in the individual car sections.

—Adjust the idle speed, mixture, and idle quality, as specified in the car sections. Final idle adjustments should be made with the air cleaner installed. CAUTION: *Due to strict emission control requirements on 1969 and later models, special test equipment (CO meter, SUN Tester) may be necessary to properly adjust idle mixture to specifications.*

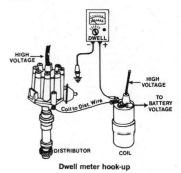

Dwell meter hook-up

Trouble-shooting

The following section is designed to aid in the rapid diagnosis of engine problems. The systematic format is used to diagnose problems ranging from engine starting difficulties to the need for engine overhaul. It is assumed that the user is equipped with basic hand tools and test equipment (tach-dwell meter, timing light, voltmeter, and ohmmeter).

Troubleshooting is divided into two sections. The first, *General Diagnosis*, is used to locate the problem area. In the second, *Specific Diagnosis*, the problem is systematically evaluated.

General Diagnosis

PROBLEM: Symptom	Begin diagnosis at Section Two, Number ——
Engine won't start:	
Starter doesn't turn	1.1, 2.1
Starter turns, engine doesn't	2.1
Starter turns engine very slowly	1.1, 2.4
Starter turns engine normally	3.1, 4.1
Starter turns engine very quickly	6.1
Engine fires intermittently	4.1
Engine fires consistently	5.1, 6.1
Engine runs poorly:	
Hard starting	3.1, 4.1, 5.1, 8.1
Rough idle	4.1, 5.1, 8.1
Stalling	3.1, 4.1, 5.1, 8.1
Engine dies at high speeds	4.1, 5.1
Hesitation (on acceleration from standing stop)	5.1, 8.1
Poor pickup	4.1, 5.1, 8.1
Lack of power	3.1, 4.1, 5.1, 8.1
Backfire through the carburetor	4.1, 8.1, 9.1
Backfire through the exhaust	4.1, 8.1, 9.1
Blue exhaust gases	6.1, 7.1
Black exhaust gases	5.1
Running on (after the ignition is shut off)	3.1, 8.1
Susceptible to moisture	4.1
Engine misfires under load	4.1, 7.1, 8.4, 9.1
Engine misfires at speed	4.1, 8.4
Engine misfires at idle	3.1, 4.1, 5.1, 7.1, 8.4

PROBLEM: Symptom	Probable Cause
Engine noises: ①	
Metallic grind while starting	Starter drive not engaging completely
Constant grind or rumble	*Starter drive not releasing, worn main bearings
Constant knock	Worn connecting rod bearings
Knock under load	Fuel octane too low, worn connecting rod bearings
Double knock	Loose piston pin
Metallic tap	*Collapsed or sticky valve lifter, excessive valve clearance, excessive end play in a rotating shaft
Scrape	*Fan belt contacting a stationary surface
Tick while starting	S.U. electric fuel pump (normal), starter brushes
Constant tick	*Generator brushes, shreaded fan belt
Squeal	*Improperly tensioned fan belt
Hiss or roar	*Steam escaping through a leak in the cooling system or the radiator overflow vent
Whistle	*Vacuum leak
Wheeze	Loose or cracked spark plug

①—It is extremely difficult to evaluate vehicle noises. While the above are general definitions of engine noises, those starred (*) should be considered as possibly originating elsewhere in the car. To aid diagnosis, the following list considers other potential sources of these sounds.

Metallic grind:
  Throwout bearing; transmission gears, bearings, or synchronizers; differential bearings, gears; something metallic in contact with brake drum or disc.

Metallic tap:
  U-joints; fan-to-radiator (or shroud) contact.

Scrape:
  Brake shoe or pad dragging; tire to body contact; suspension contacting undercarriage or exhaust; something non-metallic contacting brake shoe or drum.

Tick:
  Transmission gears; differential gears; lack of radio suppression; resonant vibration of body panels; windshield wiper motor or transmission; heater motor and blower.

Squeal:
  Brake shoe or pad not fully releasing; tires (excessive wear, uneven wear, improper inflation); front or rear wheel alignment (most commonly due to improper toe-in).

Hiss or whistle:
  Wind leaks (body or window); heater motor and blower fan.

Roar:
  Wheel bearings; wind leaks (body and window).

Specific Diagnosis

This section is arranged so that following each test, instructions are given to proceed to another, until a problem is diagnosed.

INDEX

Group		Topic
1	*	Battery
2	*	Cranking system
3	*	Primary electrical system
4	*	Secondary electrical system
5	*	Fuel system
6	*	Engine compression
7	**	Engine vacuum
8	**	Secondary electrical system
9	**	Valve train
10	**	Exhaust system
11	**	Cooling system
12	**	Engine lubrication

*—The engine need not be running.
**—The engine must be running.

SAMPLE SECTION

Test and Procedure	Results and Indications	Proceed to
4.1—Check for spark: Hold each spark plug wire approximately ¼″ from ground with gloves or a heavy, dry rag. Crank the engine and observe the spark.	→ If no spark is evident:	4.2
	→ If spark is good in some cases:	4.3
	→ If spark is good in all cases:	4.6

DIAGNOSIS

1.1—Inspect the battery visually for case condition (corrosion, cracks) and water level.	If case is cracked, replace battery:	1.4
	If the case is intact, remove corrosion with a solution of baking soda and water (CAUTION: *do not get the solution into the battery*), and fill with water:	1.2
1.2—Check the battery cable connections: Insert a screwdriver between the battery post and the cable clamp. Turn the headlights on high beam, and observe them as the screwdriver is gently twisted to ensure good metal to metal contact. **Testing battery cable connections using a screwdriver**	If the lights brighten, remove and clean the clamp and post; coat the post with petroleum jelly, install and tighten the clamp:	1.4
	If no improvement is noted:	1.3

1.3—Test the state of charge of the battery using an individual cell tester or hydrometer.

Spec. Grav. Reading	Charged Condition
1.260-1.280	Fully Charged
1.230-1.250	Three Quarter Charged
1.200-1.220	One Half Charged
1.170-1.190	One Quarter Charged
1.140-1.160	Just About Flat
1.110-1.130	All The Way Down

State of battery charge

The effect of temperature on the specific gravity of battery electrolyte

If indicated, charge the battery. NOTE: *If no obvious reason exists for the low state of charge (i.e., battery age, prolonged storage), the charging system should be tested:*   1.4

Test and Procedure	*Results and Indications*	*Proceed to*
1.4—Visually inspect battery cables for cracking, bad connection to ground, or bad connection to starter.	If necessary, tighten connections or replace the cables:	2.1

Tests in Group 2 are performed with coil high tension lead disconnected to prevent accidental starting.

Test and Procedure	*Results and Indications*	*Proceed to*
2.1—Test the starter motor and solenoid: Connect a jumper from the battery post of the solenoid (or relay) to the starter post of the solenoid (or relay).	If starter turns the engine normally:	2.2
	If the starter buzzes, or turns the engine very slowly:	2.4
	If no response, replace the solenoid (or relay).	3.1
	If the starter turns, but the engine doesn't, ensure that the flywheel ring gear is intact. If the gear is undamaged, replace the starter drive.	3.1
2.2—Determine whether ignition override switches are functioning properly (clutch start switch, neutral safety switch), by connecting a jumper across the switch(es), and turning the ignition switch to "start".	If starter operates, adjust or replace switch:	3.1
	If the starter doesn't operate:	2.3
2.3—Check the ignition switch "start" position: Connect a 12V test lamp between the starter post of the solenoid (or relay) and ground. Turn the ignition switch to the "start" position, and jiggle the key.	If the lamp doesn't light when the switch is turned, check the ignition switch for loose connections, cracked insulation, or broken wires. Repair or replace as necessary:	3.1
	If the lamp flickers when the key is jiggled, replace the ignition switch.	3.3

STARTER   STARTER RELAY

Checking the ignition switch "start" position

Test and Procedure	*Results and Indications*	*Proceed to*
2.4—Remove and bench test the starter, according to specifications in the car section.	If the starter does not meet specifications, repair or replace as needed:	3.1
	If the starter is operating properly:	2.5
2.5—Determine whether the engine can turn freely: Remove the spark plugs, and check for water in the cylinders. Check for water on the dipstick, or oil in the radiator. Attempt to turn the engine using an 18″ flex drive and socket on the crankshaft pulley nut or bolt.	If the engine will turn freely only with the spark plugs out, and hydrostatic lock (water in the cylinders) is ruled out, check valve timing:	9.2
	If engine will not turn freely, and it is known that the clutch and transmission are free, the engine must be disassembled for further evaluation:	Next Chapter

Tests and Procedures	Results and Indications	Proceed to
3.1—Check the ignition switch "on" position: Connect a jumper wire between the distributor side of the coil and ground, and a 12V test lamp between the switch side of the coil and ground. Remove the high tension lead from the coil. Turn the ignition switch on and jiggle the key.	If the lamp lights:	3.2
	If the lamp flickers when the key is jiggled, replace the ignition switch:	3.3
	If the lamp doesn't light, check for loose or open connections. If none are found, remove the ignition switch and check for continuity. If the switch is faulty, replace it:	3.3

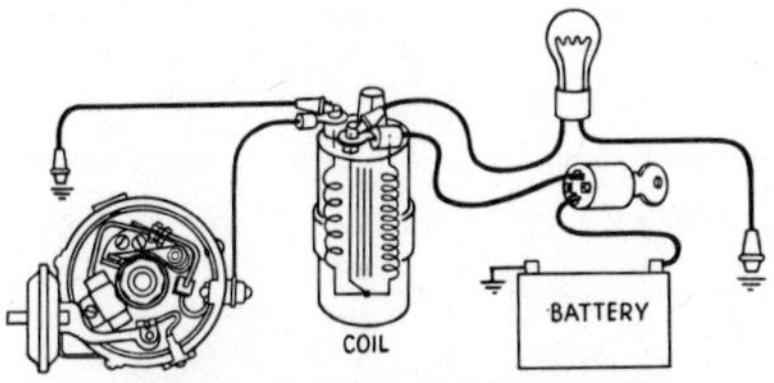

Checking the ignition switch "on" position

3.2—Check the ballast resistor or resistance wire for an open circuit, using an ohmmeter.	Replace the resistor or the resistance wire if the resistance is zero.	3.3
3.3—Visually inspect the breaker points for burning, pitting, or excessive wear. Gray coloring of the point contact surfaces is normal. Rotate the crankshaft until the contact heel rests on a high point of the distributor cam, and adjust the point gap to specifications.	If the breaker points are intact, clean the contact surfaces with fine emery cloth, and adjust the point gap to specifications. If pitted or worn, replace the points and condenser, and adjust the gap to specifications: NOTE: *Always lubricate the distributor cam according to manufacturer's recommendations when servicing the breaker points.*	3.4
3.4—Connect a dwell meter between the distributor primary lead and ground. Crank the engine and observe the point dwell angle.	If necessary, adjust the point dwell angle: NOTE: *Increasing the point gap decreases the dwell angle, and vice-versa.*	3.6
	If dwell meter shows little or no reading:	3.5

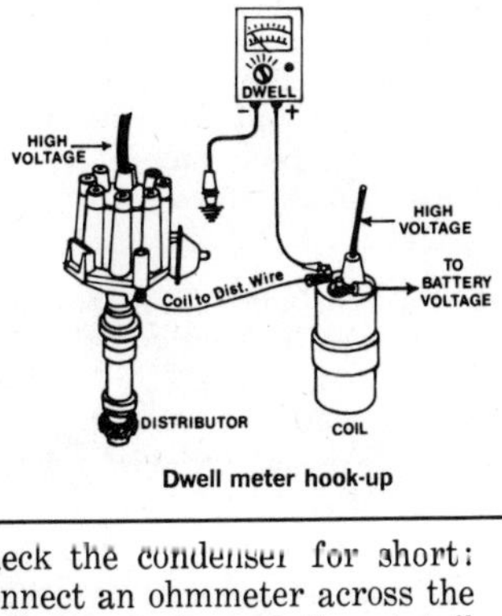

Dwell meter hook-up

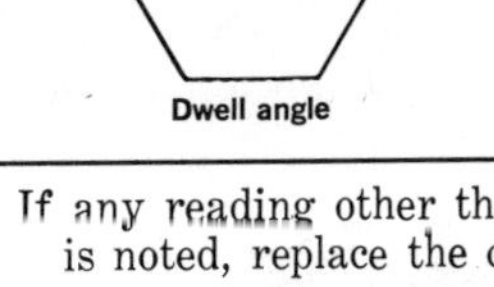

Dwell angle

| 3.5—Check the condenser for short: Connect an ohmmeter across the condenser body and the pigtail lead. | If any reading other than infinite resistance is noted, replace the condenser: | 3.6 |

Checking the condenser for short

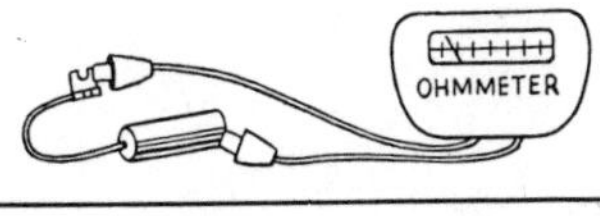

Test and Procedure	Results and Indications	Proceed to
3.6—Test the coil primary resistance: Connect an ohmmeter across the coil primary terminals, and read the resistance on the low scale. Note whether an external ballast resistor or resistance wire is utilized.	Coils utilizing ballast resistors or resistance wires should have approximately 1.0Ω resistance; coils with internal resistors should have approximately 4.0Ω resistance. If values far from the above are noted, replace the coil:	4.1
Testing the coil primary resistance		
4.1—Check for spark: Hold each spark plug wire approximately $\frac{1}{4}''$ from ground with gloves or a heavy, dry rag. Crank the engine, and observe the spark.	If no spark is evident:	4.2
	If spark is good in some cylinders:	4.3
	If spark is good in all cylinders:	4.6
4.2—Check for spark at the coil high tension lead: Remove the coil high tension lead from the distributor and position it approximately $\frac{1}{4}''$ from ground. Crank the engine and observe spark. CAUTION: *This test should not be performed on cars equipped with transistorized ignition.*	If the spark is good and consistent:	4.3
	If the spark is good but intermittent, test the primary electrical system starting at 3.3:	3.3
	If the spark is weak or non-existent, replace the coil high tension lead, clean and tighten all connections and retest. If no improvement is noted:	4.4
4.3—Visually inspect the distributor cap and rotor for burned or corroded contacts, cracks, carbon tracks, or moisture. Also check the fit of the rotor on the distributor shaft (where applicable).	If moisture is present, dry thoroughly, and retest per 4.1:	4.1
	If burned or excessively corroded contacts, cracks, or carbon tracks are noted, replace the defective part(s) and retest per 4.1:	4.1
	If the rotor and cap appear intact, or are only slightly corroded, clean the contacts thoroughly (including the cap towers and spark plug wire ends) and retest per 4.1:	
	If the spark is good in all cases:	4.6
	If the spark is poor in all cases:	4.5
4.4—Check the coil secondary resistance: Connect an ohmmeter across the distributor side of the coil and the coil tower. Read the resistance on the high scale of the ohmmeter.	The resistance of a satisfactory coil should be between $4K\Omega$ and $10K\Omega$. If the resistance is considerably higher (i.e., $40K\Omega$) replace the coil, and retest per 4.1: NOTE: *This does not apply to high performance coils.*	4.1
Testing the coil secondary resistance		

Test and Procedure	*Results and Indications*	*Proceed to*
4.5—Visually inspect the spark plug wires for cracking or brittleness. Ensure that no two wires are positioned so as to cause induction firing (adjacent and parallel). Remove each wire, one by one, and check resistance with an ohmmeter.	Replace any cracked or brittle wires. If any of the wires are defective, replace the entire set. Replace any wires with excessive resistance (over 8000Ω per foot for suppression wire), and separate any wires that might cause induction firing.	4.6
4.6—Remove the spark plugs, noting the cylinders from which they were removed, and evaluate according to the chart below.	See below.	See below.

	Condition	Cause	Remedy	*Proceed to*
	Electrodes eroded, light brown deposits.	Normal wear. Normal wear is indicated by approximately .001″ wear per 1000 miles.	Clean and regap the spark plug if wear is not excessive: Replace the spark plug if excessively worn:	4.7
	Carbon fouling (black, dry, fluffy deposits).	If present on one or two plugs:		
		Faulty high tension lead(s).	Test the high tension leads:	4.5
		Burnt or sticking valve(s).	Check the valve train: (Clean and regap the plugs in either case.)	9.1
		If present on most or all plugs: Overly rich fuel mixture, due to restricted air filter, improper carburetor adjustment, improper choke or heat riser adjustment or operation.	Check the fuel system:	5.1
	Oil fouling (wet black deposits)	Worn engine components. NOTE: *Oil fouling may occur in new or recently rebuilt engines until broken in.*	Check engine vacuum and compression: Replace with new spark plug	6.1
	Lead fouling (gray, black, tan, or yellow deposits, which appear glazed or cinder-like).	Combustion by-products.	Clean and regap the plugs. (Use plugs of a different heat range if the problem recurs.)	4.7

	Condition	Cause	Remedy	Proceed to
	Gap bridging (deposits lodged between the electrodes).	Incomplete combustion, or transfer of deposits from the combustion chamber.	Replace the spark plugs:	4.7
	Overheating (burnt electrodes, and extremely white insulator with small black spots).	Ignition timing advanced too far.	Adjust timing to specifications:	8.2
		Overly lean fuel mixture.	Check the fuel system:	5.1
		Spark plugs not seated properly.	Clean spark plug seat and install a new gasket washer: (Replace the spark plugs in all cases.)	4.7
	Fused spot deposits on the insulator.	Combustion chamber blow-by.	Clean and regap the spark plugs:	4.7
	Pre-ignition (melted or severely burned electrodes, blistered or cracked insulators, or metallic deposits on the insulator).	Incorrect spark plug heat range.	Replace with plugs of the proper heat range:	4.7
		Ignition timing advanced too far.	Adjust timing to specifications:	8.2
		Spark plugs not being cooled efficiently.	Clean the spark plug seat, and check the cooling system:	11.1
		Fuel mixture too lean.	Check the fuel system:	5.1
		Poor compression.	Check compression:	6.1
		Fuel grade too low.	Use higher octane fuel:	4.7

Test and Procedure	Results and Indications	Proceed to
4.7—Determine the static ignition timing: Using the flywheel or crankshaft pulley timing marks as a guide, locate top dead center on the *compression* stroke of the No. 1 cylinder. Remove the distributor cap.	Adjust the distributor so that the rotor points toward the No. 1 tower in the distributor cap, and the points are just opening:	4.8
4.8—Check coil polarity: Connect a voltmeter negative lead to the coil high tension lead, and the positive lead to ground (NOTE: *reverse the hook-up for positive ground cars*). Crank the engine momentarily. **Checking coil polarity**	If the voltmeter reads up-scale, the polarity is correct:	5.1
	If the voltmeter reads down-scale, reverse the coil polarity (switch the primary leads):	5.1

Test and Procedure	Results and Indications	Proceed to
5.1—Determine that the air filter is functioning efficiently: Hold paper elements up to a strong light, and attempt to see light through the filter.	Clean permanent air filters in gasoline (or manufacturer's recommendation), and allow to dry. Replace paper elements through which light cannot be seen:	5.2
5.2—Determine whether a flooding condition exists: Flooding is identified by a strong gasoline odor, and excessive gasoline present in the throttle bore(s) of the carburetor.	If flooding is not evident:	5.3
	If flooding is evident, permit the gasoline to dry for a few moments and restart. If flooding doesn't recur:	5.6
	If flooding is persistant:	5.5
5.3—Check that fuel is reaching the carburetor: Detach the fuel line at the carburetor inlet. Hold the end of the line in a cup (not styrofoam), and crank the engine.	If fuel flows smoothly:	5.6
	If fuel doesn't flow (NOTE: *Make sure that there is fuel in the tank*), or flows erratically:	5.4
5.4—Test the fuel pump: Disconnect all fuel lines from the fuel pump. Hold a finger over the input fitting, crank the engine (with electric pump, turn the ignition or pump on); and feel for suction.	If suction is evident, blow out the fuel line to the tank with low pressure compressed air until bubbling is heard from the fuel filler neck. Also blow out the carburetor fuel line (both ends disconnected):	5.6
	If no suction is evident, replace or repair the fuel pump:	5.6
	NOTE: *Repeated oil fouling of the spark plugs, or a no-start condition, could be the result of a ruptured vacuum booster pump diaphragm, through which oil or gasoline is being drawn into the intake manifold (where applicable).*	
5.5—Check the needle and seat: Tap the carburetor in the area of the needle and seat.	If flooding stops, a gasoline additive (e.g., Gumout) will often cure the problem:	5.6
	If flooding continues, check the fuel pump for excessive pressure at the carburetor (according to specifications). If the pressure is normal, the needle and seat must be removed and checked, and/or the float level adjusted:	5.6
5.6—Test the accelerator pump by looking into the throttle bores while operating the throttle.	If the accelerator pump appears to be operating normally:	5.7
	If the accelerator pump is not operating, the pump must be reconditioned. Where possible, service the pump with the carburetor(s) installed on the engine. If necessary, remove the carburetor. Prior to removal:	5.7
5.7—Determine whether the carburetor main fuel system is functioning: Spray a commercial starting fluid into the carburetor while attempting to start the engine.	If the engine starts, runs for a few seconds, and dies:	5.8
	If the engine doesn't start:	6.1

Test and Procedures	Results and Indications	Proceed to
5.8—Uncommon fuel system malfunctions: See below:	If the problem is solved: If the problem remains, remove and recondition the carburetor.	6.1

Condition	Indication	Test	Usual Weather Conditions	Remedy
Vapor lock	Car will not re-start shortly after running.	Cool the components of the fuel system until the engine starts.	Hot to very hot	Ensure that the exhaust manifold heat control valve is operating. Check with the vehicle manufacturer for the recommended solution to vapor lock on the model in question.
Carburetor icing	Car will not idle, stalls at low speeds.	Visually inspect the throttle plate area of the throttle bores for frost.	High humidity, 32-40° F.	Ensure that the exhaust manifold heat control valve is operating, and that the intake manifold heat riser is not blocked.
Water in the fuel	Engine sputters and stalls; may not start.	Pump a small amount of fuel into a glass jar. Allow to stand, and inspect for droplets or a layer of water.	High humidity, extreme temperature changes.	For droplets, use one or two cans of commercial gas dryer (Dry Gas) For a layer of water, the tank must be drained, and the fuel lines blown out with compressed air.

Test and Procedure	Results and Indications	Proceed to
6.1—Test engine compression: Remove all spark plugs. Insert a compression gauge into a spark plug port, crank the engine to obtain the maximum reading, and record.	If compression is within limits on all cylinders:	7.1
	If gauge reading is extremely low on all cylinders:	6.2
	If gauge reading is low on one or two cylinders: (If gauge readings are identical and low on two or more adjacent cylinders, the head gasket must be replaced.)	6.2

Testing compression
(© Chevrolet Div. G.M. Corp.)

Compression pressure limits
(© Buick Div. G.M. Corp.)

Maxi. Press. Lbs. Sq. In.	Min. Press. Lbs. Sq. In.	Maxi. Press. Lbs. Sq. In.	Min. Press. Lbs. Sq. In.	Max. Press. Lbs. Sq. In.	Min. Press. Lbs. Sq. In.	Max. Press. Lbs. Sq. In.	Min. Press. Lbs. Sq. In.
134	101	162	121	188	141	214	160
136	102	164	123	190	142	216	162
138	104	166	124	192	144	218	163
140	105	168	126	194	145	220	165
142	107	170	127	196	147	222	166
146	110	172	129	198	148	224	168
148	111	174	131	200	150	226	169
150	113	176	132	202	151	228	171
152	114	178	133	204	153	230	172
154	115	180	135	206	154	232	174
156	117	182	136	208	156	234	175
158	118	184	138	210	157	236	177
160	120	186	140	212	158	238	178

Test and Procedure	Results and Indications	Proceed to
6.2—Test engine compression (wet): Squirt approximately 30 cc. of engine oil into each cylinder, and retest per 6.1.	If the readings improve, worn or cracked rings or broken pistons are indicated:	Next Chapter
	If the readings do not improve, burned or excessively carboned valves or a jumped timing chain are indicated: NOTE: *A jumped timing chain is often indicated by difficult cranking.*	7.1
7.1—Perform a vacuum check of the engine: Attach a vacuum gauge to the intake manifold beyond the throttle plate. Start the engine, and observe the action of the needle over the range of engine speeds.	See below.	See below

Reading	Indications	Proceed to
Steady, from 17-22 in. Hg.	Normal.	8.1
Low and steady.	Late ignition or valve timing, or low compression:	6.1
Very low	Vacuum leak:	7.2
Needle fluctuates as engine speed increases.	Ignition miss, blown cylinder head gasket, leaking valve or weak valve spring:	6.1, 8.3
Gradual drop in reading at idle.	Excessive back pressure in the exhaust system:	10.1
Intermittent fluctuation at idle.	Ignition miss, sticking valve:	8.3, 9.1
Drifting needle.	Improper idle mixture adjustment, carburetors not synchronized (where applicable), or minor intake leak. Synchronize the carburetors, adjust the idle, and retest. If the condition persists:	7.2
High and steady.	Early ignition timing:	8.2

Test and Procedure	*Results and Indications*	*Proceed to*
7.2—Attach a vacuum gauge per 7.1, and test for an intake manifold leak. Squirt a small amount of oil around the intake manifold gaskets, carburetor gaskets, plugs and fittings. Observe the action of the vacuum gauge.	If the reading improves, replace the indicated gasket, or seal the indicated fitting or plug:	8.1
	If the reading remains low:	7.3
7.3—Test all vacuum hoses and accessories for leaks as described in 7.2. Also check the carburetor body (dashpots, automatic choke mechanism, throttle shafts) for leaks in the same manner.	If the reading improves, service or replace the offending part(s):	8.1
	If the reading remains low:	6.1
8.1—Check the point dwell angle: Connect a dwell meter between the distributor primary wire and ground. Start the engine, and observe the dwell angle from idle to 3000 rpm.	If necessary, adjust the dwell angle. NOTE: *Increasing the point gap reduces the dwell angle and vice-versa.* If the dwell angle moves outside specifications as engine speed increases, the distributor should be removed and checked for cam accuracy, shaft endplay and concentricity, bushing wear, and adequate point arm tension (NOTE: *Most of these items may be checked with the distributor installed in the engine, using an oscilloscope*):	8.2
8.2—Connect a timing light (per manufacturer's recommendation) and check the dynamic ignition timing. Disconnect and plug the vacuum hose(s) to the distributor if specified, start the engine, and observe the timing marks at the specified engine speed.	If the timing is not correct, adjust to specifications by rotating the distributor in the engine: (Advance timing by rotating distributor opposite normal direction of rotor rotation, retard timing by rotating distributor in same direction as rotor rotation.)	8.3
8.3—Check the operation of the distributor advance mechanism(s): To test the mechanical advance, disconnect all but the mechanical advance, and observe the timing marks with a timing light as the engine speed is increased from idle. If the mark moves smoothly, without hesitation, it may be assumed that the mechanical advance is functioning properly. To test vacuum advance and/or retard systems, alternately crimp and release the vacuum line, and observe the timing mark for movement. If movement is noted, the system is operating.	If the systems are functioning:	8.4
	If the systems are not functioning, remove the distributor, and test on a distributor tester:	8.4
8.4—Locate an ignition miss: With the engine running, remove each spark plug wire, one by one, until one is found that doesn't cause the engine to roughen and slow down.	When the missing cylinder is identified:	4.1

Test and Procedure	Results and Indications	Proceed to
9.1—Evaluate the valve train: Remove the valve cover, and ensure that the valves are adjusted to specifications. A mechanic's stethoscope may be used to aid in the diagnosis of the valve train. By pushing the probe on or near push rods or rockers, valve noise often can be isolated. A timing light also may be used to diagnose valve problems. Connect the light according to manufacturer's recommendations, and start the engine. Vary the firing moment of the light by increasing the engine speed (and therefore the ignition advance), and moving the trigger from cylinder to cylinder. Observe the movement of each valve.	See below	See below

Observation	Probable Cause	Remedy	Proceed to
Metallic tap heard through the stethoscope.	Sticking hydraulic lifter or excessive valve clearance.	Adjust valve. If tap persists, remove and replace the lifter:	10.1
Metallic tap through the stethoscope, able to push the rocker arm (lifter side) down by hand.	Collapsed valve lifter.	Remove and replace the lifter:	10.1
Erratic, irregular motion of the valve stem.*	Sticking valve, burned valve.	Recondition the valve and/or valve guide:	Next Chapter
Eccentric motion of the pushrod at the rocker arm.*	Bent pushrod.	Replace the pushrod:	10.1
Valve retainer bounces as the valve closes.*	Weak valve spring or damper.	Remove and test the spring and damper. Replace if necessary:	10.1

*—When observed with a timing light.

Test and Procedure	Results and Indications	Proceed to
9.2—Check the valve timing: Locate top dead center of the No. 1 piston, and install a degree wheel or tape on the crankshaft pulley or damper with zero corresponding to an index mark on the engine. Rotate the crankshaft in its direction of rotation, and observe the opening of the No. 1 cylinder intake valve. The opening should correspond with the correct mark on the degree wheel according to specifications.	If the timing is not correct, the timing cover must be removed for further investigation:	

Test and Procedure	Results and Indications	Proceed to
10.1—Determine whether the exhaust manifold heat control valve is operating: Operate the valve by hand to determine whether it is free to move. If the valve is free, run the engine to operating temperature and observe the action of the valve, to ensure that it is opening.	If the valve sticks, spray it with a suitable solvent, open and close the valve to free it, and retest.	
	If the valve functions properly:	10.2
	If the valve does not free, or does not operate, replace the valve:	10.2
10.2—Ensure that there are no exhaust restrictions: Visually inspect the exhaust system for kinks, dents, or crushing. Also note that gasses are flowing freely from the tailpipe at all engine speeds, indicating no restriction in the muffler or resonator.	Replace any damaged portion of the system:	11.1
11.1—Visually inspect the fan belt for glazing, cracks, and fraying, and replace if necessary. Tighten the belt so that the longest span has approximately ½″ play at its midpoint under thumb pressure.	Replace or tighten the fan belt as necessary:	11.2

Checking the fan belt tension
(© Nissan Motor Co. Ltd.)

Test and Procedure	Results and Indications	Proceed to
11.2—Check the fluid level of the cooling system.	If full or slightly low, fill as necessary:	11.5
	If extremely low:	11.3
11.3—Visually inspect the external portions of the cooling system (radiator, radiator hoses, thermostat elbow, water pump seals, heater hoses, etc.) for leaks. If none are found, pressurize the cooling system to 14-15 psi.	If cooling system holds the pressure:	11.5
	If cooling system loses pressure rapidly, reinspect external parts of the system for leaks under pressure. If none are found, check dipstick for coolant in crankcase. If no coolant is present, but pressure loss continues:	11.4
	If coolant is evident in crankcase, remove cylinder head(s), and check gasket(s). If gaskets are intact, block and cylinder head(s) should be checked for cracks or holes. If the gasket(s) is blown, replace, and purge the crankcase of coolant:	12.6
	NOTE: *Occasionally, due to atmospheric and driving conditions, condensation of water can occur in the crankcase. This causes the oil to appear milky white. To remedy, run the engine until hot, and change the oil and oil filter.*	

Test and Procedure	Results and Indication	Proceed to
11.4—Check for combustion leaks into the cooling system: Pressurize the cooling system as above. Start the engine, and observe the pressure gauge. If the needle fluctuates, remove each spark plug wire, one by one, noting which cylinder(s) reduce or eliminate the fluctuation. **Radiator pressure tester** (© American Motors Corp.)	Cylinders which reduce or eliminate the fluctuation, when the spark plug wire is removed, are leaking into the cooling system. Replace the head gasket on the affected cylinder bank(s).	
11.5—Check the radiator pressure cap: Attach a radiator pressure tester to the radiator cap (wet the seal prior to installation). Quickly pump up the pressure, noting the point at which the cap releases. **Testing the radiator pressure cap** (© American Motors Corp.)	If the cap releases within ± 1 psi of the specified rating, it is operating properly: If the cap releases at more than ± 1 psi of the specified rating, it should be replaced:	11.6 11.6
11.6—Test the thermostat: Start the engine cold, remove the radiator cap, and insert a thermometer into the radiator. Allow the engine to idle. After a short while, there will be a sudden, rapid increase in coolant temperature. The temperature at which this sharp rise stops is the thermostat opening temperature.	If the thermostat opens at or about the specified temperature: If the temperature doesn't increase: (If the temperature increases slowly and gradually, replace the thermostat.)	11.7 11.7
11.7—Check the water pump: Remove the thermostat elbow and the thermostat, disconnect the coil high tension lead (to prevent starting), and crank the engine momentarily.	If coolant flows, replace the thermostat and retest per 11.6: If coolant doesn't flow, reverse flush the cooling system to alleviate any blockage that might exist. If system is not blocked, and coolant will not flow, recondition the water pump.	11.6 —
12.1—Check the oil pressure gauge or warning light: If the gauge shows low pressure, or the light is on, for no obvious reason, remove the oil pressure sender. Install an accurate oil pressure gauge and run the engine momentarily.	If oil pressure builds normally, run engine for a few moments to determine that it is functioning normally, and replace the sender. If the pressure remains low: If the pressure surges: If the oil pressure is zero:	— 12.2 12.3 12.3

Test and Procedure	Results and Indications	Proceed to
12.2—Visually inspect the oil: If the oil is watery or very thin, milky, or foamy, replace the oil and oil filter.	If the oil is normal:	12.3
	If after replacing oil the pressure remains low:	12.3
	If after replacing oil the pressure becomes normal:	—
12.3—Inspect the oil pressure relief valve and spring, to ensure that it is not sticking or stuck. Remove and thoroughly clean the valve, spring, and the valve body.	If the oil pressure improves:	—
	If no improvement is noted:	12.4

Oil pressure relief valve
(© British Leyland Motors)

Test and Procedure	Results and Indications	Proceed to
12.4—Check to ensure that the oil pump is not cavitating (sucking air instead of oil): See that the crankcase is neither over nor underfull, and that the pickup in the sump is in the proper position and free from sludge.	Fill or drain the crankcase to the proper capacity, and clean the pickup screen in solvent if necessary. If no improvement is noted:	12.5
12.5—Inspect the oil pump drive and the oil pump:	If the pump drive or the oil pump appear to be defective, service as necessary and retest per 12.1:	12.1
	If the pump drive and pump appear to be operating normally, the engine should be disassembled to determine where blockage exists:	Next Chapter
12.6—Purge the engine of ethylene glycol coolant: Completely drain the crankcase and the oil filter. Obtain a commercial butyl cellosolve base solvent, designated for this purpose, and follow the instructions precisely. Following this, install a new oil filter and refill the crankcase with the proper weight oil. The next oil and filter change should follow shortly thereafter (1000 miles).		

3 · Engine and Engine Rebuilding

Engine Electrical

DISTRIBUTOR

Four types of distributors have been used: an internal point adjustment distributor used on six-cylinder engines, an external point adjustment distributor used on eight-cylinder engines, an optional capacitive discharge distributor and ignition system (1967), and beginning 1972, as an option, a transistorized unit distributor/coil.

All units perform the same basic function. They induce a high-voltage surge into the coil and time these surges with regard to piston movements. They use centrifugal and vacuum ignition timing advance mechanisms to time the surges. They then direct these high-voltage surges through the distributor rotor, distributor cap, and high-tension wiring to the spark plugs.

Removal and Installation

1. Disconnect distributor primary wire from the coil.

2. Remove distributor cap. On six-cylinder models, the cap is retained by two screws which thread into the distributor. On V8s, the cap is retained by two spring hooks. To remove the cap, use a

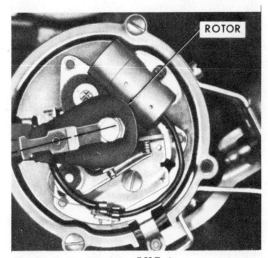

No. 1 rotor positioning—OHC six

screwdriver to depress the hooks and then swivel them out and away from the distributor.

3. Make reference marks on the block and the distributor housing which align with the tip of the rotor. Do not crank the engine after these marks have been made.

4. Disconnect the vacuum line at distributor.

5. Remove the distributor clamp screw and hold-down clamp.

6. Lift out the distributor and distributor-to-block gasket. Notice the slight

No. 1 rotor positioning—OHV six

No. 1 rotor positioning—V8

Spark plug wire positioning—OHC six

Spark plug wire positioning—OHV six

Spark plug wire positioning—V8

rotation of the rotor as the distributor is removed from the block.

7. Installation procedure is the reverse of the removal procedure. It should be noted, however, that while inserting the distributor into the block, the rotor should be moved slightly to one side. This is necessary because of the helical cut of the distributor and camshaft gears. As the distributor seats in its bore, the rotor will turn slightly so that the reference marks will once again be aligned.

Installation—If the Engine has been disturbed

1. With the No. 1 piston coming up on compression stroke, continue cranking the engine until the pulley timing mark indexes with the zero (0) mark on the engine timing scale.

2. Replace the distributor-to-block gasket.

3. Install the distributor in the block so that the vacuum diaphragm faces the left-side of the engine on V8 engines, and to the front of the engine on six-cylinder engines. The rotor should point toward the contact in the cap for the No. 1 cylinder. Move the rotor slightly to the side because, as the distributor is pressed into its bore, it will turn a small amount.

4. Remove the condenser lead and ignition primary lead from the points.

5. Install a new set of points and tighten the attaching screws.

6. Connect the condenser and primary leads to the points.

7. Apply a very small amount of grease to the distributor breaker cam.

8. Install the R.F.I. shield, if so equipped. (The half covering the points should be installed first.)

9. Install the rotor and distributor cap.

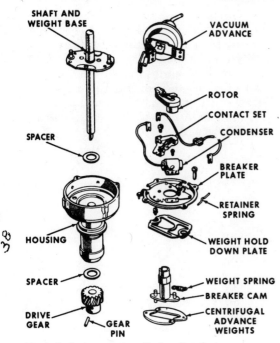

Exploded view of six-cylinder distributor

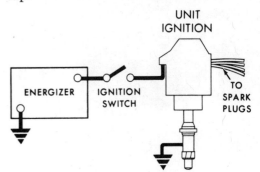

Basic wiring of the unitized distributor

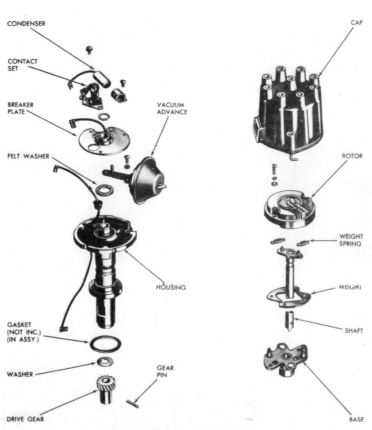

Exploded view of V8 distributor

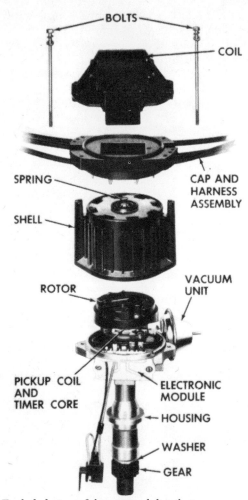

Exploded view of the unitized distributor

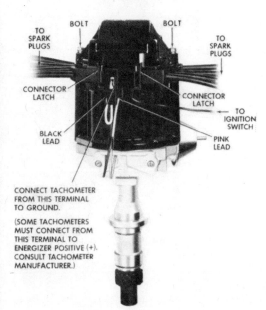

Unitized distributor connections

10. Set the dwell using a dwell meter, or set the point gap by rotating the engine until the fiber rubbing block of the point set is on a high point of the breaker cam. (The cap, rotor, and R.F.I. shield must be removed to set the points.) Using a 1/8 in. allen wrench, rotate the adjusting screw until the gap (dwell) meets the specification. Replace the cap, rotor, and R.F.I. shield.

Firing Order

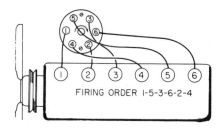

Six-cylinder

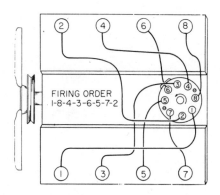

V8

ALTERNATOR

An alternating current (AC) generator is used on all Firebirds. This unit is the Delco-Remy Delcotron or after 1969, the unitized C.S.I. alternator/regulator.

Alternator Precautions

Since the alternator is designed for use on only one polarity system, the following precautions must be observed:

1. The polarity of the battery, generator and regulator must be considered before making any electrical connections with the system.

2. When connecting a booster battery, be sure to connect the negative battery

terminals respectively, and the positive battery terminals respectively.

3. When connecting a charger to the battery, connect the charger positive lead to the battery positive terminal. Connect the charger negative lead to the battery negative terminal.

4. Never operate the Delcotron on open circuit. Be sure that all connections in the circuit are clean and tight.

5. Do not short across or ground any of the terminals on the Delcotron regulator.

6. Do not attempt to polarize the Delcotron.

7. Do not use test lamps of more than 12 volts for checking diode continuity.

8. Avoid long soldering times when replacing diodes or transistors. Prolonged heat is damaging to these units.

9. Disconnect the battery ground terminal when servicing any AC system. This will prevent the possibility of accidental reversal of polarity.

Removal and Installation

1. Disconnect the positive battery cable.

2. Remove the alternator wires or connector.

3. Loosen the adjusting bolt.

4. Remove the drive belt. On cars so equipped, loosen the A.I.R. pump.

5. Remove the alternator retaining bolts or through-bolt.

6. Remove the alternator.

7. Install the alternator using the reverse of the removal procedure. Tighten the bracket bolt on non-A/C cars to 10–25 ft lbs. All other models are tightened to 25–35 ft lbs.

VOLTAGE REGULATOR

Removal and Installation

1967–69

1. Disconnect the battery cables.

2. Disconnect the wiring from the voltage regulator.

3. Remove the screws which hold the regulator to the firewall or front bulkhead, depending on the car.

4. Reverse the removal procedure to install the regulator.

1971–74

The voltage regulator is inside the alternator. If the unit is malfunctioning, have it repaired at a specialty shop or replace the alternator/regulator with a new or rebuilt unit.

Alternator and Regulator Specifications

	ALTERNATOR			REGULATOR							
					Field Relay			Regulator			
Year	Part No. or Manufacturer	Field Current @ 12 V	Output (amps)	Part No. or Manufacturer	Air Gap (in.)	Point Gap (in.)	Volts to Close	Air Gap (in.)	Point Gap (in.)	Volts @ 75°
'67–'69	1100761	2.2–2.6	37	1119515①	.015	.030	1.5–3.2	.067	.014	13.5–16.0
	1100704	2.2–2.6	37	1119515	.015	.030	1.5–3.2	.067	.014	13.5–16.0
	1100832②	4.0–4.5	37	1119515	.015	.030	1.5–3.2	.067	.014	13.5–16.0
	1100830②	4.0–4.5	37	1119515	.015	.030	1.5–3.2	.067	.014	13.5–16.0
	1100700	2.2–2.6	55	1119515	.015	.030	1.5–3.2	.067	.014	13.5–16.0
	1100760	2.2–2.6	55	1119515	.015	.030	1.5–3.2	.067	.014	13.5–16.0
'70	1100704	2.2–2.6	37	1119515①	.015	.030	1.5–3.2	.067	.014	13.5–16.0
	1100888	2.2–2.6	55	1119515	.015	.030	1.5–3.2	.067	.014	13.5–16.0

Alternator and Regulator Specifications (cont.)

Year	ALTERNATOR Part No. or Manufacturer	Field Current @ 12 V	Output (amps)	Part No. or Manufacturer	REGULATOR Field Relay Air Gap (in.)	Point Gap (in.)	Volts to Close	Regulator Air Gap (in.)	Point Gap (in.)	Volts @ 75°
'70	1100905	2.2–2.6	37	1119515	.015	.030	1.5–3.2	.067	.014	13.5–16.0
	1100700	2.2–2.6	55	1119515	.015	.030	1.5–3.2	.067	.014	13.5–16.0
	1100891	2.2–2.6	55	1119515	.015	.030	1.5–3.2	.067	.014	13.5–16.0
	1100892	2.2–2.6	55	1119515	.015	.030	1.5–3.2	.067	.014	13.5–16.0
	1100906	2.2–2.6	55	1119515	.015	.030	1.5–3.2	.067	.014	13.5–16.0
	1100895	2.2–2.6	61	1119515	.015	.030	1.5–3.2	.067	.014	13.5–16.0
'71–'74	1100927	4.0–4.5	37	Integral with Alternator						
	1100920	4.0–4.5	55	Integral with Alternator						
	1100928	4.0–4.5	55	Integral with Alternator						
	11001015	4.0–4.5	80	Integral with Alternator						
	1100497	4.0–4.9	37	Integral with Alternator						

① Transistor regulator 1116368 optional equipment until 1969
② Integrated Circuit Generator (C.S.I.—no external regulator) optional on 1969 model

—— Not applicable

STARTER

The starter circuit consists of the battery, battery cables, starting motor, starter motor solenoid switch, ignition-starter switch, the neutral safety switch used on cars with automatic transmissions, and clutch switch on manual transmission cars.

The solenoid switch closes the circuit between the battery and the starting motor. It also operates the shift lever that moves the drive pinion into mesh with the flywheel ring gear.

Removal and Installation

SIX-CYLINDER

1. Disconnect the positive battery cable.

2. Disconnect the solenoid wires.
3. Disconnect the starter brace, if so equipped.
4. Remove the starter-to-engine bolts and starter.
5. Install the starter in the reverse order of removal.

V8

1. Disconnect the positive battery cable.
2. Jack up the front of the car and support it on stands.
3. Disconnect the starter brace and swing it toward the front and out of the way.
4. Remove the two starter-to-engine bolts and let the starter swing down.
5. Disconnect the solenoid wires and battery cable.

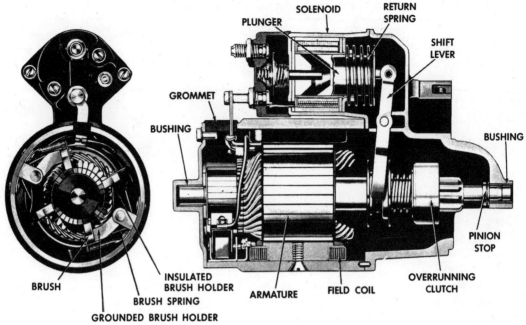

Starter cross-section

6. Remove the starter.

7. Install the starter in the reverse order of removal.

Starter Drive Replacement

1. Disconnect the field straps from the solenoid and remove the starter through-bolts.

2. Remove the commutator end frame, field frame, and armature from the drive housing.

3. To remove the overrunning clutch from the armature shaft:

a. Slide the thrust collar from the end of the armature shaft.

b. Slide a standard ½ in. pipe coupling (or an old pinion of suitable size) onto the armature shaft so that it butts against the snap-ring retainer. Tap the end of the pipe with a hammer, driving the retainer off of the snap-ring.

c. Remove the snap-ring from the groove in the armature shaft.

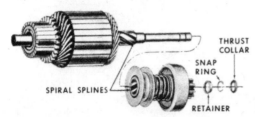

Starter drive

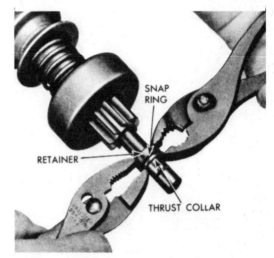

Refitting the snap-ring and thrust collar

d. Slide the retainer and clutch from the armature shaft.

4. To reassemble, reverse the above procedure, being sure to:

a. Slide the snap-ring, after it has been forced onto the armature shaft, past the grease groove to the snap-ring groove.

b. Use two pairs of pliers at the same time, on opposite sides of the armature shaft, and grip the retainer and thrust collar and squeeze until the retainer is forced over the snap-ring.

Battery and Starter Specifications

| Year | Engine Displacement (cu in.) | BATTERY | | | STARTER | | | | Brush Spring Tension (oz) |
| | | Ampere Hour Capacity | Volts | Terminal Grounded | No-Load Test | | | |
					Amps	Volts	RPM	
'67–'69	6	44①	12	Neg.	49–76	10.6	6,200–9,600	35
	8-326, 350	53①	12	Neg.	65–100	10.6	3,600–5,100	35
	8-400	61	12	Neg.	Not Recommended			35
'70–'74	6	45①	12	Neg.	Not Recommended			35
	8-350	53①	12	Neg.	Not Recommended			35
	8-400, 455	61	12	Neg.	Not Recommended			35

① 61 amp battery used w/AC or H.D. battery option.

Engine Mechanical

SIX CYLINDER

1967–69

A belt-driven overhead cam engine of 230 and 250 cu in. displacement, was offered from 1967 to 1969. It uses a cast iron block and head, and was available with a 1 or 4 bbl carburetor. A unique feature of this engine was the accessory drive housing assembly located on the front, right-hand side of the block containing the oil pump and filter, fuel pump, and distributor. The assembly is driven by the cam belt.

1970–74

The overhead cam six-cylinder engine was replaced by an overhead valve, 250 cu in. six-cylinder engine in 1970. It has a cast iron block and cylinder head, uses hydraulic valve lifters, and is basically the Chevrolet six-cylinder engine.

V8

In 1967, the two 326 cu in. V8s remained in the engine lineup, but the old 389 was replaced by the new 400 cu in. V8. In 1968 and 1969, the 400 engine was

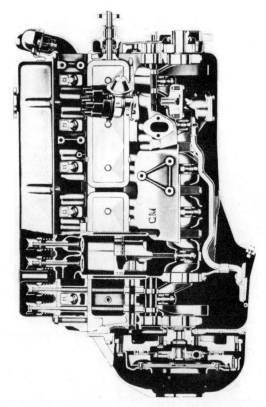

OHV six side view

retained, although the Ram Air version of this engine was given four-bolt main caps due to the increased performance. In 1968, an all-new 350 cu in. engine of Pon-

OHC six cross-section

V8 cross-section

tiac design was introduced. This engine is used as the standard base V8 right up to the present. The 455 cu in. became available in the Firebird in 1971. The basic engine lineup has remained the same through 1974 with modifications for emission control and a concurrent reduction in power output. The 1974 Super Duty 455, rated at 290 hp in the Trans Am, remains one of the most powerful engines still available in an American car.

General Engine Specifications

Year	Engine Cu In. Displacement	Carburetor Type	Advertised Horsepower @ rpm ⑤	Advertised Torque @ rpm (ft lbs) ⑤	Bore and Stroke (in.)	Advertised Compression Ratio	Oil Pressure @ 2050 rpm
'67	6-230 OHC	1 bbl	165 @ 4700	216 @ 2600	3.8762 x 3.250	9.0 : 1	31 ①
	6-230 OHC	4 bbl	215 @ 5200	240 @ 3800	3.8762 x 3.250	10.5 : 1	31 ①
	8-326	2 bbl	250 @ 4600	333 @ 3800	3.7199 x 3.750	9.2 : 1	35
	8-326 HO	4 bbl	285 @ 5000	359 @ 3200	3.7199 x 3.750	10.5 : 1	35
	8-400	4 bbl	325 @ 4800	410 @ 3400	4.1222 x 3.750	10.75 : 1	58
	8-400 Ram Air	4 bbl	325 @ 5200	410 @ 3600	4.1222 x 3.750	10.75 : 1	58
	8-400	4 bbl	360 @ 5100	438 @ 3600	4.1222 x 3.750	10.75 : 1	58
	8-400 Ram Air	4 bbl	360 @ 5400	438 @ 3800	4.1222 x 3.750	10.75 : 1	58
'68	6-250 OHC	1 bbl	175 @ 4800	240 @ 2600	3.8762 x 3.530	9.0 : 1	31 ①
	6-250 OHC	4 bbl	215 @ 5200	255 @ 3800	3.8762 x 3.530	10.5 : 1	31 ①
	8-350	2 bbl	265 @ 4600	355 @ 2800	3.8762 x 3.750	9.2 : 1	35
	8-350 HO	4 bbl	320 @ 5100	380 @ 3200	3.8762 x 3.750	10.5 : 1	35
	8-400	2 bbl	265 @ 4600	397 @ 2400	4.1212 x 3.750	8.6 : 1	58
	8-400	4 bbl	330 @ 4800	430 @ 3300	4.1212 x 3.750	10.75 : 1	58
	8-400 Ram Air	4 bbl	335 @ 5300	430 @ 3600	4.1212 x 3.750	10.75 : 1	58
	8-400	4 bbl	350 @ 5000	445 @ 3000	4.1212 x 3.750	10.75 : 1	58
	8-400 HO	4 bbl	360 @ 5100	445 @ 3600	4.1212 x 3.750	10.75 : 1	58
	8-400 Ram Air	4 bbl	360 @ 5400	445 @ 3800	4.1212 x 3.750	10.75 : 1	58

General Engine Specifications (cont.)

Year	Engine Cu In. Displacement	Carburetor Type	Advertised Horsepower @ rpm⑤	Advertised Torque @ rpm (ft lbs)⑤	Bore and Stroke (in.)	Advertised Compression Ratio	Oil Pressure @ 2050 rpm
'69	6-250 OHC	1 bbl	175 @ 4800	240 @ 2600	3.8762 x 3.530	9.0 : 1	31①
	6-250 OHC	4 bbl	215 @ 5200	255 @ 3500	3.8762 x 3.530	10.5 : 1	31①
	6-250 OHC	4 bbl	230 @ 5400	260 @ 3600	3.8762 x 3.530	10.5 : 1	31①
	8-350	2 bbl	265 @ 4600	325 @ 2800	3.8762 x 3.750	9.2 : 1	35
	8-350	4 bbl	325 @ 5100	380 @ 3200	3.8762 x 3.750	10.5 : 1	35
	8-350	4 bbl	330 @ 5100	380 @ 3200	3.8762 x 3.750	10.5 : 1	35
	8-400	2 bbl	265 @ 4600	397 @ 2400	4.1212 x 3.750	8.6 : 1	35
	8-400	4 bbl	330 @ 4800	430 @ 3300	4.1212 x 3.750	10.75 : 1	58
	8-400 HO	4 bbl	335 @ 5000	430 @ 3400	4.1212 x 3.750	10.75 : 1	58
	8-400 Ram Air	4 bbl	345 @ 5400	430 @ 3700	4.1212 x 3.750	10.75 : 1	58
	8-400 Ram Air	4 bbl	366 @ 5100	445 @ 3600	4.1212 x 3.750	10.75 : 1	58
	8-400 Ram Air IV	4 bbl	370 @ 5500	445 @ 3900	4.1212 x 3.750	10.75 : 1	58
'70	6-250	1 bbl	155 @ 4200	235 @ 1600	3.8762 x 3.530	8.5 : 1	53②
	8-350	2 bbl	255 @ 4600	355 @ 2800	3.8762 x 3.750	8.8 : 1	35
	8-400	2 bbl	265 @ 4600	397 @ 2400	4.1212 x 3.750	8.8 : 1	35
	8-400	4 bbl	330 @ 4800	430 @ 3000	4.1212 x 3.750	10.25 : 1③	35
	8-400 Ram Air	4 bbl	345 @ 5000	430 @ 3400	4.1212 x 3.750	10.5 : 1	35
	8-400	4 bbl	370 @ 5500	445 @ 3900	4.1212 x 3.750	10.5 : 1	35
'71	6-250	1 bbl	145 @ 4200	230 @ 1600	3.8750 x 3.530	8.5 : 1	38④
	8-350	2 bbl	250 @ 4400	350 @ 2400	3.8762 x 3.750	8.0 : 1	35
	8-400	2 bbl	265 @ 4400	400 @ 2400	4.1212 x 3.750	8.2 : 1	58
	8-400	4 bbl	300 @ 4800	400 @ 3600	4.1212 x 3.750	8.2 : 1	58

General Engine Specifications (cont.)

Year	Engine Cu In. Displacement	Carburetor Type	Advertised Horsepower @ rpm⑤	Advertised Torque @ rpm (ft lbs)⑤	Bore and Stroke (in.)	Advertised Compression Ratio	Oil Pressure @ 2050 rpm
'71	8-455	4 bbl	325 @ 4400	455 @ 3200	4.1522 x 4.210	8.2 : 1	35
	8-455 HO	4 bbl	335 @ 4800	480 @ 3600	4.1522 x 4.210	8.4 : 1	35
'72	6-250	1 bbl	110 @ 3800	185 @ 1600	3.8750 x 3.530	8.5 : 1	40②
	8-350	2 bbl	160 @ 4400	270 @ 2000	3.8762 x 3.750	8.2 : 1	35
	8-400	2 bbl	175 @ 4000	310 @ 2400	4.1212 x 3.750	8.2 : 1	35
	8-400	4 bbl	200 @ 4000	295 @ 2800	4.1212 x 3.750	8.2 : 1	35
	8-400	4 bbl	250 @ 4400	325 @ 3200	4.1212 x 3.750	8.2 : 1	35
	8-455	4 bbl	250 @ 3600	375 @ 2400	4.1522 x 4.210	8.2 : 1	35
	8-455	4 bbl	300 @ 4000	415 @ 3200	4.1522 x 4.210	8.4 : 1	35
'73	6-250	1 bbl	100 @ 3600	175 @ 1600	3.8750 x 3.530	8.2 : 1	50–65②
	8-350 SE	2 bbl	150 @ 4000	270 @ 2000	3.8762 x 3.750	7.6 : 1	55–60
	8-350 DE	2 bbl	175 @ 4400	280 @ 2400	3.8782 x 3.750	7.6 : 1	55–60
	8-400 SE	2 bbl	170 @ 3600	320 @ 2000	4.1212 x 3.750	8.0 : 1	55–60
	8-400 DE	2 bbl	185 @ 4000	320 @ 2400	4.1212 x 3.750	8.0 : 1	55–60
	8-400 DE	4 bbl	230 @ 4400	325 @ 3200	4.1212 x 3.750	8.0 : 1	55–60
	8-455 DE	4 bbl	250 @ 4000	370 @ 2800	4.1522 x 4.210	8.0 : 1	55–60
	8-455 SD, DE	4 bbl	310 @ 4000	390 @ 3600	4.1522 x 4.210	8.4 : 1	75–80
'74	6-250	1 bbl	100 @ 3600	175 @ 1600	3.8750 x 3.530	8.2 : 1	50–65②
	8-350 SE	2 bbl	155 @ 4000	275 @ 2400	3.8762 x 3.750	7.6 : 1	55–60
	8-350 DE	2 bbl	170 @ 4400	290 @ 2400	3.8782 x 3.750	7.6 : 1	55–60
	8-350 SE	4 bbl	170 @ 4000	280 @ 2000	3.8762 x 3.750	7.6 : 1	55–60
	8-350 DE	4 bbl	200 @ 4000	295 @ 2800	3.8762 x 3.750	7.6 : 1	55–60
	8-400 SE	2 bbl	175 @ 3600	315 @ 2000	4.1212 x 3.750	8.0 : 1	55–60

General Engine Specifications (cont.)

Year	Engine Cu In. Displacement	Carburetor Type	Advertised Horsepower @ rpm⑤	Advertised Torque @ rpm (ft lbs)⑤	Bore and Stroke (in.)	Advertised Compression Ratio	Oil Pressure @ 2050 rpm
'74	8-400 DE	2 bbl	190 @ 4000	330 @ 2400	4.1212 x 3.750	8.0 : 1	55–60
	8-400 DE	4 bbl	225 @ 4000	330 @ 2800	4.1212 x 3.750	8.0 : 1	55–60
	8-455 SE	4 bbl	215 @ 3600	355 @ 2400	4.1522 x 4.210	8.0 : 1	55–60
	8-455 DE	4 bbl	250 @ 4000	380 @ 2800	4.1522 x 4.210	8.0 : 1	55–60
	8-455 SD, DE	4 bbl	290 @ 4000	395 @ 3200	4.1522 x 4.210	8.4 : 1	75–80

① Oil pressure at 2800 rpm
② Oil pressure at 2000 rpm
③ For vehicles equipped with automatic transmissions, advertised compression ratio is 10.0 : 1
④ Oil pressure at 1500 rpm
⑤ Beginning 1972, horsepower and torque are SAE net figures. They are measured at the rear of the transmission with all accessories installed and operating. Since the figures vary when a given engine is installed in different models, some are representative, rather than exact.

HO High Output
OHC Overhead Cam
SE Single Exhaust
DE Dual Exhaust
SD Super Duty

Valve Specifications

Year	Engine No. Cyl Displacement (cu in.)	Seat Angle (deg) ⑩	Face Angle (deg) ⑪	Spring Test Pressure (lbs @ in.)	Spring Installed Height (in.)	STEM TO GUIDE Clearance (in.) Intake	STEM TO GUIDE Clearance (in.) Exhaust	STEM Diameter (in.) Intake	STEM Diameter (in.) Exhaust
'67	6-230 1 bbl	30	29	97 @ 1.58	1³⁷⁄₆₄	.0016–.0033	.0021–.0058	.3400	.3400
	6-230 4 bbl	30	29	62 @ 1.58	1³⁷⁄₆₄	.0016–.0033	.0021–.0038	.3400	.3400
	8-326	30	29	62 @ 1.59	1¹⁹⁄₃₂	.0016–.0033	.0021–.0038	.3400	.3400
	8-400 4 bbl	30	29	62 @ 1.59	1¹⁹⁄₃₂	.0016–.0033	.0021–.0038	.3400	.3400
	8-400 Ram Air	30	29	102 @ 1.59	1¹⁹⁄₃₂	.0016–.0033	.0021–.0038	.3400	.3400
'68	6-250 1 bbl	30	29	98 @ 1.63	1⅝	.0016–.0033	.0021–.0038	.3416	.3411
	6-250 4 bbl	30	29	65 @ 1.63	1⅝	.0016–.0033	.0021–.0038	.3416	.3411
	8-350	30	29	63 @ 1.58	1³⁷⁄₆₄	.0016–.0033	.0021–.0038	.3416	.3411
	8-400① 4 bbl	30	29	66 @ 1.56	1⁹⁄₁₆	.0016–.0033	.0021–.0038	.3416	.3411
	8-400 Ram Air	30	29	76 @ 1.71	1²³⁄₃₂	.0016–.0033	.0021–.0038	.3416	.3411

Valve Specifications (cont.)

Year	Engine No. Cyl Displacement (cu in.)	Seat Angle (deg) ⑩	Face Angle (deg) ⑪	Spring Test Pressure (lbs @ in.)	Spring Installed Height (in.)	STEM TO GUIDE Clearance (in.) Intake	Exhaust	STEM Diameter (in.) Intake	Exhaust
'69	6-250 1 bbl	45	44	97 @ 1.63	1⅝	.0016–.0033	.0021–.0038	.3416	.3411
	6-250 4 bbl	45	44	65 @ 1.63	1⅝	.0016–.0033	.0021–.0038	.3416	.3411
	8-350 2 bbl	45	44	63 @ 1.58	1³⁷⁄₆₄	.0016–.0033	.0021–.0038	.3416	.3411
	8-350 4 bbl	45	44	83 @ 1.59	1¹⁹⁄₃₂	.0016–.0033	.0021–.0038	.3416	.3411
	8-400 4 bbl	30	29	66 @ 1.56	1⅝	.0016–.0033	.0021–.0038	.3416	.3411
	8-400 Ram Air	30	29	83 @ 1.59	1¹⁹⁄₃₂	.0016–.0033	.0021–.0038	.3416	.3411
	8-400 Ram Air II	30	29	75 @ 1.82	1⁵³⁄₆₄	.0016–.0033	.0021–.0038	.3416	.3411
'70	6-250 1 bbl	46④	45④	60 @ 1.66	1²¹⁄₃₂	.0010–.0027	.0010–.0027	.3414	.3414
	8-350 2 bbl	45	44	63 @ 1.58	1³⁷⁄₆₄	.0016–.0033	.0021–.0038	.3416	.3416
	8-400 2 bbl	45	44	63 @ 1.58	1³⁷⁄₆₄	.0016–.0033	.0021–.0038	.3416	.3411
	8-400② 4 bbl	30	29	61 @ 1.59	1¹⁹⁄₃₂	.0016–.0033	.0021–.0038	.3416	.3411
	8-400③ 4 bbl	30	29	66 @ 1.56	1⁹⁄₁₆	.0016–.0033	.0021–.0038	.3416	.3416
	8-400 Ram Air	30	29	61 @ 1.59	1¹⁹⁄₃₂	.0016–.0033	.0021–.0038	.3416	.3411
'71	6-250 1 bbl	46④	45④	61 @ 1.66	1²¹⁄₃₂	.0010–.0027	.0010–.0027	.3414	.3414
	8-350 2 bbl	45	44	61 @ 1.57	1¹⁹⁄₃₂	.0016–.0033	.0021–.0058	.3416	.3411
	8-400②	30	29	60 @ 1.60	1¹⁹⁄₃₂	.0016–.0033	.0021–.0038	.3416	.3411
	8-400 2 bbl	45	44	61 @ 1.59	1¹⁹⁄₃₂	.0016–.0033	.0021–.0038	.3416	.3411
	8-400 4 bbl	30	29	65 @ 1.57	1⁹⁄₁₆	.0016–.0033	.0021–.0038	.3416	.3411
	8-455	30	29	65 @ 1.57	1⁹⁄₁₆	.0016–.0033	.0021–.0038	.3416	.3416
	8-455 H.O.	30	29	66 @ 1.56	1⁹⁄₁₆	.0016–.0033	.0021–.0038	.3416	.3416
'72	6-250 1 bbl	46④	45④	60 @ 1.66	1²¹⁄₃₂	.0010–.0027	.0010–.0027	.3414	.3414
	8-350 2 bbl	45	44	61 @ 1.59	1¹⁹⁄₃₂	.0016–.0033	.0021–.0038	.3414	.3411
	8-400②	30	29	60 @ 1.60	1¹⁹⁄₃₂	.0016–.0033	.0021–.0038	.3416	.3411

Valve Specifications (cont.)

Year	Engine No. Cyl Displacement (cu in.)	Seat Angle (deg) ⑩	Face Angle (deg) ⑪	Spring Test Pressure (lbs @ in.)	Spring Installed Height (in.)	STEM TO GUIDE Clearance (in.)		STEM Diameter (in.)	
						Intake	Exhaust	Intake	Exhaust
'72	8-400 2 bbl	45	44	61 @ 1.59	1¹⁹⁄₃₂	.0016–.0033	.0021–.0038	.3416	.3411
	8-400 4 bbl	30	29	65 @ 1.57	1⁹⁄₁₆	.0016–.0033	.0021–.0038	.3416	.3411
	8-455 H.O.	30	29	66 @ 1.56	1⁹⁄₁₆	.0016–.0033	.0021–.0038	.3416	.3416
'73	6-250 1 bbl	46④	45④	60 @ 1.66	1²¹⁄₃₂	.0010–.0027	.0010–.0027	.3414	.3414
	8-350 2 bbl	45	44	61 @ 1.59	1¹⁹⁄₃₂	.0016–.0033	.0021–.0038	.3414	.3411
	8-400②	30	29	60 @ 1.60	1¹⁹⁄₃₂	.0016–.0033	.0021–.0038	.3416	.3411
	8-400 2 bbl	45	44	61 @ 1.59	1¹⁹⁄₃₂	.0016–.0033	.0021–.0038	.3416	.3411
	8-400 4 bbl	30	29	65 @ 1.57⑦	1⁹⁄₁₆	.0016–.0033	.0021–.0038	.3416	.3411
	8-455	30	29	66 @ 1.56⑧	1⁹⁄₁₆	.0016–.0033	.0021–.0038	.3416	.3411⑨
'74	6-250 1 bbl	46④	45④	60 @ 1.66	1²¹⁄₃₂	.0010–.0027	.0010–.0027	.3414	.3414
	8-350 2 bbl	45	44	61 @ 1.59	1¹⁹⁄₃₂	.0016–.0033	.0021–.0038	.3414	.3411
	8-400②	30	29	60 @ 1.60	1¹⁹⁄₃₂	.0016–.0033	.0021–.0038	.3416	.3411
	8-400 2 bbl	45	44	61 @ 1.59	1¹⁹⁄₃₂	.0016–.0033	.0021–.0038	.3416	.3411
	8-400 4 bbl	30	29	65 @ 1.57⑦	1⁹⁄₁₆	.0016–.0033	.0021–.0038	.3416	.3411
	8-455	30	29	66 @ 1.56⑧	1⁹⁄₁₆	.0016–.0033	.0021–.0038	.3416	.3411⑨

① Applies to H.O. also
② Manual transmission with 400 cu in. engine
③ Automatic transmission with 400 cu in. engine
④ Exhaust valve seat and face angles are the same as intake valve seat and face angles
⑦ 59 @ 1.50 with manual transmission
⑧ 70 @ 1.82 for 455 S.D. engine
⑨ .3416 in. for 455 S.D. engine
⑩ Intake valve seat angles are shown. All exhaust valve seat angles are 45° unless otherwise indicated.
⑪ Intake valve face angles are shown. All exhaust valve face angles are 44° unless otherwise indicated.

Crankshaft and Connecting Rod Specifications

All measurements are given in inches

| Year | Engine Displacement (cu in.) | CRANKSHAFT | | | | CONNECTING ROD | | |
		Main Brg. Journal Dia	Main Brg. Oil Clearance	Shaft End-Play	Thrust on No.	Journal Diameter	Oil Clearance	Side Clearance
'67	6	2.30	.0003–.0019	.002–.006	7	2.000	.0007–.0027②	.0085–.0135
	8-326	3.00	.0002–.0017	.0035–.0085	4	2.250	.0005–.0025	.006–.011①
	8-400	3.00	.0002–.0017	.0035–.0085	4	2.250	.0005–.0026	.006–.011①
'68	6	2.30	.0003–.0019	.002–.006	7	2.000	.0007–.0027②	.0085–.0135
	8-350	3.00	.0002–.0017	.0035–.0085	4	2.250	.0005–.0025	.006–.011①
	8-400	3.00	.0002–.0017	.0035–.0085	4	2.250	.0005–.0026	.006–.011①
'69	6	2.30	.0003–.0019	.002–.006	7	2.000	.0007–.0027②	.0085–.0135
	8-350	3.00	.0002–.0017③	.0035–.0085	4	2.250	.0005–.0025	.006–.011①
	8-400	3.00	.0002–.0017③	.0035–.0085	4	2.250	.0005–.0026④	.006–.011①
'70	6	2.30	.0003–.0029	.002–.006	7	2.000	.0007–.0027	.009–.013
	8-350	3.00	.0002–.0017	.0035–.0085	4	2.250	.0005–.0025	.012–.017①
	8-400	3.00	.0002–.0017⑤	.0035–.0085	4	2.250	.0005–.0026④	.012–.017①
	8-455	3.25	.0005–.0021	.0035–.0085	4	2.250	.0010–.0031	.012–.017①
'71–'74	6	2.30	.0003–.0029	.002–.006	7	2.000	.0007–.0027	.009–.014⑦
	8-350	3.00	.0002–.0017	.003–.009	4	2.250	.0005–.0025	.012–.017①
	8-400	3.00	.0002–.0017	.003–.009	4	2.250	.0005–.0026	.012–.017①
	8-455	3.25	⑥ ⑧	.003–.009	4	2.250	.0010–.0031⑨	.012–.017①⑩

① Total for 2 connecting rods
② .0007–.0028 on 6 Cyl 4-BBL engine option
③ .0012–.0028 on Ram Air IV engine option
④ .0015–.0031 on Ram Air IV engine option
⑤ No.'s 1, 2, 3, 4 on Ram Air IV option—.0007–.0023
    No.'s 1, 2, 3, 4 on Ram Air IV option—.0012–.0028
    No. 5 on Ram Air IV option—.0007–.0022

⑥ w/small valve—.0003–.0019
    w/large valve—.0005–.0021
⑦ .007–.016 in 1973–74
⑧ 1973–74—.0005–.0021 (455); .0010–.0026 (455 S.D.)
⑨ .0015–.0031 in 455 S.D. engine
⑩ .019–.027 in 455 S.D. engine

Torque Specifications
All readings in ft lbs

Year	Engine Type	Cylinder Head Bolts	Rod Bearing Bolts	Main Bearing Bolts	Crankshaft Pulley Bolt	Flywheel to Crankshaft Bolts	MANIFOLD	
							Intake	Exhaust
'67–'69	6	85–100	30–35	60–70	Pressed on	60–70	25–40	15–25
	8	85–100	40–46	90–110③	130–190	85–100	20–35	30–45
'70–'74	6	95	35	65	Pressed on	60	25–30①	25
	8	95	43②	90–110	160	95	40	30

① End bolts 15–20 ft lbs
② 63 ft lbs on 455 S D engine
③ Rear main—120 ft lbs

Ring Gap

Year①	Engine	Compression	
		Top	Bottom
'67–'69	6-230, 250	.005–.025	.005–.025
'67–'69	All 8 cylinders	.010–.030	.010–.030
'70–'74	8-350, 400	.009–.029	.005–.025
'70–'74	8-455	.011–.031	.005–.025
'70–'74	6-250	.010–.020	.010–.020

① In '67–'74 models, the oil control for all engines is .015–.005 in.

Ring Side Clearance

Year	Engine	Compression		Oil Control
		Top	Bottom	
'67–'69	6-230, 250	.0015–.0050	.0015–.0050	.0015–.0050
'70–'74	6-250	.0012–.0027	.0012–.0032	.0001–.0050
'67–'74	8-350, 400, 455	.0015–.0050	.0015–.0050	.0015–.0050

Inner Spring Test Pressure
(lbs @ in.)

Year	Engine No. Cyl Displacement (cu in.)	Test Pressure
'67	6-230 4 bbl	31 @ 1.56
	8-326 2 bbl	31 @ 1.57
	8-326 4 bbl	31 @ 1.57
	8-440 4 bbl	31 @ 1.57①
'68	6-250 4 bbl	34 @ 1.59
	8-350	35 @ 1.54
	8-400 4 bbl	38 @ 1.52②
	8-400 Ram Air	43 @ 1.64
'69	6-250 4 bbl	34 @ 1.59
	8-350 2 bbl	35 @ 1.54
	8-350 4 bbl	45 @ 1.52
	8-400 4 bbl	38 @ 1.32
	8-400 Ram Air II	45 @ 1.52③
'70	8-350 2 bbl	35 @ 1.54
	8-400 2 bbl	35 @ 1.54
	8-400 4 bbl	57 @ 1.52④
	8-400 4 bbl	45 @ 1.52⑤
	8-400 Ram Air	57 @ 1.52
'71	8-350 2 bbl	33 @ 1.55
	8-400	56 @ 1.53④
	8-400 2 bbl	33 @ 1.55
	8-400 4 bbl	36 @ 1.53
	8-455	37 @ 1.53
	8-455 H.O.	38 @ 1.52

Inner Spring Test Pressure
(lbs @ in.)

Year	Engine No. Cyl Displacement (cu in.)	Test Pressure
'72	8-400	56 @ 1.53④
	8-400 2 bbl	33 @ 1.55
	8-400 4 bbl	36 @ 1.53
	8-455 H.O.	38 @ 1.52
'73	8-350	33 @ 1.55
	8-400	56 @ 1.53④
	8-400 2 bbl	33 @ 1.55
	8-400 4 bbl	36 @ 1.53
	8-455	36 @ 1.53⑥
'74	8-350	33 @ 1.55
	8-400	56 @ 1.53④
	8-400 2 bbl	33 @ 1.55
	8-400 4 bbl	36 @ 1.53
	8-455	36 @ 1.53⑥

① With manual transmission: 50 @ 1.57
② With manual transmission: 57 @ 1.52
③ With manual transmission: 38 @ 1.52
④ 400 cu in. engine with manual transmission
⑤ 400 cu in. engine with automatic transmission
⑥ 40 @ 1.75 for 455 S.D.

Piston Clearance

Year	Engine	Pitson-to-Bore Clearance (in.)
'67	6-230 OHC	.0022–.0028
	8-326, 400	.0022–.0028
'68	6-250 OHC	.0022–.0028
	8-350, 400	.0025–.0031
'69	6-250 OHC	.0022–.0028
	8-350, 400	.0025–.0031
	8-400 Ram Air	.0055–.0061
'70	6-250	.0005–.0015
	8-350,400	.0025–.0033
	8-400 Ram Air	.0055–.0061
'71	6-250	.0005–.0015
	8-350,400	.0025–.0033
'72	6-250	.0005–.0015
	8-350, 400, 455	.0025–.0033
'73–'74	6-250	.0005–.0015
	8-350, 400	.0029–.0037
	8-455	.0025–.0033
	8-455 S D	.0060–.0068

ENGINE REMOVAL AND INSTALLATION

1. Disconnect the battery.
2. Drain the cooling system.
3. Scribe alignment marks on the hood and remove the hood from the hinges.
4. Disconnect the engine wiring harness and ground straps, alternator wires, and the engine temperature and oil pressure sending unit wires.
5. Remove the air cleaner and fan shield or shroud.
6. Disconnect the radiator and heater hoses.
7. If the car is equipped with a manual transmission, remove the radiator.
8. Remove the fan and fan pulley.
NOTE: *If equipped with power steering and/or air conditioning, disconnect and swing the pump/compressor aside without disconnecting hoses.*

9. Disconnect the accelerator linkage and support bracket.
10. Disconnect the automatic transmission vacuum modulator line and power brake vacuum line at the carburetor.
NOTE: *On models up to 1969 with air conditioning, remove the wiper motor.*
11. Jack up the front of the car and drain the engine oil.
12. Disconnect the fuel lines at the pump.
13. Disconnect the exhaust pipes.
14. Disconnect the starter wires and remove the starter.
15. If equipped with an automatic transmission, remove the converter cover and crank the engine over and remove each of the 3 converter retaining bolts, then slide the converter to the rear.
16. If equipped with a manual transmission, disconnect the clutch linkage and remove the clutch cross-shaft.

17. Remove the lower flywheel cover. Remove the 4 lower bellhousing bolts (two per side).

18. Disconnect the transmission filler tube support (automatic) and the starter wire shield from cylinder heads.

19. Remove the two front motor mount-to-frame bracket bolts.

20. Lower the car to the floor and then, using a jack and a wood block, support the transmission.

21. Remove the two remaining bellhousing bolts.

22. Slightly raise the transmission, using the jack and wood block, then, using a chain hoist, remove the engine.

23. To install the engine, reverse the removal procedure. Install the two upper bellhousing bolts first (with the jack still under the transmission).

NOTE: *Do not lower the engine completely until the jack and wood block are removed.*

CYLINDER HEAD

Removal and Installation

OHC Six-Cylinder 1967–69

1. Remove the air cleaner and drain the cooling system. Remove the thermostat housing with the hose attached, and position it out of the way.

2. Disconnect the accelerator pedal cable and the fuel and vacuum lines from the carburetor.

3. Disconnect the exhaust pipe from the carburetor.

4. Disconnect the exhaust pipe from the manifold then remove the manifold and carburetor as an assembly.

5. Loosen the accessory drive mounting bolts to provide slack in the timing belt.

6. Remove the timing belt rear lower cover, top front cover, and the support bracket for the upper front cover. Align

OHC six-cylinder head tightening sequence

the timing marks (be sure that you use the correct illustration). Remove the timing belt.

7. Disconnect the spark plug wires.

8. Remove the rocker arms and the valve lash adjusters and tag them so that they can be returned to exactly the same location. Rocker arms are retained on the adjusters by spring clips.

9. Remove the cylinder head bolts, the cylinder head, and its gasket. The head should be placed on two blocks of wood to prevent any damage.

10. Before installing the cylinder head, the gasket surfaces on the head and on the block must be clean.

11. Apply sealer and place a new gasket over the dowel pins on the block.

12. Carefully lower the head into place on the block.

13. Install the bolts.

NOTE: *The head bolts are of two different lengths and must be placed in the proper holes. When correctly installed, they will all rise an equal length from the head. Sealer must not be used on head bolts.*

14. The head bolts should be tightened in the proper sequence a little at a time with a torque wrench. Tighten the center bolts first and then the end bolts. All bolts should be tightened to 95 ft lbs. To complete the installation, reverse the applicable steps of the removal procedures. Adjust the timing belt as outlined later in this Chapter.

OHV Six-Cylinder 1970–74

1. Remove the air cleaner and drain the cooling system.

2. Disconnect the accelerator rod from its connection on the manifold and detach the fuel and vacuum lines from the carburetor.

3. Disconnect the exhaust pipe from the manifold and then remove the manifolds and carburetor as an assembly.

4. Disconnect the wiring harness from the temperature sending unit and the coil.

5. Disconnect the radiator hose from the water outlet and detach the battery ground strap from the head.

6. Remove the spark plugs and the coil.

7. Remove the valve cover, loosen

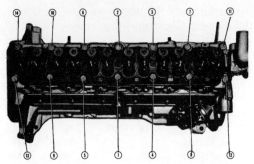

OHV six-cylinder head tightening sequence

the rocker arm nuts and remove the pushrods.

8. Remove the cylinder head bolts and then remove the head and its gasket. To prevent any damage, place the head on two blocks of wood.

9. Install a new head gasket over the dowel pins in the block.

10. Carefully lower the head into position over the dowel pins.

11. Coat the head bolt threads with a sealing compound and install them.

12. Using a torque wrench, tighten the bolts a little at a time. The bolts should be tightened in the proper sequence. Their final torque must be 95 ft lbs.

13. Install the pushrods through the head and seat them into the lifters.

14. Install the rocker arms, the balls and nuts, and tighten the nuts until pushrod play is eliminated.

15. Connect the radiator hose.

16. Install the coil, connect the temperature sending unit, and attach the battery ground cable to the head.

17. Clean the manifold gasket surfaces and install the manifold and carburetor using a new gasket. Torque the bolts as shown in the picture.

18. Connect the throttle linkage and the fuel and vacuum lines.

19. Fill the cooling system.

20. Position the rocker arms and torque the rocker arm nuts to 20 ft lbs and further tighten until any valve train play is removed. Adjust the valve lash as outlined in Chapter 2.

21. Install the spark plugs.

22. Install the valve cover being careful not to overtighten the bolts.

23. Install the spark plug wires and the air cleaner.

V8

NOTE: *Drain the cooling system including the block.*

1. Remove the intake manifold, the valley cover, and the valve covers.

2. Loosen the rocker arm retaining nuts and pivot the rockers off the pushrods.

3. Remove the pushrods and tag them as to location so that they may be returned to their same positions.

NOTE: *On 1967–70 air conditioned models, remove the compressor hold-down bolts and move the compressor aside without disconnecting the hoses. The right motor mount-to-frame bolt must be removed and the engine jacked up about 2 in. to gain access to the right rear rocker arm cover bolt and cylinder head bolt.*

4. Remove the exhaust pipe flange bolts, except when removing the left head on SD455s. On this model, it is necessary to remove the exhaust manifold retaining nuts and drop the manifold. Remove the inner side of the carburetor heat stove from the two center cylinder head bolts.

5. Remove the battery ground strap and the engine ground strap from the left head. Remove the engine ground strap and the automatic transmission oil filler tube bracket from the right head.

6. Remove the bolts and lift off the head with the exhaust manifold attached. Be careful not to damage the cylinder head surface when maneuvering it out around the power steering and brake equipment.

7. Check head surface for straightness, then place a new head gasket on the block.

NOTE: *On 1968–70 air conditioned models, install the right rear head bolt into the head before placing the head on the block. Bolts are of three different lengths on V8s. When the bolts are properly installed, they will project an equal distance from the head.*

8. Install all bolts and tighten evenly to the specified torque. Tighten the bolts in 3 stages.

9. Install the pushrods in their original positions.

10. Position the rocker arms over the

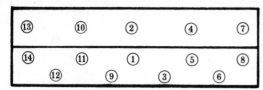

V8 cylinder head tightening sequence

pushrods and tighten the ball retaining nuts to 20 ft lbs. See below for the adjustment procedure.

11. Replace the rocker arm cover.

12. Replace the valley cover.

13. Replace the ground straps, oil filler tube bracket, intake manifold, and right motor mount bolts (on A/C models.)

14. Install the exhaust pipe flange nuts. On the 455 S.D. engine, install the left head exhaust manifold, with a new gasket.

NOTE: *Most left and right cylinder heads are interchangeable. Large and small-valve heads should not be used on the same engine.*

Rocker Arm Removal and Installation

1970–74 6 Cylinder and All V8s

1. Remove the valve covers.

2. Remove the rocker arm nut and rocker arm ball.

3. Lift the rocker arm off the rocker arm stud. Always keep the rocker arm assemblies in order and assemble them on the same stud.

4. Remove the pushrod from its bore. Make sure that the rods are returned to their original bores, with the same end in the block.

5. Reverse the removal procedure to install the rocker arms and adjust the valve on any rocker arm that was removed before installing the valve cover.

Rocker Arm Stud Removal and Installation

1970-74 OHV 6 Cylinder

1. Remove the rocker cover and rocker arm.

2. File two slots, $3/32-1/8$ in. deep, on opposite sides of the stud. The bottom of the slots should be $1/2$ in. from the top of the stud hole.

2. Place a spacer washer (or tool No. J-

6392-3) over the stud, then position a stud remover (or tool J-6329-1 on the stud and tighten it securely.

4. Place a spacer (a socket or tool No. J-6392-2) over the stud remover, then thread a $7/8$ in. nut onto the stud remover and turn it in until the stud pulls free from the head.

5. If an oversize stud is to be used (0.003 and 0.013 in. oversize studs are available), ream the stud hole to size.

6. To install, coat the press fit area of the stud with axle lube, then press or hammer it into place.

NOTE: *The factory recommends that tool No. J-6880 be used for this job. This tool is simply a sleeve that is held in place with an allen screw—it protects the threads from damage. A similar homemade tool will work if care is exercised. Do not hammer directly on the stud, because it is hardened and will fracture if subjected to shock.*

1967–74 V8

NOTE: *This procedure can be used only on engines with pressed-in rocker studs. Special high-performance engines have screwed-in rocker studs which are easily identified by their hex head lower portion. Another common aftermarket, stud-securing procedure on standard engines is "pinning" pressed-in studs by drilling through the stud boss and stud and inserting an interference-fit roll pin. Make sure that any such pins are removed before attempting the following procedure.*

1. Disconnect the battery and drain the cooling system.

2. Remove the rocker cover.

3. Pack oily rags around the stud holes and engine openings, to catch any metal chips.

4. Remove the rocker arm and pushrod, then file two slots $3/32-1/8$ in. deep on opposite sides of the stud. The top of the slots should be $1/4-3/8$ in. below thread travel.

5. Place a spacer washer (or tool No. J-8934-3) over the stud, then position a stud remover (or tool No. J-8934-1) on the stud and tighten the allen screws.

6. Place a spacer (a socket or tool No. J-8934-2) over the remover, then thread a $7/8$ in. nut on the stud remover and turn it

in until the stud pulls out from the head.

7. If an oversize stud is to be used (0.003 in. oversize studs are available), ream the stud hole to the proper size, then clean any chips from the area.

8. To install, refer to Step 6 of the OHV 6 cylinder stud replacement procedure, substituting factory tool No. J-23342 for J-6880.

NOTE: *Valve adjustment for Ram Air IV engines is covered in Chapter 2.*

SCREW-IN ROCKER STUDS

1. Remove the rocker cover.
2. Remove the rocker arm and nut.
3. Remove the stud, using a deep well socket.
4. Install the new stud and tighten it to 50 ft lbs.

Valve Guides

Pontiac engines have integral valve guides. Pontiac offers valves with oversize stems for worn guides (0.001, 0.003 and 0.005 in. being available for most engines). To fit these, enlarge the valve guide bores with valve guide reamers to an oversize that cleans up the wear. If a large oversize is required, it is best to approach that size in stages by using a series of reamers of increasing diameter. This helps to maintain the concentricity of the guide bores with the valve seats. The correct valve stem-to-guide clearance is given in the "Valve Specifications" table at the beginning of this Section. As an alternate procedure, some automotive machine shops can fit replacement guides that use standard stem valves or knurl the guides if wear permits. Valve guide procedures are provided in the "Engine Rebuilding" Section at the end of this Chapter.

Valve Adjuster and Rocker Arm Service

OHC 6 CYLINDER 1967–69

This engine is equipped with hydraulic valve lash adjusters. These adjusters are located in the cylinder head and serve as a fulcrum for the rocker arms, and locate the rocker arms accurately with the camshaft lobes. This lash adjuster is similar to the lifter used in a conventional pushrod engine. However, the lash adjuster remains stationary to main-

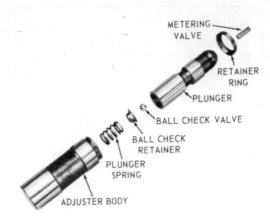

OHC six-cylinder valve lash adjuster

tain adjustment at all times. The rocker arm is attached to the adjuster with a spring clip. These adjusters are serviced in the same manner as conventional hydraulic tappets.

1. Remove the rocker cover assembly.
2. Remove the rocker arm and hydraulic lash adjuster assemblies, keeping them in proper order for correct installation in their original positions.
3. If the lash adjuster sticks in its bore, proceed as follows:
   a. Remove the rocker arm.
   b. Fill the vent hole adjacent to the lifter with SAE 30 oil.
   c. Insert a 4 in. length of $3/16$ in. diameter rod into the vent hole and strike the end of the rod sharply with a hammer.
NOTE: *The hydraulic pressure generated in this operation should be sufficient to dislodge even the most stubborn adjuster.*
4. To install, reverse the removal procedure, with the exception of Step 3.

Hydraulic Valve Lifter Disassembly

1970–74 6 CYLINDER AND ALL V8s

Lifters are disassembled for cleaning only. Lifters should slide easily from their bores. If not, use a magnet to raise the lifter in its bore and then grasp and remove it with a pair of pliers. Be careful not to gouge the lifter jacket.

1. Grasp the lockring with needlenose pliers and remove it. (Depress the plunger to gain clearance).
2. Remove the pushrod cup, metering

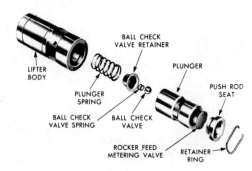

OHV six-cylinder hydraulic lifter

valve disc, and upper metering disc (if any). Do not bend the metering disc.

3. Remove the plunger assembly and plunger spring.

4. Remove the spring, check valve retainer, and check valve from the plunger.

5. Clean all parts in solvent (lacquer thinner is good) and reassemble.

NOTE: *Internal parts should not be interchanged between lifters.*

Valve Adjustment

1970–74 6 Cylinder and All V8s

The purpose of the hydraulic valve lifter is to maintain zero clearance in the valve train. It does this by expanding to take up additional clearance created as the lifter moves onto the base circle of its camshaft lobe. To perform properly, the lifter must be adjusted halfway between its fully-extended position and its collapsed position. If the lifter is adjusted too loosely, the valve will not open fully; if adjusted too tightly, any number of major mechanical failures may result.

When a rocker arm is loosened or removed, the lifter will expand to its fully-extended position. Upon reassembly, it is necessary to be sure that the lifter is on its camshaft lobe base circle before adjusting the lifter. This is the purpose of the preliminary valve adjustment. Perform the final valve adjustment after the engine is running.

Preliminary Valve Adjustment

1. Rotate the crankshaft until the No. 1 piston is at TDC on the compression stroke and the distributor rotor points to the No. 1 spark plug wire cap tower. The timing mark should be aligned with zero (0°) on the timing cover.

2. Tighten the adjusting nut until the play just disappears. Adjust both valves. On Ram Air and Super Duty engines, adjust the valves to obtain a 0.008 in. clearance between the rocker arms and valve stems, then tighten the adjusting nut an additional ⅛ turn and tighten the locknut.

3. On V8s, rotate the crankshaft 90°, in the normal direction of rotation, to bring the next piston in the firing order to TDC on the compression stroke. Repeat Step 2 until all of the valves are done. On six-cylinder engines, bring each cylinder to TDC on its compression stroke and repeat Step 2.

Final Valve Adjustment

NOTE: *On Ram Air and Super Duty engines, refer to the valve "Lash Adjustment" procedure in Chapter 2 for the final adjustment.*

1. Start the engine and retighten the rocker arm on any valve that is clattering. Tighten until the noise disappears.

2. Allow the engine to run until the normal operating temperature is reached, then loosen each rocker arm adjusting nut until clattering begins. Retighten the nut until the noise disappears. On all V8s tighten the nut, very slowly, to 20 ft lbs. On the 1970–72 six-cylinder engines, very slowly tighten the nut ½–1 revolution further.

NOTE: *The purpose of tightening the adjusting nut slowly is to give the lifter time to adjust its height.*

Overhaul

A general discussion of cylinder head overhaul, including checking, repair, and refinishing, may be found in the "Engine Rebuilding" Section at the end of this Chapter.

INTAKE MANIFOLD

Removal and Installation

V8

1. Drain the cooling system.

2. Remove the air cleaner assembly.

3. Remove the water outlet fitting allowing the radiator hose to remain attached.

4. As necessary, disconnect the heater hose from its fitting.

5. Disconnect the wire from the temperature gauge sending unit.

6. Remove the spark plug wire bracket.

7. If equipped with power brakes, remove the vacuum pipe from the carburetor.

8. Disconnect the fuel line and the vacuum hoses.

9. Disconnect the crankcase vent hose from the manifold.

10. Disconnect the throttle linkage from the carburetor.

11. Remove the screws from the throttle control bracket.

12. Remove the manifold bolts and lift off the manifold.

NOTE: *It may be necessary to remove the distributor for clearance.*

13. Install new gaskets on the heads keeping them in position with plastic gasket retainers.

14. Lower the intake manifold onto the engine and the install the O-ring seal.

15. Loosely install the bolts and nuts.

16. Install the throttle control bracket assembly.

17. Install a new O-ring seal (use the old one if undamaged) between the timing chain cover and the intake manifold and tighten the bolt to 15 ft lbs.

18. Tighten all bolts and nuts evenly to 40 ft lbs, starting from the center and working out.

19. To complete the installation, reverse the removal procedures.

COMBINATION MANIFOLD

Removal and Installation

SIX-CYLINDER

1. Remove the air cleaner.

2. Disconnect the throttle linkage or cable and the return spring.

3. Disconnect the fuel and vacuum lines and the choke coil rod, if so equipped.

4. If the manifold is to be replaced, remove the carburetor and, if so equipped, the heat shield.

5. Disconnect the exhaust pipe from the manifold.

6. Remove the manifold bolts and then the manifolds as an assembly.

7. Clean the mating surfaces of the manifold.

8. To separate the manifolds, remove

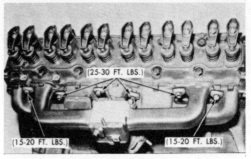

Six-cylinder combination manifold—torque sequence

the single bolt and two nuts at the center. Use a new gasket when reassembling. Tighten the fasteners to 25 ft lbs.

9. Install the manifold on the cylinder head with new gaskets.

10. Hold the manifold in place and install the clamp and bolts.

11. Tighten the center clamp bolts to 30 ft lbs and the end bolts to 20 ft lbs on 1970–74 models; 20 ft lbs for all bolts on the 1967–69 OHC 6.

12. Connect the exhaust pipe to the manifold using a new packing seal.

13. To complete the installation, reverse the remaining removal steps.

EXHAUST MANIFOLD

Removal and Installation

V8

1. Remove the alternator and bracket as an assembly.

2. Disconnect the exhaust pipe from the manifold.

3. Remove the carburetor air preheater shroud from the manifold.

4. Straighten the tabs on the manifold bolt locks, remove the bolts and the manifold.

5. To install, clean the gasket surfaces and position the manifold on the engine, holding it in place with the two end bolts.

6. Insert the gasket between the manifold and the head.

7. Install the remaining bolts with new bolt locks and torque them evenly to 30 ft lbs. Bolt locks go only on the front and rear bolts.

8. Install the carburetor air preheater shroud.

9. Connect the exhaust pipe to the manifold and tighten to 30 ft lbs.

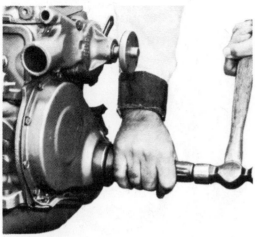

Timing cover seal installation

Apply sealer to oil pan—timing cover mating surfaces

TIMING GEAR COVER AND OIL SEAL

Replacement

OHV SIX-CYLINDER 1970–74

1. Drain the cooling system and disconnect the radiator hoses at the radiator.

2. Remove the fan and the water pump pulley.

3. Remove the radiator.

4. Using a puller, remove the harmonic balancer.

5. Loosen the oil pan bolts and allow the pan to rest against the front crossmember.

6. Remove the timing gear cover bolts and remove the cover and its gasket.

7. Using a screwdriver, remove the oil seal.

NOTE: *The seal can be replaced with the cover installed.*

8. Install the new seal with the lip toward the inside of the cover. Drive it into place using a proper seal installer or an old wheel bearing outer race.

9. Inspect the oil nozzle for any damage and replace as necessary; clean all gasket surfaces.

10. Install the cover and its gasket making sure that the cover is properly centered on the crankshaft end.

11. Tighten the cover bolts to 7 ft lbs.

V8

1. Drain the radiator and the block.

2. Remove the fan belt and the accessory belt.

3. Remove the fan and the pulley from the water pump.

4. As necessary, remove the water pump.

5. Disconnect the lower radiator hose.

6. Remove the fuel pump.

NOTE: *It is not necessary to remove the fuel pump if only the seal is to be replaced.*

7. Remove the harmonic balancer.

NOTE: *Do not pry on the rubber mounted balancers. The seal can be removed at this time with a screwdriver. Install the new seal with the lip inward.*

8. Remove the cover bolts and remove the cover.

9. Remove the O-ring from its recess in the intake manifold and then clean all gasket surfaces.

10. If damaged, replace the front oil pan gasket using gasket cement.

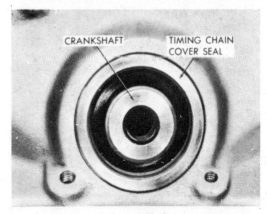

CRANKSHAFT   TIMING CHAIN COVER SEAL

V8 timing cover seal—installed positioning

11. To replace the seal, pry it out of the cover with a screwdriver. Install the new seal with the lip inward.

12. To install, reverse the removal procedure, making sure that all gaskets are replaced. Tighten the 4 oil pan bolts to 12 ft lbs, the harmonic balancer bolt to 160 ft lbs and the fan pulley bolts to 20 ft lbs.

TIMING BELT, CRANKSHAFT SPROCKET, OR LOWER CRANKCASE COVER SEAL

Removal and Installation

OHC 6 CYLINDER 1967–69

Radiator removal, at this point, is a distinct advantage for this operation.

1. Remove the upper front timing cover.

2. Align the timing marks.

NOTE: *There are three sets of timing marks that must be aligned. One set is located on the harmonic balancer and the lower front belt cover. A second set is located on the accessory drive housing pulley and the lower front belt cover. The third set is the camshaft pulley set.*

The mark on the harmonic balancer must be aligned with zero (0°) on the cover with the No. 1 cylinder on TDC of the compression stroke. The mark on the drive pulley should point toward the water pump and align with its mark on the belt cover. The mark on the camshaft pulley, on 1967–68 models, aligns with a mark on the cover behind the pulley. In 1969, the camshaft pulley mark aligns with a mark on a bolt head located directly below the camshaft pulley.

1967–68 OHC six timing mark alignment

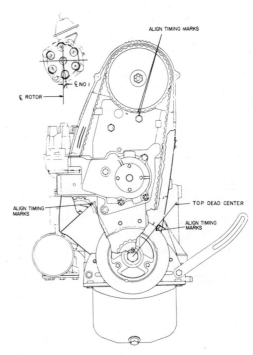

1969 OHC six timing mark alignment

All three sets of marks must be aligned at the same time when replacing the camshaft drive belt.

3. Remove the fan and water pump pulley.

OHC six timing cover

4. Remove the harmonic balancer.

5. Remove the timing belt lower front cover.

6. Loosen the accessory drive mounting bolts to provide slack in the timing belt.

7. Remove the timing belt.

8. Remove the crankshaft timing belt flange and sprocket.

9. Carefully remove the seal from the crankcase cover.

10. Install a new seal, with the lip of the seal inward.

11. Replace the crankshaft timing belt sprocket and flange.

12. Align the timing marks and replace the timing belt.

13. Replace the timing belt lower cover and harmonic balancer.

14. Adjust the timing belt tension.

15. Replace the water pump pulley and fan.

16. Replace the timing belt upper front cover.

FRONT CRANKCASE COVER AND GASKET

Removal and Installation

OHC 6 CYLINDER 1967–69

1. Remove the timing belt sprocket, as described above.

2. Remove the 4 front oil pan-to-crankcase cover retaining bolts.

3. Loosen the remaining oil pan bolts, as necessary, to provide clearance between the crankcase cover and oil pan.

4. Remove the 5 front crankcase cover attaching bolts.

5. Remove the front crankcase cover and gasket, clean off the old gasket.

6. Inspect the cover seal for wear or distortion.

7. Using new gasket installed over dowels and, as necessary, new seal, reverse removal procedures, torque oil pan and crankcase cover bolts to 10–15 ft lbs.

TIMING BELT

Adjustment

OHC 6 CYLINDER 1967–69

NOTE: *Pontiac special tools, numbers J-22232-1 and J-22232-2, or commercial substitutes, are necessary for this adjustment.*

1. Remove the timing belt top front cover.

2. Using the J-22232-2 calibration bar, set the pointer of the timing belt tension fixture J-22232-1 to zero.

NOTE: *This calibration must be performed before each use of J-22232 fixture to insure an accurate timing belt adjustment.*

3. Remove the camshaft sprocket-to-camshaft bolt and install J-22232-1 (tension fixture) on the belt with the roller on the outside (smooth) surface of the belt. Thread the fixture mounting bolt into the

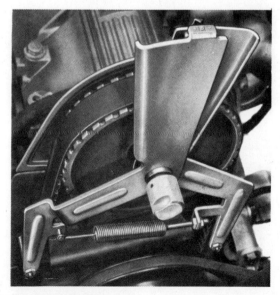

OHC six timing belt tension adjustment

camshaft sprocket bolt location, finger-tight.

4. Squeeze the indicator end (upper) of fixture and quickly release so that the fixture assumes a released or relaxed position.

5. With J-22232-1 installed, as above, adjust the accessory drive housing up or down, as required, to obtain a tension adjustment indicator reading centered in the green range, with the drive housing mounting bolts torqued to 15 ± 3 ft lbs.

6. Remove the tension fixture and install the sprocket retaining bolt, making sure that the bolt threads and washers are free of dirt.

Accessory drive mounting

ASSEMBLY, OIL PUMP, DISTRIBUTOR AND FUEL PUMP—OHC 6 CYLINDER

This housing is unique to the OHC 6 and consists of the oil pump, distributor and the fuel pump. The oil filter is also attached to this housing. The housing carries the drive sprocket for the above units and is used as a tensioner for the timing belt.

Oil Pressure Regulator Removal and Installation

1. Remove the cap washer and spring from the housing assembly.

2. Using a magnet, remove the valve from the housing assembly.

3. Install the valve on the spring and install as an assembly.

4. Install the cap washer.

Oil Pump Removal and Installation

1. Remove the oil pump cover and gasket.

2. Remove the drive gear and driven gear.

3. Install the gears.

4. Replace the cover using a new gas-

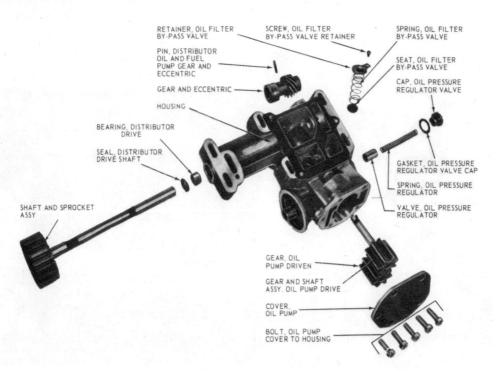

Exploded view of accessory drive housing

ket. Torque the attaching bolts to 20 ft lbs.

Housing Assembly Removal and Installation

1. Remove the timing belt top front cover.
2. Align the timing marks.
3. Loosen the six housing assembly retaining bolts from the cylinder block.
4. Remove the timing belt from camshaft sprocket and distributor drive.
5. Disconnect the fuel lines from the fuel pump.
6. Remove the cap, vacuum lines and wires from the distributor.
7. Remove the housing by removing the six retaining bolts.
8. Using a new gasket, loosely install the housing assembly to the cylinder block with the six retaining bolts.
9. Align the timing marks and install the timing belt.
10. Connect the fuel lines to the fuel pump.
11. Replace the distributor cap, vacuum lines and wires.
12. Adjust the timing belt tension. See "Timing Belt Adjustment."
13. Replace the timing belt top front cover.

CAMSHAFT

Removal and Installation

OHC 6 Cylinder

1. Remove the camshaft sprocket and seal.
2. Remove the rocker cover assembly.
3. Using an adapter (Pontiac special tool No. J-22284 or a substitute) and a slide hammer, drive the camshaft to the rear. Be careful that the bearing surfaces are not damaged during this operation.

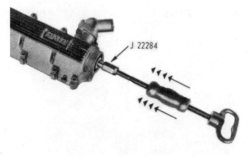

Overhead camshaft removal

4. Disconnect the slide hammer and remove the camshaft from the rear of the rocker cover.
5. Remove the thrust washer, retaining washer, and bolt from the rear of the camshaft.
6. Clean and inspect all parts for wear or damage, then inspect the bearing surfaces for wear or scoring.
7. Clean the camshaft oil passages.
8. To install, reverse the removal procedure making sure that the thrust washer is installed as illustrated. Tighten the retaining bolt to 40 ft lbs.

INDEX THRUST WASHER TANG IN HOLE IN ROCKER ARM COVER

9. Check the camshaft end-play, using a dial indicator on the front sprocket; end-play should be 0.003–0.009 in. and is controlled by the camshaft bore plug.

NOTE: *Lubricate the camshaft lobes and rockers with special break-in lubricant or gear oil. Tighten the locker cover bolts and nuts to 15 ft lbs from the center outward.*

OHV 6 Cylinder 1970–74

1. Drain the cooling system.
2. Remove the radiator, fan, and water pump pulley.
3. Remove the grille.
4. Remove the valve cover and gasket. Loosen the rocker arm nuts and move the rocker arms out of the way.
5. Remove the pushrods.
6. Remove the distributor, fuel pump, and spark plugs.
7. Remove the ignition coil, pushrod covers, and gasket. Remove the valve

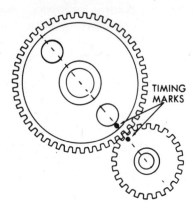

OHV six timing mark alignment

lifters making sure to note their positions for reinstallation.

8. Remove the harmonic balancer, then loosen the oil pan bolts and allow the pan to drop.

9. Remove the timing gear cover.

10. Remove the two camshaft thrust plate bolts.

11. Remove the camshaft by pulling it straight out the front. If the cam gear is to be replaced, press it off.

CAUTION: *The thrust plate must be positioned so that the woodruff key does not damage it during removal.*

12. Install the camshaft into the engine, turn it so that the timing marks align, and tighten the thrust plate bolts to 5–8 ft lbs.

13. Reverse the remaining procedures to complete the installation.

V8

1. Drain the cooling system and remove the air cleaner.

2. Disconnect all water hoses, vacuum lines, and spark plug wires. Remove the radiator.

3. Disconnect the accelerator linkage, temperature gauge wire, and fuel lines.

4. Remove the hood latch brace.

5. Remove the PCV hose, then remove the rocker covers.

NOTE: *On air-conditioned models, remove the alternator and its bracket.*

6. Remove the distributor, then remove the intake manifold.

7. Remove the valley cover.

8. Loosen the rocker arm nuts and pivot the rockers out of the way.

9. Remove the pushrods and lifters, keeping them in proper order.

10. Remove the harmonic balancer, fuel pump, and 4 oil pan-to-timing cover bolts.

11. Remove the timing cover and gasket, then remove the fuel pump eccentric and the bushing.

12. Align the timing marks, then remove the timing chain and sprockets.

13. Remove the camshaft thrust plate.

14. Remove the camshaft by pulling it straight forward, being careful not to damage the cam bearings in the process.

1967–68 timing mark alignment

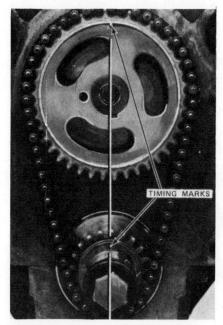

1969–74 timing mark alignment

15. Install the new camshaft (with the lobes and journals coated with heavy (SAE 50–60 oil) into the engine, being careful not to damage the cam bearings.

16. Install the camshaft thrust plate and tighten the bolts to 20 ft lbs.

NOTE: *Before installing the timing cover, make sure that the No. 1 piston is at TDC of its compression stroke and that the timing marks are correctly aligned for your year engine.*

17. To install, reverse Steps 1–12, tightening the sprocket bolts to 40 ft lbs, timing cover bolts and nuts to 30 ft lbs, oil pan bolts to 12 ft lbs, and harmonic balancer bolt to 160 ft lbs.

PISTON AND CONNECTING RODS

Removal and Installation

OHC 6 CYLINDER 1967–69

1. Remove the rocker arm cover.

2. Disconnect the fuel and vacuum lines from the carburetor.

3. Remove the cylinder head and the intake and exhaust manifold as an assembly.

4. Remove the ring ridge, using an appropriate cutter.

5. Remove the oil pan.

6. Mark the connecting rod and piston assembly to make sure that they go into the same cylinder and that the same piston face is pointing toward the front of the engine upon reassembly. Do not reverse the bearing caps on the end of the connecting rods.

7. Remove the bearing cap and carefully push the piston and rod from its

bore. Do not allow the piston and rod assembly to be scratched, nicked, or struck against a hard surface.

8. Using a ring compressor, insert the rod and piston assembly into the cylinder.

9. Pull the assembly into place against the crankpin, install the bearing cap and torque it to 33 ft lbs.

10. Install the oil pan.

11. Install the cylinder head assembly.

12. Connect the fuel and vacuum lines and install the rocker arm cover.

OHV 6 CYLINDER 1970–74

Piston and piston ring removal and installation are the same as for the OHC six-cylinder engine. However, ring-clearances are different. These are 0.010–0.020 in. end clearance for the upper and lower compressing rings and 0.015–0.055 in. for the oil ring. Side clearance is: 0.0012–0.0027 in. for the upper compression ring; 0.0012–0.0032 in. for the lower compression ring; 0.001–0.005 in. for the oil ring.

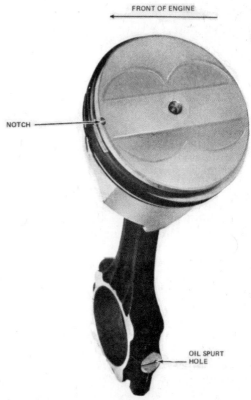

V8 piston and rod positioning—oil spurt holes always face the camshaft

Six-cylinder piston and rod positioning—oil spurt hole always faces distributor

V8 Engine

1. Remove the oil pan, oil baffle, and oil pump.

2. Remove the intake manifold, exhaust manifolds, and cylinder heads.

3. Rotate the crankshaft to allow access to the rods being removed.

4. Remove the ring ridge, using a reamer.

5. Remove the bearing cap.

6. Push the piston and rod assembly from the cylinder.

7. To install, reverse the removal procedures. Torque the bearing caps to specification.

Engine Lubrication

OIL PAN

Removal and Installation

OHC 6 Cylinder 1967–69

1. Disconnect the battery.

2. Remove the air cleaner assembly.

3. On air conditioned cars, remove the compressor from the mounting brackets and position it to one side.

4. Inspect all water hoses and wiring harness for routing and possible interference. (Engine will be raised at least 2 in.).

NOTE: *Before raising the car, prop the hood open at least 6 in. to ensure enough clearance between the timing belt cover and the inner hood panel.*

5. Raise the car and drain the crankcase.

6. Remove the starter assembly and flywheel cover.

7. Reroute or disconnect any wiring between the bellhousing and floor pan to insure against damage when the bellhousing contacts the pan.

8. Loosen the transmission insulator-to-crossmember retaining bolts.

9. Remove the right and left engine insulator-to-frame bracket through-bolts.

10. Rotate the harmonic balancer until the timing mark is at bottom. (This properly positions the crankshaft counterweights).

11. With suitable equipment, raise the engine until the insulators clear the frame brackets.

12. Remove the oil pan bolts.

13. Raise the engine. Apply a rearward force on the engine-transmission assembly until the oil pan clears the flywheel housing. Remove the oil pan.

14. Reverse the removal procedure to install the oil pan.

OHV 6 Cylinder 1970–74

1. Remove the upper radiator shield assembly.

2. Disconnect the positive battery cable.

3. Jack up the front of the car and drain the engine oil.

4. Disconnect the exhaust pipe at the manifold flange.

5. Remove the starter motor and flywheel cover.

6. Raise the engine slightly, using a chain hoist, and then remove both the front motor mount-to-frame bolts and the right motor mount.

7. Remove the oil pan bolts, then raise the engine and remove the oil pan.

8. To install, reverse the removal procedure.

NOTE: *Install the bolts into timing gear cover last. They are installed at an angle and holes line up after rest of oil pan bolts are tightened finger-tight.*

1967–69 V8

1. Disconnect the battery cable.

2. Remove the distributor cap and fan shield.

3. Remove the fan and fan pulley on air conditioned models.

4. Disconnect the engine ground straps.

5. On air conditioned models, remove the compressor and swing it out of the way without disconnecting the hoses.

6. Jack up the front of car and drain the engine oil.

7. Disconnect the steering idle arm from the frame.

8. Remove the exhaust crossover pipe on single exhaust cars; disconnect the exhaust pipes at the manifold flanges on dual exhaust cars.

9. Remove the starter, starter bracket, and flywheel cover.

10. Support the engine with a chain hoist, then remove the motor mounts and loosen the rear transmission mount.

NOTE: *It may be necessary, in some*

cases, to remove the rear transmission mount.

11. Remove the oil pan bolts, raise the engine about 4½ in., and move the engine forward about 1½ in.

12. Remove the oil pan by rotating it clockwise (to clear oil pump) and pulling it down.

13. To install, reverse the removal procedure.

1970–74 V8

1. Rotate the engine until the timing mark is at the 2 o'clock position.

2. Disconnect the battery cables.

3. Remove the fan.

4. Move all water hoses and wiring out of the way.

5. Raise the car and drain the engine oil. Disconnect the idler arm from the frame and the pitman arm from the shaft.

6. Disconnect the exhaust pipe(s) at the manifold.

7. Remove the starter and bracket, and then remove the flywheel inspection cover.

8. Support the engine with a wood-padded jack.

9. Remove both the frame-to-motor mount bolts.

10. Jack up the engine for clearance, then remove the oil pan bolts and pan.

11. To install, reverse the removal procedure. Tighten the pan bolts to 12 ft lbs.

OIL PUMP

Removal and Installation

ALL EXCEPT OHC 6 CYLINDER

1. Remove the engine oil pan. (See the previous procedure).

2. Remove the pump attaching screws and carefully lower the pump, while removing the pump driveshaft.

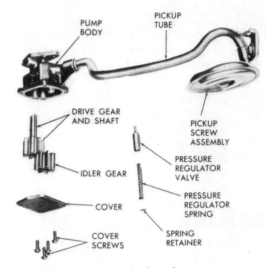

Exploded view of six-cylinder oil pump

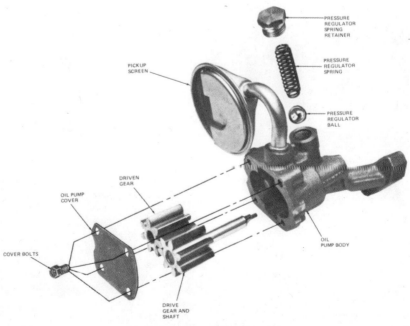

Exploded view of V8 oil pump

3. Reinstall in the reverse order of removal.

NOTE: *OHC 6 cylinder oil pump removal is covered earlier in this Chapter.*

REAR MAIN OIL SEAL
Removal and Installation
ALL 6 CYLINDER ENGINES 1967–74

Always replace both the upper and lower seal halves. It is not necessary to remove the crankshaft to install the seal.

1. Remove the engine oil pan.
2. Remove the rear main bearing cap.
3. Remove the oil seal from the groove in the cap by prying from the bottom with a small screwdriver.
4. Insert a new seal, well lubricated

Removing upper half of six-cylinder seal

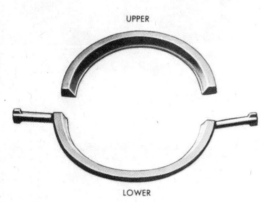

Six-cylinder rear main seals

with engine oil, into the bearing cap groove.

5. Remove the upper half of the seal. Use a small hammer and brass pin and tap one end of the oil seal until it protrudes far enough to be removed with pliers.

6. Install a new seal with the lip toward the front of the engine.

7. Install the bearing cap and torque it to specification.

V8 1967–74

1. Remove the oil pan, baffle, and oil pump.
2. Remove the rear main bearing cap.
3. Make a seal tool similar to the one illustrated.
4. Insert the tool against one end of the oil seal in the block and drive the seal gently into the groove a distance of ¾ in. Repeat on the other end of the seal.
5. Form a new seal in the cap. Cut four ⅜ in. long pieces from this seal.
6. Work two of the pieces into each of the gaps which have been made at the end of the seal in the block. Do not cut off any material to make them fit.
7. Form a new seal in the bearing cap.
8. Apply a 1/16 in. bead of sealer from the center of the seal across to the external cork groove.
9. Reassemble the cap and torque to specification.

Forming V8 rear main seal

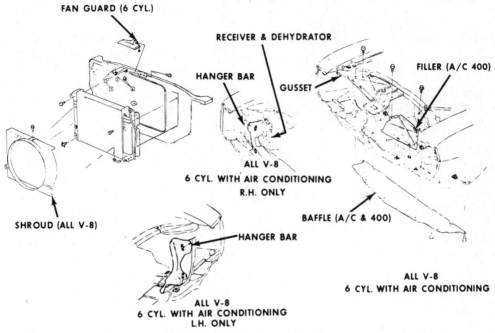

FAN GUARD (6 CYL.)

RECEIVER & DEHYDRATOR

HANGER BAR

GUSSET

FILLER (A/C 400)

SHROUD (ALL V-8)

ALL V-8
6 CYL. WITH AIR CONDITIONING
R.H. ONLY

BAFFLE (A/C & 400)

HANGER BAR

ALL V-8
6 CYL. WITH AIR CONDITIONING

ALL V-8
6 CYL. WITH AIR CONDITIONING
L.H. ONLY

Typical 1967–69 radiator mounting

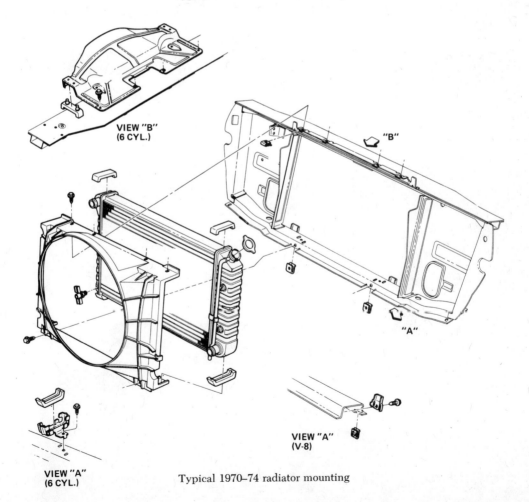

VIEW "B"
(6 CYL.)

"B"

"A"

VIEW "A"
(V-8)

VIEW "A"
(6 CYL.)

Typical 1970–74 radiator mounting

Engine Cooling

The cooling system consists of the radiator cap, radiator, hoses, water pump, cooling fan, thermostat, and water passages in the block.

RADIATOR

A crossflow radiator is used instead of a conventional down-flow and center type. With the crossflow design, coolant flows horizontally through the core and the tanks are located on each side.

Advantages of the crossflow radiators are improved cooling capability, more effective cooling surface area, and a lower silhouette.

Automatic transmission radiators have an oil cooler built into the right-hand tank. Air conditioned and high-performance models have greater cooling capacity than standard. The drain cock is located at the inside, lower left-hand corner of the radiator.

Removal and Installation

1. Disconnect the battery.
2. Drain the coolant, then disconnect the upper and lower hoses.
3. Disconnect and plug the oil cooler lines, if equipped with automatic transmission.
4. Remove the upper fan shield (six-cylinder) or upper shroud bracket (V8).
5. Remove the radiator hold-down bolts and lift the radiator and shroud assembly from the car.
6. To install, reverse the removal procedure, making sure that the automatic transmission fluid level is correct. Tighten the hold-down bolts to 12 ft lbs.

WATER PUMP

This is a centrifugal-type water pump. It is die-cast, with sealed bearings and pressed together. It is serviced as a unit.

Removal and Installation

1. Disconnect the battery and drain the radiator.
2. Loosen the generator and remove the fan belt.
3. Remove the power steering and air conditioning belts, if so equipped.
4. Remove the fan and water pump pulley.
5. Remove the front generator bracket.
6. Remove the heater hose and radiator hose at the pump.

NOTE: *Remove the upper front timing cover and the two accessory drive housing bolts on OHC six engines.*

7. Remove the water pump retaining bolts and the pump.
8. Install the pump by reversing the above steps. Make sure that all gasket surfaces are clean and smooth. Always use a gasket sealer on both sides of the gasket. Torque the retaining bolts to 20 ft lbs on six-cylinder engines and 15 ft lbs on V8 engines.

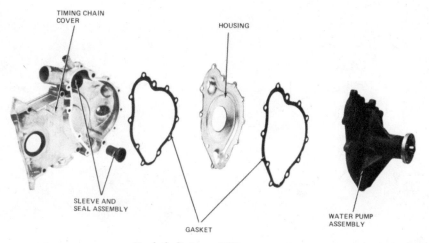

TIMING CHAIN COVER

HOUSING

SLEEVE AND SEAL ASSEMBLY

GASKET

WATER PUMP ASSEMBLY

Exploded view of V8 water pump

THERMOSTAT

Removal and Installation

1. Drain the coolant to below thermostat level.

2. Disconnect the upper hose and remove the water outlet assembly.

3. Replace the thermostat by reversing the above Steps. Install the new thermostat "spring side" down. Torque the attaching bolts to 20–30 ft lbs. Clean the gasket surfaces and use a gasket sealer and a new gasket.

4. Refill the radiator to 3 in. below the filler neck and bleed the cooling system.

Engine Rebuilding

This section describes, in detail, the procedures involved in rebuilding a typical engine. The procedures specifically refer to an inline engine, however, they are basically identical to those used in rebuilding engines of nearly all design and configurations. Procedures for servicing atypical engines (i.e., horizontally opposed) are described in the appropriate section, although in most cases, cylinder head reconditioning procedures described in this chapter will apply.

The section is divided into two sections. The first, Cylinder Head Reconditioning, assumes that the cylinder head is removed from the engine, all manifolds are removed, and the cylinder head is on a workbench. The camshaft should be removed from overhead cam cylinder heads. The second section, Cylinder Block Reconditioning, covers the block, pistons, connecting rods and crankshaft. It is assumed that the engine is mounted on a work stand, and the cylinder head and all accessories are removed.

Procedures are identified as follows:

Unmarked—Basic procedures that must be performed in order to successfully complete the rebuilding process.

Starred (*)—Procedures that should be performed to ensure maximum performance and engine life.

Double starred (**)—Procedures that may be performed to increase engine performance and reliability. These procedures are usually reserved for extremely heavy-duty or competition usage.

In many cases, a choice of methods is also provided. Methods are identified in the same manner as procedures. The choice of method for a procedure is at the discretion of the user.

The tools required for the basic rebuilding procedure should, with minor exceptions, be those

TORQUE (ft. lbs.)*

U.S.

Bolt Diameter (inches)	Bolt Grade (SAE)				Wrench Size (inches)	
	⬡ 1 and 2	⬡ 5	⬡ 6	⬡ 8	Bolt	Nut
1/4	5	7	10	10.5	3/8	7/16
5/16	9	14	19	22	1/2	9/16
3/8	15	25	34	37	9/16	5/8
7/16	24	40	55	60	5/8	3/4
1/2	37	60	85	92	3/4	13/16
9/16	53	88	120	132	7/8	7/8
5/8	74	120	167	180	15/16	1
3/4	120	200	280	296	1-1/8	1-1/8
7/8	190	302	440	473	1-5/16	1-5/16
1	282	466	660	714	1-1/2	1-1/2

Metric

Bolt Diameter (mm)	Bolt Grade				Wrench Size (mm)
	5D 5D	8G 8G	10K 10K	12K 12K	Bolt and Nut
6	5	6	8	10	10
8	10	16	22	27	14
10	19	31	40	49	17
12	34	54	70	86	19
14	55	89	117	137	22
16	83	132	175	208	24
18	111	182	236	283	27
22	182	284	394	464	32
24	261	419	570	689	36

*—Torque values are for lightly oiled bolts. CAUTION: Bolts threaded into aluminum require much less torque.

General Torque Specifications

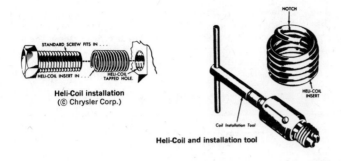

Heli-Coil installation
(© Chrysler Corp.)

Heli-Coil and installation tool

Heli-Coil Insert			Drill	Tap	Insert. Tool	Extract- ing Tool
Thread Size	Part No.	Insert Length (In.)	Size	Part No.	Part No.	Part No.
1/2 -20	1185-4	3/8	17/64(.266)	4 CPB	528-4N	1227-6
5/16-18	1185-5	15/32	Q(.332)	5 CPB	528-5N	1227-6
3/8 -16	1185-6	9/16	X(.397)	6 CPB	528-6N	1227-6
7/16-14	1185-7	21/32	29/64(.453)	7 CPB	528-7N	1227-16
1/2 -13	1185-8	3/4	33/64(.516)	8 CPB	528-8N	1227-16

Heli-Coil Specifications

included in a mechanic's tool kit. An accurate torque wrench, and a dial indicator (reading in thousandths) mounted on a universal base should be available. Bolts and nuts with no torque specification should be tightened according to size (see chart). Special tools, where required, all are readily available from the major tool suppliers (i.e., Craftsman, Snap-On, K-D). The services of a competent automotive machine shop must also be readily available.

When assembling the engine, any parts that will be in frictional contact must be pre-lubricated, to provide protection on initial start-up. Vortex Pre-Lube, STP, or any product specifically formulated for this purpose may be used. NOTE: *Do not use engine oil.* Where semi-permanent (locked but removable) installation of bolts or nuts is desired, threads should be cleaned and coated with Loctite. Studs may be permanently installed using Loctite Stud and Bearing Mount.

Aluminum has become increasingly popular for use in engines, due to its low weight and excellent heat transfer characteristics. The following precautions

must be observed when handling aluminum engine parts:
—Never hot-tank aluminum parts.
—Remove all aluminum parts (identification tags, etc.) from engine parts before hot-tanking (otherwise they will be removed during the process).
—Always coat threads lightly with engine oil or anti-seize compounds before installation, to prevent seizure.
—Never over-torque bolts or spark plugs in aluminum threads. Should stripping occur, threads can be restored according to the following procedure, using Heli-Coil thread inserts:

Tap drill the hole with the stripped threads to the specified size (see chart). Using the specified tap (NOTE: *Heli-Coil tap sizes refer to the size thread being replaced, rather than the actual tap size*), tap the hole for the Heli-Coil. Place the insert on the proper installation tool (see chart). Apply pressure on the insert while winding it clockwise into the hole, until the top of the insert is one turn below the surface. Remove the installation tool, and break the installation tang from the bottom of the in-

sert by moving it up and down. If the Heli-Coil must be removed, tap the removal tool firmly into the hole, so that it engages the top thread, and turn the tool counter-clockwise to extract the insert.

Snapped bolts or studs may be removed, using a stud extractor (unthreaded) or Vise-Grip pliers (threaded). Penetrating oil (e.g., Liquid Wrench) will often aid in breaking frozen threads. In cases where the stud or bolt is flush with, or below the surface, proceed as follows:

Drill a hole in the broken stud or bolt, approximately ½ its diameter. Select a screw extractor (e.g., Easy-Out) of the proper size, and tap it into the stud or bolt. Turn the extractor counterclockwise to remove the stud or bolt.

Magnaflux and Zyglo are inspection techniques used to locate material flaws, such as stress cracks. Magnafluxing coats the part with fine magnetic particles, and subjects the part to a magnetic field. Cracks cause breaks

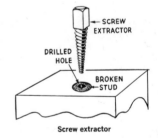

Screw extractor

in the magnetic field, which are outlined by the particles. Since Magnaflux is a magnetic process, it is applicable only to ferrous materials. The Zyglo process coats the material with a fluorescent dye penetrant, and then subjects it to blacklight inspection, under which cracks glow bright-

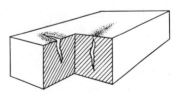

Magnaflux indication of cracks

ly. Parts made of any material may be tested using Zyglo. While Magnaflux and Zyglo are excellent for general inspection, and locating hidden defects, specific checks of suspected cracks may be made at lower cost and more readily using spot check dye. The dye is sprayed onto the suspected area, wiped off, and the area is then sprayed with a developer. Cracks then will show up brightly. Spot check dyes will only indicate surface cracks; therefore, structural cracks below the surface may escape detection. When questionable, the part should be tested using Magnaflux or Zyglo.

CYLINDER HEAD RECONDITIONING

Procedure	Method
Identify the valves: 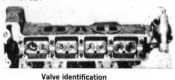 **Valve identification** (© SAAB)	Invert the cylinder head, and number the valve faces front to rear, using a permanent felt-tip marker.
Remove the rocker arms:	Remove the rocker arms with shaft(s) or balls and nuts. Wire the sets of rockers, balls and nuts together, and identify according to the corresponding valve.
Remove the valves and springs:	Using an appropriate valve spring compressor (depending on the configuration of the cylinder head), compress the valve springs. Lift out the keepers with needlenose pliers, release the compressor, and remove the valve, spring, and spring retainer.
Check the valve stem-to-guide clearance:  **Checking the valve stem-to-guide clearance** (© American Motors Corp.)	Clean the valve stem with lacquer thinner or a similar solvent to remove all gum and varnish. Clean the valve guides using solvent and an expanding wire-type valve guide cleaner. Mount a dial indicator so that the stem is at 90° to the valve stem, as close to the valve guide as possible. Move the valve off its seat, and measure the valve guide-to-stem clearance by moving the stem back and forth to actuate the dial indicator. Measure the valve stems using a micrometer, and compare to specifications, to determine whether stem or guide wear is responsible for excessive clearance.
De-carbon the cylinder head and valves: 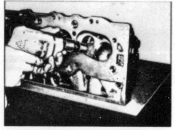 **Removing carbon from the cylinder head** (© Chevrolet Div. G.M. Corp.)	Chip carbon away from the valve heads, combustion chambers, and ports, using a chisel made of hardwood. Remove the remaining deposits with a stiff wire brush. NOTE: *Ensure that the deposits are actually removed, rather than burnished.*

Procedure	Method
Hot-tank the cylinder head:	Have the cylinder head hot-tanked to remove grease, corrosion, and scale from the water passages. NOTE: *In the case of overhead cam cylinder heads, consult the operator to determine whether the camshaft bearings will be damaged by the caustic solution.*
Degrease the remaining cylinder head parts:	Using solvent (i.e., Gunk), clean the rockers, rocker shaft(s) (where applicable), rocker balls and nuts, springs, spring retainers, and keepers. Do not remove the protective coating from the springs.
Check the cylinder head for warpage:  **Checking the cylinder head for warpage** (© Ford Motor Co.)	Place a straight-edge across the gasket surface of the cylinder head. Using feeler gauges, determine the clearance at the center of the straight-edge. Measure across both diagonals, along the longitudinal centerline, and across the cylinder head at several points. If warpage exceeds .003″ in a 6″ span, or .006″ over the total length, the cylinder head must be resurfaced. NOTE: *If warpage exceeds the manufacturers maximum tolerance for material removal, the cylinder head must be replaced.* When milling the cylinder heads of V-type engines, the intake manifold mounting position is altered, and must be corrected by milling the manifold flange a proportionate amount.
** Porting and gasket matching:  **Marking the cylinder head for gasket matching** (© Petersen Publishing Co.)  **Port configuration before and after gasket matching** (© Petersen Publishing Co.)	** Coat the manifold flanges of the cylinder head with Prussian blue dye. Glue intake and exhaust gaskets to the cylinder head in their installed position using rubber cement and scribe the outline of the ports on the manifold flanges. Remove the gaskets. Using a small cutter in a hand-held power tool (i.e., Dremel Moto-Tool), gradually taper the walls of the port out to the scribed outline of the gasket. Further enlargement of the ports should include the removal of sharp edges and radiusing of sharp corners. Do not alter the valve guides. NOTE: *The most efficient port configuration is determined only by extensive testing. Therefore, it is best to consult someone experienced with the head in question to determine the optimum alterations.*

Procedure	*Method*
** Polish the ports:	** Using a grinding stone with the above mentioned tool, polish the walls of the intake and exhaust ports, and combustion chamber. Use progressively finer stones until all surface imperfections are removed. NOTE: *Through testing, it has been determined that a smooth surface is more effective than a mirror polished surface in intake ports, and vice-versa in exhaust ports.*

Relieved and polished ports
(© Petersen Publishing Co.)

Polished combustion chamber
(© Petersen Publishing Co.)

| * Knurling the valve guides: | * Valve guides which are not excessively worn or distorted may, in some cases, be knurled rather than replaced. Knurling is a process in which metal is displaced and raised, thereby reducing clearance. Knurling also provides excellent oil control. The possibility of knurling rather than replacing valve guides should be discussed with a machinist. |

Cut-away view of a knurled valve guide
(© Petersen Publishing Co.)

| Replacing the valve guides: NOTE: *Valve guides should only be replaced if damaged or if an oversize valve stem is not available.* | Depending on the type of cylinder head, valve guides may be pressed, hammered, or shrunk in. In cases where the guides are shrunk into the head, replacement should be left to an equipped machine shop. In other cases, the guides are replaced as follows: Press or tap the valve guides out of the head using a stepped drift (see illustration). Determine the height above the boss that the guide must extend, and obtain a stack of washers, their I.D. similar to the guide's O.D., of that height. Place the stack of washers on the guide, and insert the guide into the boss. NOTE: *Valve guides are often tapered or beveled for installation.* Using the stepped installation tool (see illustration), press or tap the guides into position. Ream the guides according to the size of the valve stem. |

A - VALVE GUIDE I.D.
B - SLIGHTLY SMALLER THAN VALVE GUIDE O.D.

Valve guide removal tool

WASHERS

A - VALVE GUIDE I.D.
B - LARGER THAN THE VALVE GUIDE O.D.

Valve guide installation tool (with washers used during installation)

Procedure	Method
Replacing valve seat inserts:	Replacement of valve seat inserts which are worn beyond resurfacing or broken, if feasible, must be done by a machine shop.
Resurfacing (grinding) the valve face:  **Grinding a valve** (© Subaru) 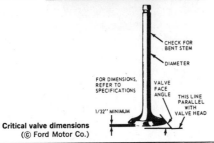 **Critical valve dimensions** (© Ford Motor Co.)	Using a valve grinder, resurface the valves according to specifications. CAUTION: *Valve face angle is not always identical to valve seat angle.* A minimum margin of 1/32″ should remain after grinding the valve. The valve stem tip should also be squared and resurfaced, by placing the stem in the V-block of the grinder, and turning it while pressing lightly against the grinding wheel.
Resurfacing the valve seats using reamers:  **Reaming the valve seat** (© S.p.A. Fiat) **Valve seat width and centering** (© Ford Motor Co.)	Select a reamer of the correct seat angle, slightly larger than the diameter of the valve seat, and assemble it with a pilot of the correct size. Install the pilot into the valve guide, and using steady pressure, turn the reamer clockwise. CAUTION: *Do not turn the reamer counter-clockwise.* Remove only as much material as necessary to clean the seat. Check the concentricity of the seat (see below). If the dye method is not used, coat the valve face with Prussian blue dye, install and rotate it on the valve seat. Using the dye marked area as a centering guide, center and narrow the valve seat to specifications with correction cutters. NOTE: *When no specifications are available, minimum seat width for exhaust valves should be 5/64″, intake valves 1/16″.* After making correction cuts, check the position of the valve seat on the valve face using Prussian blue dye.
* Resurfacing the valve seats using a grinder:  **Grinding a valve seat** (© Subaru)	Select a pilot of the correct size, and a coarse stone of the correct seat angle. Lubricate the pilot if necessary, and install the tool in the valve guide. Move the stone on and off the seat at approximately two cycles per second, until all flaws are removed from the seat. Install a fine stone, and finish the seat. Center and narrow the seat using correction stones, as described above.

Procedure	*Method*
Checking the valve seat concentricity:  **Checking the valve seat concentricity using a dial gauge** (© American Motors Corp.)	Coat the valve face with Prussian blue dye, install the valve, and rotate it on the valve seat. If the entire seat becomes coated, and the valve is known to be concentric, the seat is concentric.
	* Install the dial gauge pilot into the guide, and rest the arm on the valve seat. Zero the gauge, and rotate the arm around the seat. Run-out should not exceed .002″.
* Lapping the valves: NOTE: *Valve lapping is done to ensure efficient sealing of resurfaced valves and seats. Valve lapping alone is not recommended for use as a resurfacing procedure.*  **Hand lapping the valves**  HAND DRILL — ROD — SUCTION CUP **Home made mechanical valve lapping tool**	* Invert the cylinder head, lightly lubricate the valve stems, and install the valves in the head as numbered. Coat valve seats with fine grinding compound, and attach the lapping tool suction cup to a valve head (NOTE: *Moisten the suction cup*). Rotate the tool between the palms, changing position and lifting the tool often to prevent grooving. Lap the valve until a smooth, polished seat is evident. Remove the valve and tool, and rinse away all traces of grinding compound.
	** Fasten a suction cup to a piece of drill rod, and mount the rod in a hand drill. Proceed as above, using the hand drill as a lapping tool. CAUTION: *Due to the higher speeds involved when using the hand drill, care must be exercised to avoid grooving the seat.* Lift the tool and change direction of rotation often.
Check the valve springs: 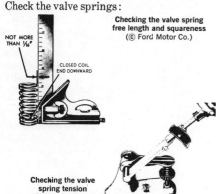 **Checking the valve spring free length and squareness** (© Ford Motor Co.) NOT MORE THAN 1/16″ CLOSED COIL END DOWNWARD **Checking the valve spring tension** (© Chrysler Corp.)	Place the spring on a flat surface next to a square. Measure the height of the spring, and rotate it against the edge of the square to measure distortion. If spring height varies (by comparison) by more than 1/16″ or if distortion exceeds 1/16″, replace the spring.
	** In addition to evaluating the spring as above, test the spring pressure at the installed and compressed (installed height minus valve lift) height using a valve spring tester. Springs used on small displacement engines (up to 3 liters) should be ± 1 lb. of all other springs in either position. A tolerance of ± 5 lbs. is permissible on larger engines.

Procedure	Method
* Install valve stem seals:  **Valve stem seal installation** (© Ford Motor Co.) SEAL	* Due to the pressure differential that exists at the ends of the intake valve guides (atmospheric pressure above, manifold vacuum below), oil is drawn through the valve guides into the intake port. This has been alleviated somewhat since the addition of positive crankcase ventilation, which lowers the pressure above the guides. Several types of valve stem seals are available to reduce blow-by. Certain seals simply slip over the stem and guide boss, while others require that the boss be machined. Recently, Teflon guide seals have become popular. Consult a parts supplier or machinist concerning availability and suggested usages. NOTE: *When installing seals, ensure that a small amount of oil is able to pass the seal to lubricate the valve guides; otherwise, excessive wear may result.*
Install the valves:	Lubricate the valve stems, and install the valves in the cylinder head as numbered. Lubricate and position the seals (if used, see above) and the valve springs. Install the spring retainers, compress the springs, and insert the keys using needlenose pliers or a tool designed for this purpose. NOTE: *Retain the keys with wheel bearing grease during installation.*
Checking valve spring installed height: 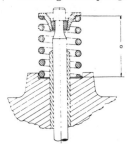  **Valve spring installed height dimension** (© Porsche) **Measuring valve spring installed height** (© Petersen Publishing Co.)	Measure the distance between the spring pad and the lower edge of the spring retainer, and compare to specifications. If the installed height is incorrect, add shim washers between the spring pad and the spring. CAUTION: *Use only washers designed for this purpose.*
** CC'ing the combustion chambers:	** Invert the cylinder head and place a bead of sealer around a combustion chamber. Install an apparatus designed for this purpose (burette mounted on a clear plate; see illustration) over the combustion chamber, and fill with the specified fluid to an even mark on the burette. Record the burette reading, and fill the combustion chamber with fluid. (NOTE: *A hole drilled in the plate will permit air to escape*). Subtract the burette reading, with the combustion chamber filled, from the previous reading, to determine combustion chamber volume in cc's. Duplicate this procedure in all combustion

Procedure	Method

CC'ing the combustion chamber
(© Petersen Publishing Co.)

chambers on the cylinder head, and compare the readings. The volume of all combustion chambers should be made equal to that of the largest. Combustion chamber volume may be increased in two ways. When only a small change is required (usually), a small cutter or coarse stone may be used to remove material from the combustion chamber. NOTE: *Check volume frequently.* Remove material over a wide area, so as not to change the configuration of the combustion chamber. When a larger change is required, the valve seat may be sunk (lowered into the head). NOTE: *When altering valve seat, remember to compensate for the change in spring installed height.*

Inspect the rocker arms, balls, studs, and nuts (where applicable):

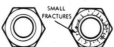

Stress cracks in rocker nuts
(© Ford Motor Co.)

Visually inspect the rocker arms, balls, studs, and nuts for cracks, galling, burning, scoring, or wear. If all parts are intact, liberally lubricate the rocker arms and balls, and install them on the cylinder head. If wear is noted on a rocker arm at the point of valve contact, grind it smooth and square, removing as little material as possible. Replace the rocker arm if excessively worn. If a rocker stud shows signs of wear, it must be replaced (see below). If a rocker nut shows stress cracks, replace it. If an exhaust ball is galled or burned, substitute the intake ball from the same cylinder (if it is intact), and install a new intake ball. NOTE: *Avoid using new rocker balls on exhaust valves.*

Replacing rocker studs:

Reaming the stud bore for oversize rocker studs
(© Buick Div. G.M. Corp.)

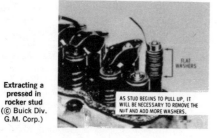

Extracting a pressed in rocker stud
(© Buick Div. G.M. Corp.)

In order to remove a threaded stud, lock two nuts on the stud, and unscrew the stud using the lower nut. Coat the lower threads of the new stud with Loctite, and install.

Two alternative methods are available for replacing pressed in studs. Remove the damaged stud using a stack of washers and a nut (see illustration). In the first, the boss is reamed .005-.006″ oversize, and an oversize stud pressed in. Control the stud extension over the boss using washers, in the same manner as valve guides. Before installing the stud, coat it with white lead and grease. To retain the stud more positively, drill a hole through the stud and boss, and install a roll pin. In the second method, the boss is tapped, and a threaded stud installed. Retain the stud using Loctite Stud and Bearing Mount.

Procedure	Method
Inspect the rocker shaft(s) and rocker arms (where applicable):  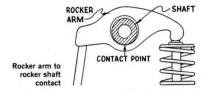 Disassembled rocker shaft parts arranged for inspection (© American Motors Corp.)	Remove rocker arms, springs and washers from rocker shaft. NOTE: *Lay out parts in the order they are removed.* Inspect rocker arms for pitting or wear on the valve contact point, or excessive bushing wear. Bushings need only be replaced if wear is excessive, because the rocker arm normally contacts the shaft at one point only. Grind the valve contact point of rocker arm smooth if necessary, removing as little material as possible. If excessive material must be removed to smooth and square the arm, it should be replaced. Clean out all oil holes and passages in rocker shaft. If shaft is grooved or worn, replace it. Lubricate and assemble the rocker shaft.

ROCKER ARM — SHAFT — CONTACT POINT

Rocker arm to rocker shaft contact

Procedure	Method
Inspect the camshaft bushings and the camshaft (overhead cam engines):	See next section.
Inspect the pushrods:	Remove the pushrods, and, if hollow, clean out the oil passages using fine wire. Roll each pushrod over a piece of clean glass. If a distinct clicking sound is heard as the pushrod rolls, the rod is bent, and must be replaced.
	* The length of all pushrods must be equal. Measure the length of the pushrods, compare to specifications, and replace as necessary.
Inspect the valve lifters: 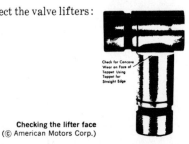 Check for Concave Wear on Face of Toppet Using Toppet for Straight Edge Checking the lifter face (© American Motors Corp.)	Remove lifters from their bores, and remove gum and varnish, using solvent. Clean walls of lifter bores. Check lifters for concave wear as illustrated. If face is worn concave, replace lifter, and carefully inspect the camshaft. Lightly lubricate lifter and insert it into its bore. If play is excessive, an oversize lifter must be installed (where possible). Consult a machinist concerning feasibility. If play is satisfactory, remove, lubricate, and reinstall the lifter.
* Testing hydraulic lifter leak down: 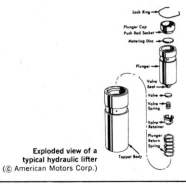 Lock Ring, Plunger Cap, Push Rod Socket, Metering Disc, Plunger, Valve Seat, Valve, Valve Spring, Valve Retainer, Plunger Return Spring, Toppet Body Exploded view of a typical hydraulic lifter (© American Motors Corp.)	Submerge lifter in a container of kerosene. Chuck a used pushrod or its equivalent into a drill press. Position container of kerosene so pushrod acts on the lifter plunger. Pump lifter with the drill press, until resistance increases. Pump several more times to bleed any air out of lifter. Apply very firm, constant pressure to the lifter, and observe rate at which fluid bleeds out of lifter. If the fluid bleeds very quickly (less than 15 seconds), lifter is defective. If the time exceeds 60 seconds, lifter is sticking. In either case, recondition or replace lifter. If lifter is operating properly (leak down time 15-60 seconds), lubricate and install it.

CYLINDER BLOCK RECONDITIONING

Procedure	*Method*
Checking the main bearing clearance:  Plastigage installed on main bearing journal (© Chevrolet Div. G.M. Corp.)  Measuring Plastigage to determine main bearing clearance (© Chevrolet Div. G.M. Corp.)  Causes of bearing failure (© Ford Motor Co.)	Invert engine, and remove cap from the bearing to be checked. Using a clean, dry rag, thoroughly clean all oil from crankshaft journal and bearing insert. NOTE: *Plastigage is soluble in oil; therefore, oil on the journal or bearing could result in erroneous readings.* Place a piece of Plastigage along the full length of journal, reinstall cap, and torque to specifications. Remove bearing cap, and determine bearing clearance by comparing width of Plastigage to the scale on Plastigage envelope. Journal taper is determined by comparing width of the Plastigage strip near its ends. Rotate crankshaft 90° and retest, to determine journal eccentricity. NOTE: *Do not rotate crankshaft with Plastigage installed.* If bearing insert and journal appear intact, and are within tolerances, no further main bearing service is required. If bearing or journal appear defective, cause of failure should be determined before replacement.
	* Remove crankshaft from block (see below). Measure the main bearing journals at each end twice (90° apart) using a micrometer, to determine diameter, journal taper and eccentricity. If journals are within tolerances, reinstall bearing caps at their specified torque. Using a telescope gauge and micrometer, measure bearing I.D. parallel to piston axis and at 30° on each side of piston axis. Subtract journal O.D. from bearing I.D. to determine oil clearance. If crankshaft journals appear defective, or do not meet tolerances, there is no need to measure bearings; for the crankshaft will require grinding and/or undersize bearings will be required. If bearing appears defective, cause for failure should be determined prior to replacement.
Checking the connecting rod bearing clearance:  Plastigage installed on connecting rod bearing journal (© Chevrolet Div. G.M. Corp.)	Connecting rod bearing clearance is checked in the same manner as main bearing clearance, using Plastigage. Before removing the crankshaft, connecting rod side clearance also should be measured and recorded.
	* Checking connecting rod bearing clearance, using a micrometer, is identical to checking main bearing clearance. If no other service

Procedure	Method
 **Measuring Plastigage to determine connecting rod bearing clearance** (© Chevrolet Div. G.M. Corp.)	is required, the piston and rod assemblies need not be removed.
Removing the crankshaft:  **Connecting rod matching marks** (© Ford Motor Co.)	Using a punch, mark the corresponding main bearing caps and saddles according to position (i.e., one punch on the front main cap and saddle, two on the second, three on the third, etc.). Using number stamps, identify the corresponding connecting rods and caps, according to cylinder (if no numbers are present). Remove the main and connecting rod caps, and place sleeves of plastic tubing over the connecting rod bolts, to protect the journals as the crankshaft is removed. Lift the crankshaft out of the block.
Remove the ridge from the top of the cylinder: 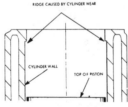 **Cylinder bore ridge** (© Pontiac Div. G.M. Corp.)	In order to facilitate removal of the piston and connecting rod, the ridge at the top of the cylinder (unworn area; see illustration) must be removed. Place the piston at the bottom of the bore, and cover it with a rag. Cut the ridge away using a ridge reamer, exercising extreme care to avoid cutting too deeply. Remove the rag, and remove cuttings that remain on the piston. CAUTION: *If the ridge is not removed, and new rings are installed, damage to rings will result.*
Removing the piston and connecting rod:  **Removing the piston** (© SAAB)	Invert the engine, and push the pistons and connecting rods out of the cylinders. If necessary, tap the connecting rod boss with a wooden hammer handle, to force the piston out. CAUTION: *Do not attempt to force the piston past the cylinder ridge* (see above).

Procedure	Method
Service the crankshaft:	Ensure that all oil holes and passages in the crankshaft are open and free of sludge. If necessary, have the crankshaft ground to the largest possible undersize.
	** Have the crankshaft Magnafluxed, to locate stress cracks. Consult a machinist concerning additional service procedures, such as surface hardening (e.g., nitriding, Tuftriding) to improve wear characteristics, cross drilling and chamfering the oil holes to improve lubrication, and balancing.
Removing freeze plugs:	Drill a hole in the center of the freeze plugs, and pry them out using a screwdriver or drift.
Remove the oil gallery plugs:	Threaded plugs should be removed using an appropriate (usually square) wrench. To remove soft, pressed in plugs, drill a hole in the plug, and thread in a sheet metal screw. Pull the plug out by the screw using pliers.
Hot-tank the block:	Have the block hot-tanked to remove grease, corrosion, and scale from the water jackets. NOTE: *Consult the operator to determine whether the camshaft bearings will be damaged during the hot-tank process.*
Check the block for cracks:	Visually inspect the block for cracks or chips. The most common locations are as follows: Adjacent to freeze plugs. Between the cylinders and water jackets. Adjacent to the main bearing saddles. At the extreme bottom of the cylinders. Check only suspected cracks using spot check dye (see introduction). If a crack is located, consult a machinist concerning possible repairs.
	** Magnaflux the block to locate hidden cracks. If cracks are located, consult a machinist about feasibility of repair.
Install the oil gallery plugs and freeze plugs:	Coat freeze plugs with sealer and tap into position using a piece of pipe, slightly smaller than the plug, as a driver. To ensure retention, stake the edges of the plugs. Coat threaded oil gallery plugs with sealer and install. Drive replacement soft plugs into block using a large drift as a driver.
	* Rather than reinstalling lead plugs, drill and tap the holes, and install threaded plugs.

Procedure	*Method*

Check the bore diameter and surface:

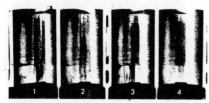

1, 2, 3 Piston skirt seizure resulted in this pattern. Engine must be rebored

4. Piston skirt and oil ring seizure caused this damage. Engine must be rebored

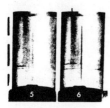

5, 6 Score marks caused by a split piston skirt. Damage is not serious enough to warrant reboring

7. Ring seized longitudinally, causing a score mark 1 3/16" wide, on the land side of the piston groove. The honing pattern is destroyed and the cylinder must be rebored

8. Result of oil ring seizure. Engine must be rebored

9. Oil ring seizure here was not serious enough to warrant reboring. The honing marks are still visible

Cylinder wall damage
(© Daimler-Benz A.G.)

Visually inspect the cylinder bores for roughness, scoring, or scuffing. If evident, the cylinder bore must be bored or honed oversize to eliminate imperfections, and the smallest possible oversize piston used. The new pistons should be given to the machinist with the block, so that the cylinders can be bored or honed exactly to the piston size (plus clearance). If no flaws are evident, measure the bore diameter using a telescope gauge and micrometer, or dial gauge, parallel and perpendicular to the engine centerline, at the top (below the ridge) and bottom of the bore. Subtract the bottom measurements from the top to determine taper, and the parallel to the centerline measurements from the perpendicular measurements to determine eccentricity. If the measurements are not within specifications, the cylinder must be bored or honed, and an oversize piston installed. If the measurements are within specifications the cylinder may be used as is, with only finish honing (see below). NOTE: *Prior to submitting the block for boring, perform the following operation(s).*

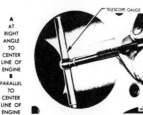

Cylinder bore measuring positions
(© Ford Motor Co.)

Measuring the cylinder bore with a telescope gauge
(© Buick Div. G.M. Corp.)

Determining the cylinder bore by measuring the telescope gauge with a micrometer
(© Buick Div. G.M. Corp.)

Measuring the cylinder bore with a dial gauge
(© Chevrolet Div. G.M. Corp.)

Procedure	Method
Check the block deck for warpage:	Using a straightedge and feeler gauges, check the block deck for warpage in the same manner that the cylinder head is checked (see Cylinder Head Reconditioning). If warpage exceeds specifications, have the deck resurfaced. NOTE: *In certain cases a specification for total material removal (Cylinder head and block deck) is provided. This specification must not be exceeded.*
* Check the deck height:	The deck height is the distance from the crankshaft centerline to the block deck. To measure, invert the engine, and install the crankshaft, retaining it with the center main cap. Measure the distance from the crankshaft journal to the block deck, parallel to the cylinder centerline. Measure the diameter of the end (front and rear) main journals, parallel to the centerline of the cylinders, divide the diameter in half, and subtract it from the previous measurement. The results of the front and rear measurements should be identical. If the difference exceeds .005″, the deck height should be corrected. NOTE: *Block deck height and warpage should be corrected concurrently.*
Check the cylinder block bearing alignment: Checking main bearing saddle alignment (© Petersen Publishing Co.)	Remove the upper bearing inserts. Place a straightedge in the bearing saddles along the centerline of the crankshaft. If clearance exists between the straightedge and the center saddle, the block must be align-bored.
Clean and inspect the pistons and connecting rods:  Piston ring expander Removing the piston rings (© Subaru)	Using a ring expander, remove the rings from the piston. Remove the retaining rings (if so equipped) and remove piston pin. NOTE: *If the piston pin must be pressed out, determine the proper method and use the proper tools; otherwise the piston will distort.* Clean the ring grooves using an appropriate tool, exercising care to avoid cutting too deeply. Thoroughly clean all carbon and varnish from the piston with solvent. CAUTION: *Do not use a wire brush or caustic solvent on pistons.* Inspect the pistons for scuffing, scoring, cracks, pitting, or excessive ring groove wear. If wear is evident, the piston must be replaced. Check the connecting rod length by measuring the rod from the inside of the large end to the inside of the small end using calipers (see

Procedure	*Method*

 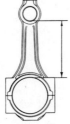

Cleaning the piston ring grooves
(© Ford Motor Co.)

Connecting rod length checking dimension

illustration). All connecting rods should be equal length. Replace any rod that differs from the others in the engine.

*   Have the connecting rod alignment checked in an alignment fixture by a machinist. Replace any twisted or bent rods.

*   Magnaflux the connecting rods to locate stress cracks. If cracks are found, replace the connecting rod.

Fit the pistons to the cylinders:

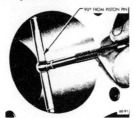

Measuring the cylinder with a telescope gauge for piston fitting
(© Buick Div. G.M. Corp.)

Measuring the piston for fitting
(© Buick Div. G.M. Corp.)

Using a telescope gauge and micrometer, or a dial gauge, measure the cylinder bore diameter perpendicular to the piston pin, 2½″ below the deck. Measure the piston perpendicular to its pin on the skirt. The difference between the two measurements is the piston clearance. If the clearance is within specifications or slightly below (after boring or honing), finish honing is all that is required. If the clearance is excessive, try to obtain a slightly larger piston to bring clearance within specifications. Where this is not possible, obtain the first oversize piston, and hone (or if necessary, bore) the cylinder to size.

Assemble the pistons and connecting rods:

Installing piston pin lock rings
(© Nissan Motor Co., Ltd.)

Inspect piston pin, connecting rod small end bushing, and piston bore for galling, scoring, or excessive wear. If evident, replace defective part(s). Measure the I.D. of the piston boss and connecting rod small end, and the O.D. of the piston pin. If within specifications, assemble piston pin and rod. CAUTION: *If piston pin must be pressed in, determine the proper method and use the proper tools; otherwise the piston will distort.* Install the lock rings; ensure that they seat properly. If the parts are not within specifications, determine the service method for the type of engine. In some cases, piston and pin are serviced as an assembly when either is defective. Others specify reaming the piston and connecting rods for an oversize pin. If the connecting rod bushing is worn, it may in many cases be replaced. Reaming the piston and replacing the rod bushing are machine shop operations.

Procedure	Method
Clean and inspect the camshaft: 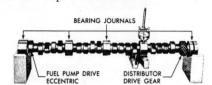 Checking the camshaft for straightness (© Chevrolet Motor Div. G.M. Corp.) 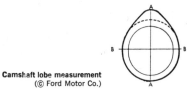 Camshaft lobe measurement (© Ford Motor Co.)	Degrease the camshaft, using solvent, and clean out all oil holes. Visually inspect cam lobes and bearing journals for excessive wear. If a lobe is questionable, check all lobes as indicated below. If a journal or lobe is worn, the camshaft must be reground or replaced. NOTE: *If a journal is worn, there is a good chance that the bushings are worn.* If lobes and journals appear intact, place the front and rear journals in V-blocks, and rest a dial indicator on the center journal. Rotate the camshaft to check straightness. If deviation exceeds .001″, replace the camshaft. * Check the camshaft lobes with a micrometer, by measuring the lobes from the nose to base and again at 90° (see illustration). The lift is determined by subtracting the second measurement from the first. If all exhaust lobes and all intake lobes are not identical, the camshaft must be reground or replaced.
Replace the camshaft bearings: 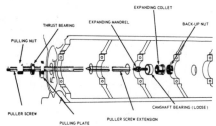 Camshaft removal and installation tool (typical) (© Ford Motor Co.)	If excessive wear is indicated, or if the engine is being completely rebuilt, camshaft bearings should be replaced as follows: Drive the camshaft rear plug from the block. Assemble the removal puller with its shoulder on the bearing to be removed. Gradually tighten the puller nut until bearing is removed. Remove remaining bearings, leaving the front and rear for last. To remove front and rear bearings, reverse position of the tool, so as to pull the bearings in toward the center of the block. Leave the tool in this position, pilot the new front and rear bearings on the installer, and pull them into position. Return the tool to its original position and pull remaining bearings into position. NOTE: *Ensure that oil holes align when installing bearings.* Replace camshaft rear plug, and stake it into position to aid retention.
Finish hone the cylinders:  Finish honed cylinder (© Chrysler Corp.)	Chuck a flexible drive hone into a power drill, and insert it into the cylinder. Start the hone, and move it up and down in the cylinder at a rate which will produce approximately a 60° cross-hatch pattern (see illustration). NOTE: *Do not extend the hone below the cylinder bore.* After developing the pattern, remove the hone and recheck piston fit. Wash the cylinders with a detergent and water solution to remove abrasive dust, dry, and wipe several times with a rag soaked in engine oil.

Procedure	*Method*

Check piston ring end-gap:

Checking ring end-gap
(© Chevrolet Motor Div. G.M. Corp.)

Compress the piston rings to be used in a cylinder, one at a time, into that cylinder, and press them approximately 1″ below the deck with an inverted piston. Using feeler gauges, measure the ring end-gap, and compare to specifications. Pull the ring out of the cylinder and file the ends with a fine file to obtain proper clearance. CAUTION: *If inadequate ring end-gap is utilized, ring breakage will result.*

Install the piston rings:

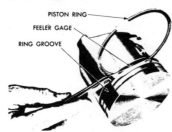

PISTON RING
FEELER GAGE
RING GROOVE

Checking ring side clearance
(© Chrysler Corp.)

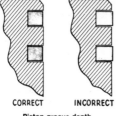 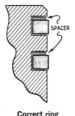

SPACER

CORRECT   INCORRECT
Piston groove depth

Correct ring spacer installation

Inspect the ring grooves in the piston for excessive wear or taper. If necessary, recut the groove(s) for use with an overwidth ring or a standard ring and spacer. If the groove is worn uniformly, overwidth rings, or standard rings and spacers may be installed without recutting. Roll the outside of the ring around the groove to check for burrs or deposits. If any are found, remove with a fine file. Hold the ring in the groove, and measure side clearance. If necessary, correct as indicated above. NOTE: *Always install any additional spacers above the piston ring.* The ring groove must be deep enough to allow the ring to seat below the lands (see illustration). In many cases, a "go-no-go" depth gauge will be provided with the piston rings. Shallow grooves may be corrected by recutting, while deep grooves require some type of filler or expander behind the piston. Consult the piston ring supplier concerning the suggested method. Install the rings on the piston, lowest ring first, using a ring expander. NOTE: *Position the ring markings as specified by the manufacturer (see car section).*

Install the camshaft:

Liberally lubricate the camshaft lobes and journals, and slide the camshaft into the block. CAUTION: *Exercise extreme care to avoid damaging the bearings when inserting the camshaft.* Install and tighten the camshaft thrust plate retaining bolts.

Check camshaft end-play:

Checking camshaft end-play with a feeler gauge
(© Ford Motor Co.)

Using feeler gauges, determine whether the clearance between the camshaft boss (or gear) and backing plate is within specifications. Install shims behind the thrust plate, or reposition the camshaft gear and retest end-play.

Procedure	*Method*

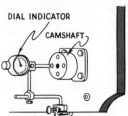

Checking camshaft end-play with a dial indicator

* Mount a dial indicator stand so that the stem of the dial indicator rests on the nose of the camshaft, parallel to the camshaft axis. Push the camshaft as far in as possible and zero the gauge. Move the camshaft outward to determine the amount of camshaft end-play. If the end-play is not within tolerance, install shims behind the thrust plate, or reposition the camshaft gear and retest.

Install the rear main seal (where applicable):

Seating the rear main seal
(© Buick Div. G.M. Corp.)

Position the block with the bearing saddles facing upward. Lay the rear main seal in its groove and press it lightly into its seat. Place a piece of pipe the same diameter as the crankshaft journal into the saddle, and firmly seat the seal. Hold the pipe in position, and trim the ends of the seal flush if required.

Install the crankshaft:

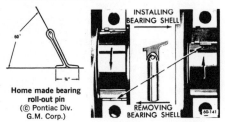

Home made bearing roll-out pin
(© Pontiac Div. G.M. Corp.)

Removal and installation of upper bearing insert using a roll-out pin
(© Buick Div. G.M. Corp.)

Thoroughly clean the main bearing saddles and caps. Place the upper halves of the bearing inserts on the saddles and press into position. NOTE: *Ensure that the oil holes align.* Press the corresponding bearing inserts into the main bearing caps. Lubricate the upper main bearings, and lay the crankshaft in position. Place a strip of Plastigage on each of the crankshaft journals, install the main caps, and torque to specifications. Remove the main caps, and compare the Plastigage to the scale on the Plastigage envelope. If clearances are within tolerances, remove the Plastigage, turn the crankshaft 90°, wipe off all oil and retest. If all clearances are correct, remove all Plastigage, thoroughly

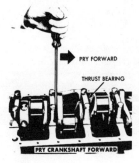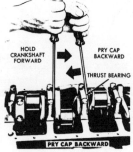

Aligning the thrust bearing
(© Ford Motor Co.)

Procedure	Method
	lubricate the main caps and bearing journals, and install the main caps. If clearances are not within tolerance, the upper bearing inserts may be removed, without removing the crankshaft, using a bearing roll out pin (see illustration). Roll in a bearing that will provide proper clearance, and retest. Torque all main caps, excluding the thrust bearing cap, to specifications. Tighten the thrust bearing cap finger tight. To properly align the thrust bearing, pry the crankshaft the extent of its axial travel several times, the last movement held toward the front of the engine, and torque the thrust bearing cap to specifications. Determine the crankshaft end-play (see below), and bring within tolerance with thrust washers.
Measure crankshaft end-play:  **Checking crankshaft end-play with a dial indicator** (© Ford Motor Co.)  **Checking crankshaft end-play with a feeler gauge** (© Chevrolet Div. (G.M. Corp.)	Mount a dial indicator stand on the front of the block, with the dial indicator stem resting on the nose of the crankshaft, parallel to the crankshaft axis. Pry the crankshaft the extent of its travel rearward, and zero the indicator. Pry the crankshaft forward and record crankshaft end-play. NOTE: *Crankshaft end-play also may be measured at the thrust bearing, using feeler gauges* (see illustration).
Install the pistons:	Press the upper connecting rod bearing halves into the connecting rods, and the lower halves into the connecting rod caps. Position the piston ring gaps according to specifications (see car section), and lubricate the pistons. Install a ring compresser on a piston, and press two long (8″) pieces of plastic tubing over the rod bolts. Using the plastic tubes as a guide, press the pistons into the bores and onto the crankshaft with a wooden hammer handle. After seating the rod on the crankshaft journal, remove the tubes and install the cap finger tight. Install the remaining pistons in the same man-

Procedure	Method

Tubing used as guide when installing a piston
(© Oldsmobile Div. G.M. Corp.)

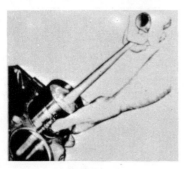

Installing a piston
(© Chevrolet Div. G.M. Corp.)

ner. Invert the engine and check the bearing clearance at two points (90° apart) on each journal with Plastigage. NOTE: *Do not turn the crankshaft with Plastigage installed.* If clearance is within tolerances, remove *all* Plastigage, thoroughly lubricate the journals, and torque the rod caps to specifications. If clearance is not within specifications, install different thickness bearing inserts and recheck. CAUTION: *Never shim or file the connecting rods or caps.* Always install plastic tube sleeves over the rod bolts when the caps are not installed, to protect the crankshaft journals.

Check connecting rod side clearance:

Checking connecting rod side clearance
(© Chevrolet Div. G.M. Corp.)

Determine the clearance between the sides of the connecting rods and the crankshaft, using feeler gauges. If clearance is below the minimum tolerance, the rod may be machined to provide adequate clearance. If clearance is excessive, substitute an unworn rod, and recheck. If clearance is still outside specifications, the crankshaft must be welded and reground, or replaced.

Inspect the timing chain:

Visually inspect the timing chain for broken or loose links, and replace the chain if any are found. If the chain will flex sideways, it must be replaced. Install the timing chain as specified. NOTE: *If the original timing chain is to be reused, install it in its original position.*

Procedure	*Method*
Check timing gear backlash and runout:	Mount a dial indicator with its stem resting on a tooth of the camshaft gear (as illustrated). Rotate the gear until all slack is removed, and zero the indicator. Rotate the gear in the opposite direction until slack is removed, and record gear backlash. Mount the indicator with its stem resting on the edge of the camshaft gear, parallel to the axis of the camshaft. Zero the indicator, and turn the camshaft gear one full turn, recording the runout. If either backlash or runout exceed specifications, replace the worn gear(s).

Checking camshaft gear backlash
(© Chevrolet Div. G.M. Corp.)

Checking camshaft gear runout
(© Chevrolet Div. G.M. Corp.)

Completing the Rebuilding Process

Following the above procedures, complete the rebuilding process as follows:

Fill the oil pump with oil, to prevent cavitating (sucking air) on initial engine start up. Install the oil pump and the pickup tube on the engine. Coat the oil pan gasket as necessary, and install the gasket and the oil pan. Mount the flywheel and the crankshaft vibrational damper or pulley on the crankshaft. NOTE: *Always use new bolts when installing the flywheel.* Inspect the clutch shaft pilot bushing in the crankshaft. If the bushing is excessively worn, remove it with an expanding puller and a slide hammer, and tap a new bushing into place.

Position the engine, cylinder head side up. Lubricate the lifters, and install them into their bores. Install the cylinder head, and torque it as specified in the car section. Insert the pushrods (where applicable), and install the rocker shaft(s) (if so equipped) or position the rocker arms on the pushrods. If solid lifters are utilized, adjust the valves to the "cold" specifications.

Mount the intake and exhaust manifolds, the carburetor(s), the distributor and spark plugs. Adjust the point gap and the static ignition timing. Mount all accessories and install the engine in the car. Fill the radiator with coolant, and the crankcase with high quality engine oil.

Break-in Procedure

Start the engine, and allow it to run at low speed for a few minutes, while checking for leaks. Stop the engine, check the oil level, and fill as necessary. Restart the engine, and fill the cooling system to capacity. Check the point dwell angle and adjust the ignition timing and the valves. Run the engine at low to medium speed (800-2500 rpm) for approximately ½ hour, and retorque the cylinder head bolts. Road test the car, and check again for leaks.

Follow the manufacturer's recommended engine break-in procedure and maintenance schedule for new engines.

4 · Emission Controls and Fuel System

Emission Controls

Pollutants from your Firebird fall into three categories: crankcase fumes, terminal exhaust gases, and gasoline evaporation. The various methods used to limit these pollutants are usually grouped under the heading of emission controls. Since the methods and equipment used to control emissions have varied so much, a year-by-year discussion follows. This allows you to understand exactly what equipment is on your Firebird and then to proceed to the individual component sections for servicing and troubleshooting.

1967

Pontiac controlled crankcase emissions in 1967 with the positive crankcase ventilation (PCV) system. The PCV system connects the crankcase to the intake manifold. Crankcase gases are returned to the intake manifold to be reburned.

The Air Injection Reactor (A.I.R.) system was used to treat exhaust emissions. It consists of an air pump, a special air cleaner, a by-pass valve, and tubes and hoses used to inject the air into the exhaust manifolds. The pump, driven by

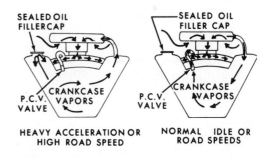

Positive crankcase ventilation

the engine, compresses, distributes, and injects clean air at the exhaust port for each cylinder. The air combines in the exhaust manifolds with the unburned hydrocarbons and carbon monoxide to produce a low-emission exhaust.

A dual diaphragm vacuum advance mechanism is used with the A.I.R. system. It is located on the distributor and takes the place of the single diaphragm unit. The outer diaphragm functions as a normal vacuum advance unit at any engine speed above idle. Vacuum for this diaphragm is supplied from a port above the carburetor throttle plate, since, at higher engine speeds, intake manifold vacuum is low and carburetor vacuum is high.

The inner diaphragm is used to retard

the spark at idle. Vacuum is supplied to the diaphragm from a port below the throttle because, at idle vacuum, conditions are reversed. Retarding the spark at idle combined with leaner mixtures gives cleaner exhaust at idle.

1968–69

General Motors Corporation had elected to adopt a special system of terminal exhaust treatment. This plan supersedes (in most cases) the method used to conform to 1966–67 California laws. The new system cancels out (except with stick shift and special purpose engine applications) the use of the A.I.R. method previously used.

The new concept, Combustion Control System (C.C.S.) utilizes engine modification. Essentially the C.C.S. increases combustion efficiency through carburetor and distributor calibrations and by increasing engine operating temperature.

Carburetors are calibrated leaner and initial ignition timing is retarded. Another carburetor feature is the idle fuel mixture limiting orifice. It is located at the base of the idle mixture screw and makes sure that, even if the idle mixture screw is turned too far, the fuel enrichment will not greatly affect exhaust emissions.

The C.C.S. also incorporates a higher engine operating temperature. A 195° thermostat is used. Engines that run hotter provide a more complete vaporization of the fuel and reduce quench area in the combustion chamber. Quench area is the relatively cool area near the cylinder wall and combustion chamber surfaces. Fuel in these areas does not burn properly because of the lower temperatures. This increases emissions.

The C.C.S. uses a thermostatically controlled air cleaner called the Auto-Therm air cleaner. It is designed to keep the temperature of the air entering the carburetor at approximately 100°F. This allows the lean carburetor to work properly, minimizes carburetor icing, and improves engine warm-up characteristics. A sensor unit located on the clean air side of the air filter senses the temperature of the air passing over it and regulates the vacuum supplied to a vacuum diaphragm in the inlet tube of the air cleaner. The colder the air, the greater the amount of

vacuum supplied to the vacuum diaphragm. The vacuum diaphragm, depending on the vacuum supplied to it, opens or closes a damper door in the inlet tube of the air cleaner. If the door is open, it allows air from the engine compartment to go to the carburetor. If the door is closed, air flows from the heat stove located on the exhaust manifold into the carburetor. In this way, heated air is supplied to the carburetor on cold days, and when first starting the engine and warming it up.

Since 1968, all car manufacturers have posted idle speeds and other pertinent data relative to the specific engine-car application in a conspicuous place in the engine compartment.

1970

The more stringent 1970 laws required tighter control of emissions. Crankcase emissions are controlled by the Positive Crankcase Ventilation System, and exhaust emissions by the engine Controlled Combustion System (C.C.S.), in conjunction with the new Transmission Controlled Spark System (T.C.S.)

In addition, cars sold in California are equipped with an Evaporation Control System that limits the amount of gasoline vapor discharged into the atmosphere (usually from the carburetor and fuel tank).

The T.C.S. system consists of a transmission switch, a solenoid valve, and a temperature switch. Under normal conditions, the system permits the vacuum distributor (spark) advance to operate only in High gear (both manual and automatic transmissions) and Reverse.

The transmission switch is located on the transmission and senses when the transmission is in one of the lower gears. When it is in a lower gear, the switch activates the vacuum solenoid valve. This valve is located in the vacuum line that runs from the carburetor to the distributor and it shuts off vacuum to the distributor advance when it is activated. There is also an engine-temperature sensing switch which overrides the transmission switch. It will allow vacuum advance in the lower gears when engine temperature is below 85°F or above 220°F. There is always vacuum advance in High gear and Reverse.

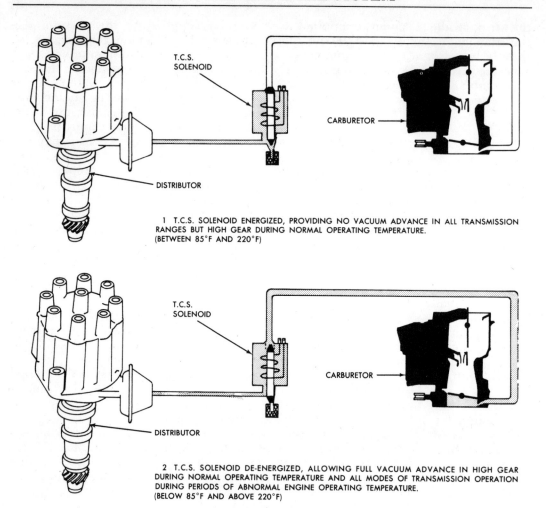

1 T.C.S. SOLENOID ENERGIZED, PROVIDING NO VACUUM ADVANCE IN ALL TRANSMISSION RANGES BUT HIGH GEAR DURING NORMAL OPERATING TEMPERATURE. (BETWEEN 85°F AND 220°F)

2 T.C.S. SOLENOID DE-ENERGIZED, ALLOWING FULL VACUUM ADVANCE IN HIGH GEAR DURING NORMAL OPERATING TEMPERATURE AND ALL MODES OF TRANSMISSION OPERATION DURING PERIODS OF ABNORMAL ENGINE OPERATING TEMPERATURE. (BELOW 85°F AND ABOVE 220°F)

1970 T.C.S. operation

1971

In 1971, the Combination Emission Control System (C.E.C.), was introduced. It uses the C.C.S. of 1968–69 and incorporates several, but not all, of the features in the T.C.S. of 1970. Although distributor vacuum advance is eliminated in the lower gears, as in the T.C.S. system, it is eliminated in a different manner. A C.E.C. solenoid valve is used to regulate distributor vacuum advance.

The C.E.C. solenoid valve is mounted on the carburetor. Vacuum from the intake manifold passes through a port at the base of the solenoid before it reaches the distributor. When the solenoid receives an electrical signal, the plunger extends, opening the port, which allows vacuum to the distributor. At the same time, the plunger head contacts the carburetor

throttle lever increasing the idle speed. When the solenoid is de-energized, the spring-loaded plunger returns to its unextended position closing the port and allowing the throttle lever to rest against the idle speed adjusting screw.

The switch is energized by two switches and one relay.

The time-delay relay is used to energize the C.E.C. solenoid and provide vacuum advance for the first 15 seconds after the ignition is turned on. This happens regardless of engine temperature. After the 15 seconds, the solenoid is again regulated by the temperature switch and the transmission switch.

One of the controlling switches is an engine temperature switch. It allows vacuum advance in all gears, by energizing the C.E.C. solenoid, when the engine temperature is below 82°F or above

220° F. In between 82° F and 220° F, this switch will allow no vacuum advance and the solenoid will be de-energized.

The other switch is the transmission switch. When the transmission is in the lower gears, this switch keeps the C.E.C. solenoid in the de-energized position eliminating vacuum advance. In High gear, the solenoid is energized by current from the battery and vacuum advance is supplied.

Engine dieseling is controlled by use of lower throttle plate openings (lower carburetor idle speeds).

On air-conditioned (A/C), automatic transmission cars, a solid-state time device engages the A/C compressor for about three seconds after the ignition is turned off. The load from the compressor effectively stalls the engine and prevents dieseling or overrrun.

The evaporation control system was added to all cars in 1971. This system limits the amount of gasoline vapor discharged into the air from the gas tank and carburetor. The fuel tank has a non-vented cap. As vapors are generated in the fuel tank, they flow through a liquid vapor separator to a canister where they are stored. From the canister, the vapors are routed to the carburetor where they are burned when the engine is running.

1972

All six-cylinder models with manual transmissions use the C.E.C. system. A description of this system can be found under the above 1971 discussion. All six-cylinder models with automatic transmissions use the A.I.R. system. A description of this system can be found under the above 1968 section. All V8s equipped with a manual four-speed transmission use the T.C.S. system which is described under "1970." All V8 models equipped with a three-speed manual transmission or an automatic transmission use the new Speed Control Spark System (S.C.S.).

Every engine/transmission combination uses the Auto-Therm air cleaner, P.C.V. system, and the evaporation control system of 1971.

The Speed Controlled Spark (S.C.S.), system uses a solenoid valve in the vacuum line running between the carburetor and the distributor. This valve is the same as the transmission-controlled

spark valve. The difference in this system is that the valve is regulated by vehicle speed using a speed control spark switch. The S.C.S. solenoid valve is energized below 38 mph in any gear, under normal operating temperature, allowing no vacuum advance. Above 38 mph, in any gear, or any time engine temperature is higher or lower than normal operating temperature, the solenoid valve is de-energized allowing full vacuum advance to the distributor.

Normal S.C.S. engine operating temperatures range from 95° to 230°F. An engine-temperature sensing switch is located in the head and de-energizes the solenoid until operating temperature is reached regardless of vehicle speed.

1973

The Controlled Combustion System (C.C.S.) is standard on all engines. The C.E.C./E.G.R. (Exhaust Gas Recirculation) system is used on all 6 cyl engines with manual transmission. The Air Injection Reactor (A.I.R.) is used on all 6 cyl, 350 with manual transmission, and 350/400 California engines. A combination of the Transmission Controlled Spark and Exhaust Gas Recirculation (E.G.R.) is found on all V8 engines.

E.G.R. is a system used to reduce nitrous oxide (NO_x) emissions. It functions by allowing a small amount of exhaust gas into the air fuel mixture in the intake manifold, under certain conditions.

The EGR TCS system consists of a temperature switch which senses when the engine temperature is under 71°F or over 230°F, a second temperature switch sensing engine temperature between 140°F and 230°F, an EGR solenoid, a vacuum advance solenoid, a transmission switch, and a time delay relay.

The under 71°F and over 230°F switch is mounted on the left cyl head. The 140°F to 230°F switch is mounted in the right cyl head. The time delay relay is mounted on the vacuum advance solenoid.

The 71°F to 230°F switch grounds the circuit for the solenoids below 71°F and above 230°F. The 140°F switch passes current to the transmission switch when engine temperature is between 140°F and 230°F. The transmission switch then grounds the circuit for the solenoids in

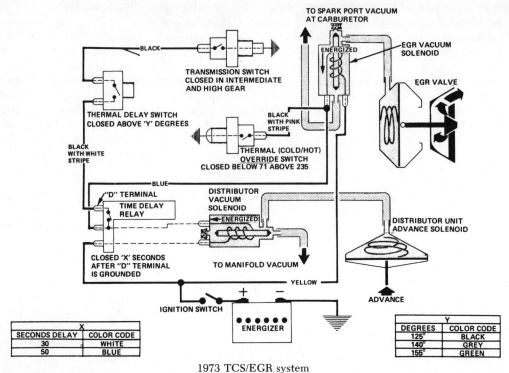

X		
SECONDS DELAY	COLOR CODE	
30	WHITE	
50	BLUE	

Y		
DEGREES	COLOR CODE	
125°	BLACK	
140°	GREY	
155°	GREEN	

1973 TCS/EGR system

First gear only. Between 71°F and 140°F the temperature switches are both open and the solenoids are in the normal positions.

The vacuum advance solenoid is normally closed, allowing no vacuum advance. The EGR solenoid is normally open, allowing exhaust gas recirculation.

Below 71°F there is a complete circuit and both solenoids are energized, allowing vacuum advance and cutting off EGR.

From 71°F to 140°F there is an open circuit, the solenoids return to their normal positions, and vacuum advance is cut off and EGR is allowed.

From 140°F to 230°F, in First gear, there is an open circuit and the solenoids are in their normal positions. The time delay relay maintains the open circuit for 33 to 55 seconds after the transmission shifts into Second gear. However, after the time delay in Second and Third gear, the solenoids are energized to allow vacuum advance and cut off EGR.

Over 235°F, the solenoids are energized and vacuum advance occurs and there is no EGR.

The C.E.C. system operates as for 1971, except that the time-delay relay now provides 20 seconds of vacuum

advance before the solenoid is de-energized, and the engine temperature switch provides vacuum advance when engine coolant temperature is below 93°F.

1973½

A mid-year redesign of the emission control system was necessitated by newly-announced Federal standards. On cars equipped with A.I.R., A.I.R. is not supplied to Nos. 3 and 6 cylinders. This is done by internal changes in the cylinder heads. Mid-year A.I.R. cylinder heads can usually be identified by the absence of a drilled passage and metal sealing ball at the Nos. 3 and 6 cylinder locations.

The new engines have a relocated vacuum source for the air cleaner. Vacuum is supplied through a tee in the hose feeding vacuum to the distributor vacuum spark thermal valve.

The mid-year EGR system operates basically on the same principle as the 1973 system, except for two major differences:

1. The EGR and TCS systems now work completely independent from each other.

2. A new EGR thermal vacuum valve

is used to sense the temperature of the intake manifold coolant. Below 95°F, no EGR; above 95°F, ported EGR.

In the TCS system, full vacuum advance is provided below 62°F. When the temperature rises above 62°F, the distributor vacuum spark thermal valve closes and from this point on the distributor solenoid must be energized to get vacuum advance. The upper temperature limit for vacuum advance cut-in is now 240°F.

The Start-Up Relay Switch gives full advance (ported for manual transmission) in any gear for 20 seconds after all engine starts. After the 20 seconds has elapsed, the switch breaks ground and the distributor solenoid is de-energized, shutting off the vacuum advance.

1974

The A.I.R. system is carried over from 1973 and is used on all manual transmission and California six-cylinder engines, 350 2 bbl manual transmission V8s, all 350 cu in. California engines and 400 cu in. 2 bbl California engines.

The EGR/TCS system is once again together, as in pre-1973½ systems, and consists of a thermal vacuum valve, vacuum advance solenoid, EGR valve, hot coolant switch, cold feed switch and a time-delay relay for engine starting. The system is found on all V8s. Pontiac six-cylinder engines have the EGR valve located on the intake manifold directly beneath the carburetor.

On the EGR/TCS system, the distributor spark-EGR thermal vacuum valve senses the temperature of the air/fuel mixture inside the intake manifold. Below 62°F, EGR is off and full vacuum advance is provided. When the temperature rises above 62°F, EGR is on (operated by a port above the throttle blade, so that it only comes on above idle). From this point on the distributor vacuum advance solenoid must be energized by the other components and switches to provide vacuum advance.

When the cylinder head metal temperature goes above 125°, 140°, 155°F (depending on use), the cold feed switch closes. This sends the 12V current to the TCS switch looking for a ground. The TCS switch provides a ground only when the transmission shifts into High gear.

There is no time delay after shifting into High gear.

Any time the coolant temperature goes over 240°F, the hot coolant switch provides a ground for the distributor solenoid. Since the hot coolant switch will ground whether the TCS switch does or not, vacuum advance will be supplied to the distributor in any gear when the coolant temperature reaches 240°F or above.

There is a distributor vacuum spark delay valve on some models, between the distributor solenoid and the distributor acting as a restrictor on vacuum supplied to the distributor. This merely slows down the rate vacuum is initially supplied to the distributor. Full vacuum is eventually supplied.

The function of the start-up relay switch is identical to that used in 1973½.

EMISSION SYSTEMS DESCRIPTIONS

Positive Crankcase Ventilation (PCV) Systems

A simple valve, operated by intake manifold vacuum, is used to meter the flow of air and vapors through the crankcase. Air is drawn in through either the breather cap, on pre-1968 cars (open system), or, on cars made after 1968, through the carburetor air cleaner (closed system). When the car is decelerating or the engine is idling, high manifold vacuum closes the valve; this restricts the flow of crankcase vapor into the intake manifold. During acceleration or at a constant speed, the intake manifold vacuum drops, the valve spring forces the valve open and more vapors flow into the intake manifold from the crankcase. If a backfire occurs the valve closes, preventing the vapor in the crankcase from being ignited. If the vapor is ignited, an explosion will result.

Air Injection System

A belt-driven air pump supplies air to an injection manifold which has a nozzle positioned behind each exhaust valve. Injection of air at this point causes combustion of any unburned hydrocarbons in the exhaust manifold rather than allowing them to escape into the atmosphere. An antibackfire valve controls the flow of air from the pump to prevent backfires resulting from an overly rich mixture

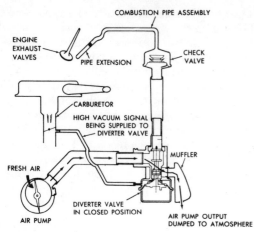

A.I.R. schematic

under closed throttle conditions. A check valve, sometimes an integral part of the air injection manifold, functions to prevent hot exhaust gas backflow into the pump and hoses in case of pump failure or when the antibackfire valve is working.

Thermostatically Controlled Air Cleaner

Thermostatically controlled air cleaners are used to improve operation of the engine and to prevent carburetor icing during warm-up in cold weather.

A movable door in the air cleaner snorkle allows air to be drawn in from either a manifold heat stove (cold operation) or from under the hood (normal operation). The door may be operated by a bimetallic spring or a vacuum motor. Doors of both types may use a vacuum override to provide cold air intake during periods of hard acceleration when stove-heated air is normally being supplied.

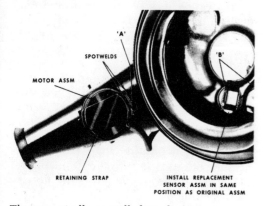

Thermostatically controlled air cleaner

Distributor Controls

There are three basic types of distributor controls:

1. Engine vacuum controls.
2. Transmission-controlled spark—transmission gear selected and/or temperature.
3. Speed-controlled spark—vehicle speed and/or temperature.

It is easier to consider these three types separately, although some of them perform similar functions and may be used in conjunction with one another.

ENGINE VACUUM CONTROLS

Many small valves and solenoids fall into this class of emission controls. Some distributors are equipped with a dual-diaphragm vacuum unit which retards the spark during closed throttle deceleration and idle. On some distributors, solenoids may be used to either advance or retard the timing under predetermined conditions.

A deceleration valve may be used to provide maximum vacuum advance when the car is slowing down, by sending intake manifold vacuum to the distributor vacuum unit. By doing this, emissions may be better controlled during deceleration.

Because emission-controlled engines run hotter, it is often necessary to use a coolant temperature vacuum valve to provide additional vacuum advance when the engine is overheated. The valve is threaded into an engine coolant passage. If the engine overheats, the additional vacuum advance causes the engine speed to increase, allowing it to cool down quite rapidly. A similar valve may also be used to determine the temperature at which a TCS, SCS, or EGR system operates (see below).

A spark delay valve is installed on some engines to prevent the vacuum advance from working immediately under heavy acceleration.

TRANSMISSION-CONTROLLED SPARK (TCS) SYSTEM

Many variations of transmission-controlled spark (TCS) systems are used to control vehicle emissions. The basic components of these systems are: a transmission switch, which is operated either by oil pressure (automatic transmissions) or by the gear selected (manual transmission); and a vacuum solenoid. The solenoid allows a vacuum to be supplied to the distributor vacuum unit or ports it into the atmosphere. Usually vacuum is supplied only in High gear and is ported in the lower gears. However, few TCS systems are quite this simple.

For example, most TCS systems use some type of temperature switch to control their operation, i.e., the system will not function below a specified air or engine temperature. In some cases it will not work above a specified temperature either. Some cars use a coolant temperature-operated vacuum valve in conjunction with the TCS system.

Various reversing and time delay relays may also be used, depending upon the needs of the engine and transmission.

SPEED-CONTROLLED SPARK (SCS) SYSTEMS

Speed-controlled spark (SCS) systems perform a similar function to the transmission-controlled systems above. Many of the components are the same and used in a similar way in both of the systems. The major difference lies in the switch which is activated by the speed, rather than the gear.

In its simplest form, this switch is noth-ing more than a centrifugal switch, connected to the speedometer drive, which completes the SCS circuit at or above a predetermined speed. A more complicated type of switch uses a small speedometer gear (or speedometer cable) driven pulse generator to send a signal to an amplifier, which, in turn, completes the SCS system circuit at predetermined speed.

Once the circuit has been completed, vacuum is allowed to flow to the distributor vacuum unit. When the circuit is not energized, vacuum is ported into the atmosphere.

Like the transmission-controlled spark systems, SCS systems use temperature switches and various relays.

Carburetor Controls

Because of the increase in engine speed necessary to control emissions at idle, dieseling has become a problem. As a result, many carburetors use a solenoid to allow the throttle to close when the ignition is shut off, thus reducing engine speed which, in turn, prevents dieseling.

To prevent dieseling on some air-conditioned cars, a signal from an amplifer engages the A/C compressor clutch momentarily when the engine is shut off. This puts a load on the engine, thus slowing it down.

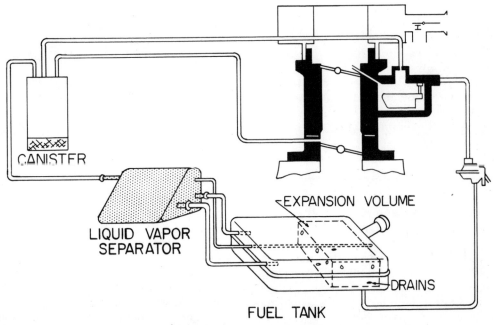

CANISTER

LIQUID VAPOR SEPARATOR

EXPANSION VOLUME

DRAINS

FUEL TANK

Evaporative control schematic

Evaporative Emission Control Systems

To control emissions resulting from fuel evaporation, all cars made after 1971 use a closed fuel supply system. Instead of fuel vapor being vented into the atmosphere, it goes into a vapor/liquid separator and is routed from there, either directly through a charcoal storage canister, or into the crankcase. To prevent vapor loss at other points, the carburetor has controlled vents and a PCV system (see above) is used along with the evaporative emission control system.

Exhaust Gas Recirculation (EGR)

Exhaust gas recirculation (EGR) systems are used to reduce NO_x emissions by lowering peak flame temperature during combustion. Exhaust gases are routed into the intake manifold via intake manifold passages and an EGR control valve.

EGR systems use coolant temperature-operated vacuum valves or air temperature-operated valves to determine when they function. In addition, a vacuum amplifier (mechanical) may be provided if a weak vacuum signal is being supplied to the EGR valve.

TROUBLESHOOTING

Positive Crankcase Ventilation (PCV) System

VALVE TESTS

1. See if any deposits are present in the carburetor passages, the oil filler cap, or the hoses. Clean these as required.
2. Connect a tachometer, as instructed by its manufacturer, to the engine.
3. With the engine idling, do one of the following:
   a. Remove the PCV valve hose from the crankcase or the oil filler connection.
   b. On cars with the PCV valve located in a grommet on the valve cover, remove both the valve and the grommet.
   NOTE: *If the valve and the hoses are not clogged-up, a hissing sound should be present.*
4. Check the tachometer reading. Place a finger over the valve or hose opening (a suction should be felt).

5. Check the tachometer again. The engine speed should have dropped at least 50 rpm. It should return to normal when the finger is removed from the opening.
6. If the engine does not change speed or if the change is less than 50 rpm, the hose is clogged or the valve is defective. Check the hose first. If the hose is not clogged replace, do not attempt to repair, the PCV valve.
7. Test the new valve in the above manner, to make sure that it is operating properly.
NOTE: *There are several commercial PCV valve testers available. Be sure that the one used is suitable for the valve to be tested, as the testers are not universal. Follow the manufacturer's instructions.*

Air Injection Systems

AIR PUMP TESTS

CAUTION: *Do not hammer on, pry, or bend the pump housing while tightening the drive belt or testing the pump.*

Belt Tension and Air Leaks

1. Before proceeding with the tests, check the pump drive belt tension to see if it is within specifications.
2. Turn the pump by hand. If it has seized, the belt will slip, producing noise. Disregard any chirping, squealing, or rolling sounds from inside the pump; these are normal when it is turned by hand.
3. Check the hoses and connections for leaks. Hissing or a blast of air is indicative of a leak. Soapy water, applied lightly around the area in question, is a good method for detecting leaks.

Air Output Tests

1. Disconnect the air supply hose at the antibackfire valve.
2. Connect a vacuum gauge, using a suitable adaptor, to the air supply hose.
NOTE: *If there are two hoses plug the second one up.*
3. With the engine at normal operating temperature, increase the idle speed and watch the vacuum gauge.
4. The airflow from the pump should be steady and fall between 2–6 psi. If it is

unsteady or falls below this, the pump is defective and must be replaced.

Pump Noise Diagnosis

The air pump is normally noisy; as engine speed increases, the noise of the pump will rise in pitch. The rolling sound the pump bearings make is normal, however if this sound becomes objectionable at certain speeds, the pump is defective and will have to be replaced.

A continual hissing sound from the air pump pressure relief valve at idle, indicates a defective valve. Replace the relief valve.

If the pump rear bearing fails, a continual knocking sound will be heard. Since the rear bearing is not separately replaceable, the pump will have to be replaced as an assembly.

ANTIBACKFIRE VALVE TESTS

There are two different types of antibackfire valves used with air injection systems. A by-pass (diverter) valve is used on most current engines, while most older engines use a gulp type antibackfire valve. Test procedures for both types are given below.

Gulp Valve

1. Detach the air supply hose which runs between the pump and the gulp valve.
2. Connect a tachometer and run the engine between 1500–2000 rpm.
3. Allow the throttle to snap closed. This should produce a loud sucking sound from the gulp valve.
4. Repeat this operation several times. If no sound is present, the valve is not working or the vacuum connections are loose.
5. Check the vacuum connections. If they are secure, replace the gulp valve.

By-pass (Diverter) Valve

1. Detach the hose, which runs from the by-pass valve to the check valve, at the by-pass valve hose connection.
2. Connect a tachometer to the engine. With the engine running at normal idle speed, check to see that air is flowing from the by-pass valve hose connection.
3. Speed the engine up, so that it is running at 1500–2000 rpm. Allow the throttle to snap shut. The flow of air from the by-pass valve at the check valve hose connection should stop momentarily and

Air Injection System Diagnosis Chart

Problem	Cause	Cure
1. Noisy drive belt	1a Loose belt 1b Seized pump	1a Tighten belt 1b Replace
2. Noisy pump	2a Leaking hose 2b Loose hose 2c Hose contacting other parts 2d Diverter or check valve failure 2e Pump mounting loose 2g Defective pump	2a Trace and fix leak 2b Tighten hose clamp 2c Reposition hose 2d Replace 2e Tighten securing bolts 2g Replace
3. No air supply	3a Loose belt 3b Leak in hose or at fitting 3c Defective anti-backfire valve 3d Defective check valve 3e Defective pump	3a Tighten belt 3b Trace and fix leak 3c Replace 3d Replace 3e Replace
4. Exhaust backfire	4a Vacuum or air leaks 4b Defective anti-backfire valve 4c Sticking choke 4d Choke setting rich	4a Trace and fix leak 4b Replace 4c Service choke 4d Adjust choke

air should then flow from the exhaust port on the valve body or the silencer assembly.

4. Repeat Step 3 several times. If the flow of air is not diverted into the atmosphere from the valve exhaust port or if it fails to stop flowing from the hose connection, check the vacuum lines and connections. If these are tight, the valve is defective and requires replacement.

5. A leaking diaphragm will cause the air to flow out both the hose connection and the exhaust port at the same time. If this happens, replace the valve.

CHECK VALVE TEST

1. Before starting the test, check all of the hoses and connections for leaks.

2. Detach the air supply hose(s) from the check valve(s).

3. Insert a suitable probe into the check valve and depress the plate. Release it; the plate should return to its original poisiton against the valve seat. If binding is evident, replace the valve.

4. Repeat Step 3 if two valves are used.

5. With the engine running at normal operating temperature, gradually increase its speed to 1500 rpm. Check for exhaust gas leakage. If any is present, replace the valve assembly.

NOTE: *Vibration and flutter of the check valve at idle speed is a normal condition and does not mean that the valve should be replaced.*

Thermostatically Controlled Air Cleaner

AIR DOOR TESTS

Non-Vacuum-Operated

1. Unfasten the temperature sensing valve and snorkle assembly from the air cleaner. Place it in a container of cold water. Make sure that the thermostat is completely covered with water.

2. Place a thermometer, of known accuracy, in the water. Heat the water slowly and watch the temperature.

3. At 105°F, or less, the door should be closed (manifold heat position).

4. Continue heating the water until it reaches 130°F. The door should be fully open to the outside air position.

5. If the door does not open at or near this temperature, check it for binding or a detached spring. If neither of these situa-

tions exist, the sensor is defective and must be replaced.

NOTE: *This usually means that the entire snorkle assembly must be replaced.*

Vacuum-Operated Door

1. Either start with a cold engine or remove the air cleaner from the engine for at least half an hour. While cooling the air cleaner, leave the engine compartment hood open.

2. Tape a thermometer, of known accuracy, to the inside of the air cleaner so that it is near the temperature sensor unit. Install the air cleaner on the engine but do not fasten its securing nut.

3. Start the engine. With the engine cold and the outside temperature less than 90°F., the door should be in the "heat on" position (closed to outside air).

NOTE: *Due to the position of the air cleaner on some cars, a mirror may be necessary when observing the position of the air door.*

4. Operate the throttle lever rapidly to ½–¾ of its opening and release it. The air door should open to allow outside air to enter and then close again.

5. Allow the engine to warm up to normal temperature. Watch the door. When it opens to the outside air, remove the cover from the air cleaner. The temperature should be over 90°F and no more than 130°F; 115°F is about normal. If the door does not work within these temperature ranges, or fails to work at all, check for linkage or door binding.

If binding is not present and the air door is not working, proceed with the vacuum tests, given below. If these indicate no faults in the vacuum motor and the door is not working, the temperature sensor is defective and must be replaced.

VACUUM MOTOR TEST

NOTE: *Be sure that the vacuum hose that runs between the temperature switch and the vacuum motor is not pinched by the retaining clip under the air cleaner. This could prevent the air door from closing.*

1. Check all of the vacuum lines and fittings for leaks. Correct any leaks. If none are found, proceed with the test.

2. Remove the hose which runs from

the sensor to the vacuum motor. Run a hose directly from the manifold vacuum source to the vacuum motor.

3. If the motor closes the air door, it is functioning properly and the temperature sensor is defective.

4. If the motor does *not* close the door and no binding is present in its operation, the vacuum motor is defective and must be replaced.

NOTE: *If an alternate vacuum source is applied to the motor, insert a vacuum gauge in the line by using a T-fitting. Apply at least 9 in. Hg of vacuum in order to operate the motor.*

Distributor Controls

DUAL DIAPHRAGM DISTRIBUTOR TESTS

1. Connect a timing light to the engine. Check the ignition timing.

NOTE: *Before proceeding with the tests, disconnect any spark control devices, distributor vacuum valves, etc. If these are left connected, inaccurate results may be obtained.*

2. Remove the retard hose from the distributor and plug it. Increase the engine speed. The timing should advance. If it fails to do so, then the vacuum unit is faulty and must be replaced.

3. Check the timing with the engine at normal idle speed. Unplug the retard hose and connect it to the vacuum unit. The timing should instantly be retarded from 4–10°. If this does not occur, the retard diaphragm has a leak and the vacuum unit must be replaced.

COOLANT TEMPERATURE OPERATED VACUUM VALVE TESTS

NOTE: *On some cars equipped with distributor control systems, this valve also is used to override the control system under overheating conditions. If a malfunction of the distributor control system occurs, remember to check the vacuum valve.*

1. Check all of the vacuum hoses for proper installation and routing.

2. Connect a tachometer to the engine.

3. Run the engine until it reaches normal operating temperature, but do not allow it to overheat. Be sure that the choke is open.

4. Check engine rpm with the carburetor at curb idle.

5. Detach the vacuum line from the intake manifold at the valve end. Plug this hose.

6. Check the idle speed; there should be no change. If the idle speed drops 100 rpm or more, the valve is defective and must be replaced.

7. Check the coolant level and radiator cap. Reconnect the intake manifold hose to the temperature valve.

8. Cover the radiator to increase the coolant temperature. Then do one of the following.

   a. If the car is equipped with a temperature gauge, run the engine until the gauge registers near the top of the "Normal" range.

   b. On cars equipped with warning lights, run the engine until the red temperature light comes on.

CAUTION: *Do not run the engine at an abnormally high temperature for any longer than is required to test the valve. It is not necessary, nor desirable, to overheat an engine when the car uses a temperature gauge, i.e., the gauge should never be allowed to register "H" (Hot) when testing the valve.*

9. If the engine speed has increased by at least 100 rpm, the valve is functioning properly. If there is little or no increase in engine speed, the valve is faulty and must be replaced.

10. Uncover the radiator and allow the car to cool by running the engine at idle.

TRANSMISSION CONTROLLED SPARK SYSTEM TESTS

NOTE: *The components used on the transmission-controlled spark (TCS) systems vary from model to model. For a description of the components used for each model, see the appropriate year description.*

System Test

1. Connect a vacuum gauge to the vacuum source for the vacuum solenoid. With the transmission in Neutral and the engine idling, vacuum should be present.

2. If there is no vacuum present, check for a clogged vacuum port, dam-

aged vacuum lines or loose hose connections.

3. Disconnect the vacuum gauge and reconnect the vacuum line.

4. Detach the vacuum line from the distributor vacuum unit and connect it to the vacuum gauge. This is the line which contains the vacuum advance solenoid or CEC solenoid.

5. With engine temperature above 95°F and the transmission in Neutral, run the engine for at least 25 seconds. The vacuum gauge should read zero.

6. Do one of the following:

a. Manual transmission—Depress the clutch pedal and move the shift lever through the gears. Increase engine speed in each gear, enough to cause vacuum advance. A vacuum should be present only in High gear.

NOTE: *On 1970–71 models with four-speed transmissions, vacuum should also be present in Third gear.*

b. Automatic transmission—Raise the rear wheels of the car off the ground. Support the car and block the front wheels, so that it cannot roll forward. Place the transmission in Drive and speed the engine up enough so that the transmission will shift into High gear; vacuum should only be present when the transmission enters High gear, and not while it is in lower gears.

NOTE: *Some cars are equipped with a time-delay device, so it may take 20–25 seconds before vacuum is present once the proper gear has been reached. Do not run the engine any longer than necessary to complete the test.*

7. If no vacuum is present when it should be or if it is present when it should not be, first check the TCS system fuse (if so equipped) and then proceed with the individual tests outlined blow.

Vacuum Advance Solenoid Tests

NOTE: *There are two different types of vacuum advance solenoids used; look at the chart to determine the proper model usage.*

Type A—Normally Opened

1. Disconnect the vacuum line from the vacuum advance solenoid to the distributor vacuum unit, at the distributor end. Connect a vacuum gauge to the line

after making sure that it is not broken or clogged.

2. Detach the electrical leads from the solenoid. With the engine running, the vacuum gauge should register a vacuum. If it does not, the solenoid is faulty and must be replaced.

3. Using care to observe the proper polarity, connect one solenoid terminal to a 12 V power source. Using a jumper wire, connect the transmission switch terminal on the vacuum solenoid to ground. The solenoid should energize and the vacuum gauge reading should return to zero. If vacuum is still present, the solenoid is jammed and should be replaced.

4. If the solenoid is not defective, connect it in the original manner and go on to the next appropriate test.

Type C—CEC Solenoid and Relays

Being careful to observe correct polarity, connect the "hot" lead of the solenoid to a 12 V power source and ground the other lead. With 12 V applied to the CEC solenoid, its plunger should extend. With no power applied to the solenoid, the plunger should retract. If it fails to do either properly, the solenoid is defective and must be replaced. If it is not defective, reconnect it.

NOTE: *A defective CEC solenoid will also affect the operation of the throttle. For further details, see "Carburetor Modifications."*

Models made prior to 1972 which are equipped with a CEC solenoid, use a reversing relay to provide proper switching action for the solenoid. To test relay operation:

1. By-pass the relay by grounding its single wire connector.

2. If the CEC solenoid plunger will now extend, and it did not extend in the above test, the reversing relay is defective.

A time-delay relay is used on some models equipped with a CEC solenoid to provide vacuum advance for 15–20 seconds after the ignition is switched on. To check its operation, proceed as follows:

1. Disconnect the electrical lead from the temperature switch.

2. Allow the relay to cool. Turn the ignition on. The CEC solenoid should energize (plunger extend) for about 15–20 seconds and then go off.

3. If it fails to go off, detach the blue

lead from the time-delay relay. If the CEC solenoid now de-energizes, then the relay is faulty and must be replaced.

If none of the CEC system components which were tested are defective, go on to the next applicable test.

Vacuum Delay Relay Tests

This relay is a solid-state unit which is used on some 1972 models. (It is not used with the CEC solenoid and should not be confused with the *time*-delay relay, above.) It is located underneath the dashboard, inside the passenger compartment. To test it proceed in the following manner:

1. Turn the ignition on. Then, using a lower amperage test lamp, check to see that the relay is getting power. If it is not, check its wiring.
2. Disconnect and ground the black lead.
3. Wait for 26 seconds. The vacuum advance solenoid should then energize. If it does not, the relay is faulty and must be replaced. If it does, reconnect the vacuum delay relay and proceed with the next applicable test.

Temperature Switch Test

1. Connect a vacuum gauge to the vacuum advance solenoid to the distributor vacuum unit.
2. Allow the engine to cool to around 75° F and then start it. The gauge should indicate the presence of a vacuum.
3. If it does not, ground the lead from the cold terminal of the temperature switch.
4. On temperature controls with an additional hot terminal, repeat Step 3—this time grounding the hot terminal.
5. If vacuum is not present when either terminal is grounded, the temperature switch is defective. If vacuum still is not present, reconnect the temperature switch leads and vacuum line. Proceed with the next applicable test.

Transmission Switch Tests

NOTE: *There are several different types of transmission switches used on Firebirds. Check the chart below for proper model usage and then proceed with the applicable test.*

Vacuum Advance Solenoid and Transmission Switch Usage

| | | Test Section Used For: | |
Year	Model	Vacuum Advance Solenoid	Transmission Switch
1970–71	All	A	E, F
1972–73	6 Cyl.	C	D
1972	V8	A	E, F

Type D—Normally Opened

This test should be performed last, once all the other TCS system components are known to be in proper working order.

1. Repeat Steps 4–6 of the "System Test." There should be vacuum to the distributor in High gear.
2. If there is none, disconnect the lead from the transmission switch and ground it.
3. If vacuum is now present, i.e., the vacuum advance solenoid has energized, then the transmission switch is faulty and must be replaced.

Type E—Manual Transmission/ Normally Closed

NOTE: *Some models with manual transmissions use a two-terminal transmission switch. Before proceeding with the test, ground the extra terminal.*

1. Detach the switch connector at the side of the transmission.
2. Connect a test lamp in series with the switch and 12 V power source.
CAUTION: *Do not use a bulb any larger than 0.8 amp (No. 1803), the switch contacts will be damaged at a higher amperage.*
3. With the engine and ignition off, move the gearshift lever through all of the gears. The test lamp should remain lighted in every gear except Third and Fourth (if so equipped).
NOTE: *On 1972 models with four-speed transmissions, the lamp should remain lighted in Third gear and not go out until Fourth is selected.*

4. If the test lamp fails to go out when it should, the switch is defective.

5. If the test lamp fails to come on at all, the switch is broken or the wiring is faulty.

6. If the switch is not defective, reconnect it when finished testing.

Type F—Automatic Transmission Normally Closed

1. Connect a test lamp as detailed in Steps 1–2 of the test for Type E switch above. Pay particular attention to the "Caution."

2. Raise the rear wheels of the car so they are off the ground and support the car so that it cannot move forward.

3. Start the engine. Shift the transmission into Drive. Increase engine speed so that the transmission shifts into High gear, the test lamp should go out when the transmission enters High gear.

4. Allow the engine to return to idle and apply the brakes. Shift into Reverse. The light should go out again, except on cars equipped with Powerglide.

5. In all other gears the lamp should remain on. If it does not or if it fails to go out when it should, replace the switch.

1973 COMBINATION T.C.S.-E.G.R. SYSTEM

NOTE: *Cars produced on or after 15 March 1973 do not use the combined TCS-EGR system, instead two separate systems are used. For test procedures on the TCS system, see the following section. EGR system tests are included below. Engines with the new systems may be identified by the darker blue paint on the engine and the two thermal valves threaded into the intake manifold, just ahead of the carburetor.*

System Test

1. Apply parking brake, and securely block wheels. Connect a vacuum gauge to the distributor end of the vacuum line that runs from the T.C.S. solenoid to the distributor. Observe the position of the stem under the E.G.R. valve, this should be in the closed position.

2. The engine must be "overnight" cold with the ambient temperature below 71°F. If this condition cannot be duplicated, follow the instructions below, skipping Step 4, and then use the "Simulated

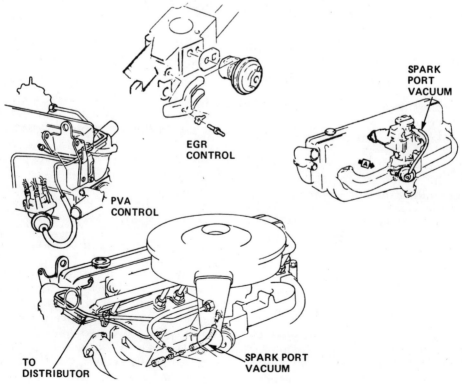

Early 1973 TCS/EGR system components

Temperature Switch Test" which follows the normal testing procedures.

3. Depress accelerator to set choke and place throttle linkage on fast idle cam. Start the engine and allow throttle to remain on fast idle cam.

4. Vacuum gauge should indicate a high manifold vacuum and E.G.R. valve should remain fully closed.

5. When the engine reaches 71°F, manifold vacuum should disappear and the E.G.R. valve should open.

6. Shut off the engine. Raise the rear of the car and place it on jackstands so that the wheels are off the floor. Release parking brake. Put automatic transmission in Drive, manual transmission in highest gear. Place throttle on fast idle cam. Make sure that the automatic transmission shifts out of First gear.

7. When engine temperature reaches 140°F (well before coolant flows through radiator), the E.G.R. valve should close fully, and manifold vacuum should again show on the vacuum gauge. Shift transmission out of gear for several seconds, then put it back in gear. Vacuum should disappear and E.G.R. valve should open. 33–55 seconds after the transmission shifts out of First gear, vacuum should come back and the E.G.R. valve should close.

8. Restrict the flow of air across the radiator core. Shift the transmission into Neutral. Vacuum will disappear, and E.G.R. valve will open. At 235°F (before temperature light comes on) vacuum should be restored and the E.G.R. valve should close.

NOTE: *If the EGR valve is not operating properly, perform Steps 5–7 of the EGR valve test, below.*

Simulated Temperature Switch Test

If the other parts of the system function, but conditions would not permit testing the low temperature function, remove the temperature sensor from the rear of the left head as follows:

1. Allow engine to cool until radiator cap can be safely removed, then remove the cap.

2. Place a clean container under the drain cock and begin draining coolant.

3. Disconnect wiring and loosen switch at rear of left cylinder head to check for presence of coolant. As soon as

switch can be removed without loss of coolant, close the radiator drain cock and remove the switch. Test the switch as follows:

1. Prepare a container of cold water or water and ice. Check with a thermometer to make sure that the temperature is below 60°F.

2. Immerse the threaded portion of the switch in the water, and allow it to cool until it has reached the temperature of the water.

3. Remove the switch from the bath and immediately check for continuity between the electrical prong and the threaded portion of the switch. Replace a switch which shows no continuity under these conditions.

Symptoms and Appropriate Checks

1. System responds normally at operating temperatures, but does not supply advance and deny EGR below 71°F and/or above 235°F. Operate engine at fast idle with transmission in Neutral until normal operating temperature is reached. Jump the switch at the rear of the left cylinder head by grounding the wire which goes to the switch. If this produces vacuum and shuts off the EGR valve, replace the switch. Otherwise, check for defects in the wiring between this switch and the solenoids.

2. System responds to temperature changes, but does not provide vacuum advance and deny EGR after transmission shifts to Second gear. Operate engine at fast idle with transmission in Neutral until operating temperature is reached. Ground the switch on the right-side of the transmission, by grounding the wire connected to it. Keep wire grounded one minute. If this produces vacuum advance and denies EGR, replace the transmission switch. Otherwise, by-pass the switch on the right cylinder head and ground the wire to the transmission switch. If this produces vacuum advance and denies EGR after one minute, replace the sensor in the right head. Otherwise, the Time Delay Relay or associated wiring is defective. By-pass each to locate the defective component.

3. System responds normally except that EGR is denied and vacuum advance established as soon as transmission shifts

to Second gear. Replace the Time Delay Relay.

4. Only one function responds as required, or system provides EGR and denies vacuum advance at all times; check wiring. Replace if defective. Otherwise, solenoid(s) are at fault.

1973½ TCS System

A new TCS system is used on 1973 models, beginning with cars produced on or after 15 March 1973. For testing the combined TCS-EGR system used before this date, see the preceding Section.

System Test

NOTE: *The following conditions must be met before beginning the TCS system test:*

The car must be run for ten minutes, if it is at room temperature. If the car is cold, it must be run until it has reached normal operating temperature. This will allow the air/fuel mixture and the engine block to reach 62°F and 155°F, respectively.

At no time during the test should the coolant temperature be allowed to go over 240°F (the temperature warning light will come on if it does).

1. Hook up a vacuum gauge to the vertical fitting at the back of the vacuum advance solenoid or, if the engine is equipped with a spark delay valve, hook up the gauge to the "DIST" port on the delay valve.

2. Place the vacuum gauge on the cowl, so that it can be seen from the driver's seat.

3. Run the engine until it is warmed-up. See the "Note" at the beginning of this Section.

4. After the engine reaches normal operating temperature, turn it off.

5. Place the gearshift in Park or Neutral, and start the engine.

a. The gauge should indicate vacuum for about 20 seconds, unless the car is equipped with a spark delay valve.

b. The vacuum gauge reading will slowly rise to a peak in 10–15 seconds on spark delay valve equipped models. The vacuum reading should disappear on all models after 20 seconds.

NOTE: *In order to get a vacuum reading on cars having a manual transmis-*

sion, open the throttle slightly in order to uncover the carburetor vacuum port.

6. If no vacuum is registered on the gauge, check for a faulty time delay relay, as outlined under "Type C—CEC Solenoid and Relays," above. If the time delay relay is working properly, check the vacuum advance solenoid to see if it is defective. If both are working properly, go on to the next step.

7. On manual transmission-equipped cars, depress the clutch pedal, open the throttle slightly and shift into High gear, the gauge should show a vacuum. Remember to wait 10–15 seconds on spark delay valve equipped engines.

8. On cars having an automatic transmission, shift into Reverse. The gauge should register vacuum in at least 10–15 seconds.

CAUTION: *Before shifting into Reverse, be sure that the parking brake is on and the service brake is fully applied to prevent the car from moving. Do not keep the car in Reverse any longer than necessary.*

9. If no vacuum is present, check for clogged, broken or misrouted vacuum lines. If the lines are in good condition, check the transmission switch or the vacuum advance solenoid, as outlined in the appropriate section, above.

10. If vacuum advance is always present, then check the following:

a. If the vacuum advance solenoid is always energized, check the red temperature warning light on the instrument panel. If it is on, either coolant temperature has reached 240°F or the temperature sensor is defective, which will cause the solenoid to remain energized. Allow the engine to cool to test the sensor's operation.

b. If the dash temperature light is not on, the engine block temperature is above 155°F, but the vacuum advance solenoid is still energized, the "cold feed" switch is probably defective and should be replaced.

c. If vacuum is always present, but the vacuum advance solenoid is NOT energized, then the air/fuel sensing valve is probably defective and should be replaced.

NOTE: *This valve will provide vacuum advance all the time, unless the air/fuel mixture temperature is above 62°F.*

SPEED CONTROLLED SPARK SYSTEMS

System Test

This test should be performed with the engine temperature between 95° and 230°F.

1. Raise the rear wheels off the ground and support the car so that it cannot roll forward.

2. Disconnect the vacuum hose which runs between the distributor vacuum unit and the vacuum advance solenoid at the distributor or valve end. Connect a vacuum gauge to the hose.

3. Start the engine and shift into Drive. Accelerate until the speedometer registers 38 mph.

4. Until the specified speed is reached, the vacuum reading should be zero. Once this speed is reached, vacuum should be present.

5. If no vacuum is registered at or above the specified speed, check the vacuum lines and connections first. Examine the carburetor port to be sure that it is not clogged.

NOTE: *Remember to check the coolant temperature vacuum override valve, if so equipped, as its failure could cause a loss of vacuum. Test procedures for it are given earlier in this section.*

6. If there is nothing wrong with the vacuum supply, disconnect the gauge, reconnect the hose and proceed with the next test.

Transmission Switch Test

1. Leave the rear wheels of the car off the ground as in the system test above.

2. Disconnect the transmission switch leads. Connect a low-amperage test lamp in series with the switch and the positive side of the battery.

3. Accelerate to the specified speed (see chart below) and watch the test lamp. It should remain on until the specified speed is reached. If the lamp fails to go out or if it does not light at all, the switch is defective and must be replaced.

4. If the switch is working properly, reconnect it and go on with the next test.

Vacuum Advance Solenoid Test

1. Disconnect the vacuum advance solenoid leads. Connect a vacuum gauge to the solenoid hose as in the system test.

2. Place the transmission in Neutral and start the engine. Increase engine speed. The gauge should indicate the presence of a vacuum.

3. Connect the hot lead to a 12 V

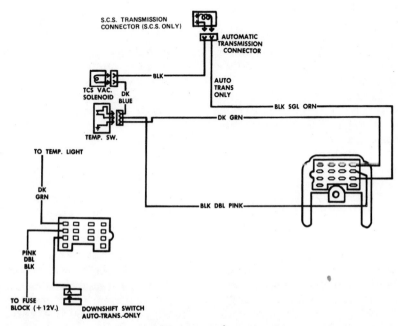

SCS system schematic

power source. Ground the other lead. Increase the engine speed again. The solenoid should energize, resulting in a vacuum reading of zero.

4. Replace the vacuum advance solenoid if it is faulty. If it is not, reconnect the wiring and go on with the next appropriate test.

Engine Temperature Switch

If vacuum advance is present when it should not be, i.e., below the speed specified in the chart, the temperature switch is defective if the other SCS System components are functioning properly and the engine temperature is 95–230°F. Replace it and repeat the system test.

If, on the other hand, vacuum is not being supplied when it should be, with the engine temperature below 95°F or above 230°F, and the other components are functioning properly, the fault again lies in the temperature switch. Replace it and repeat the system test with the engine below 95°F (cold). Vacuum advance should be present at all speeds.

Carburetor Controls

CEC Solenoid Operation

The CEC solenoid is used on some models. It has two functions; one is to regulate distributor vacuum and the other is to operate as a throttle positioner. When the solenoid is energized, the throttle blade is held off its seat by a plunger located at one end of the CEC solenoid. This provides higher engine rpm during the deceleration, thus reducing exhaust emissions.

Because of its dual function, failure of this valve can lead to higher emission levels or an idle which is considerably faster than normal. If the CEC solenoid is suspected of not working properly, follow the complete set of test procedures for it in "Distributor Controls."

Evaporative Emission Control System

There are several things to check for if a malfunction of the evaporative emission control system is suspected.

1. Leaks may be traced by using an infrared hydrocarbon tester. Run the test probe along the lines and connections. The meter will indicate the presence of a leak by a high hydrocarbon (HC) reading.

This method is much more accurate than a visual inspection which would indicate only the presence of a leak large enough to pass liquid.

2. Leaks may be caused by any of the following, so always check these areas when looking for them:
   a. Defective or worn lines;
   b. Disconnected or pinched lines;
   c. Improperly routed lines;
   d. A defective filler cap.

NOTE: *If it becomes necessary to replace any of the lines used in the evaporative emission control system, use only those hoses which are fuel resistant or are marked "EVAP."*

3. If the fuel tank has collapsed, it may be the fault of clogged or pinched vent lines, a defective vapor separator, or a plugged or incorrect fuel filler cap.

4. To test the filler cap, clean it and place it against the mouth. Blow into the relief valve housing. If the cap passes pressure with light blowing or if it fails to release with hard blowing, it is defective and must be replaced.

NOTE: *Replace the cap with one marked "pressure/vacuum" only. An incorrect cap will render the system inoperative or damage its components.*

Exhaust Gas Recirculation (EGR) Systems

1973 EGR Valve Tests

NOTE: *See TCS section above for further tests.*

1. Test the valve diaphragm by disconnecting the vacuum line and applying an outside vacuum source to the valve. The shaft should raise between 8–10 in. Hg. It should retain the pressure and not leak down.

2. If the valve shaft is frozen in the raised position, the valve is defective.

3. If the valve fails any of the above tests, it is defective. Replace it as an assembly; the valve cannot be disassembled and repaired.

4. In some cases the valve may be cleaned with a wire brush or in a spark plug cleaning machine, to loosen deposits which may cause the valve to stick.

NOTE: *If the engine is to be tested by "shorting out" the cylinders when it is equipped with an EGR valve, first disconnect the vacuum hose at the valve and plug it. Failure to do this will cause uneven idling and indicate false test results.*

1973½ AND 1974 EGR SYSTEM

NOTE: *Firebirds made on or after 15 March 1973 use separate systems for TCS and EGR. For TCS system checking procedures, see the appropriate Section above.*

The testing procedure for the EGR valve is basically the same as that outlined in the preceding Section. However, there are several points which should be noted:

1. The engine must be warmed up until the coolant temperature is above 95°F.

2. The air cleaner must be removed in order to see the EGR valve shaft.

3. If the EGR valve is not getting vacuum, check the vacuum hoses, then check the coolant temperature operated vacuum valve as outlined in the appropriate Section above. The valve should work when the coolant temperature is above 95°F.

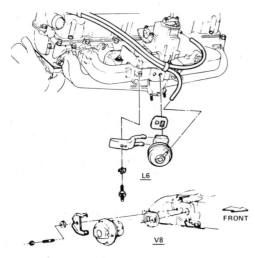

1974 EGR valve mounting

Fuel System

FUEL PUMP

Removal and Installation

The six-cylinder fuel pump is located on the right-side of the engine, adjacent to the distributor. The V8 fuel pump is located on the lower left at the front.

1. Disconnect the fuel inlet, outlet, and vapor return lines at the pump and plug the pump inlet line.

2. Remove the two pump mounting bolts and lockwashers; remove the pump and gasket.

3. Install the pump with a new gasket coated with sealer. Coat the mounting bolts threads with sealer and tighten the bolts.

4. Connect the inlet and outlet lines, start the engine, and check for leaks.

Fuel Pump Testing

To test the fuel pump, remove the gas inlet line at the carburetor, hold the line over a cup, and crank the engine to see if gas is being pumped. Then attach the line to a pressure gauge, crank the engine, and check for pressure. (See "Tune-Up Chart" for specifications.)

CARBURETORS

Removal and Installation

1. Remove the air cleaner.

2. Remove all hoses, linkage, and fuel lines.

3. Remove the retaining bolts or nuts and remove the carburetor.

4. Reverse the removal order to install.

Overhaul

ALL TYPES

Efficient carburetion depends greatly on careful cleaning and inspection during overhaul since dirt, gum, water, or varnish in or on the carburetor parts are often responsible for poor performance.

Overhaul your carburetor in a clean, dust-free area. Carefully disassemble the carburetor, referring often to the exploded views. Keep all similar and look-alike parts segregated during disassembly and cleaning to avoid accidental interchange during assembly. Make a note of all jet sizes.

When the carburetor is disassembled, wash all parts (except diaphragms, electric choke units, pump plunger, and any other plastic, leather, fiber, or rubber parts) in clean carburetor solvent. Do not leave parts in the solvent any longer than is necessary to sufficiently loosen the deposits. Excessive cleaning may remove the special finish from the float bowl and choke valve bodies, leaving these parts unfit for service. Rinse all parts in clean solvent and blow them dry with compressed air or allow them to air dry. Wipe clean all cork, plastic, leather, and fiber parts with a clean, lint-free cloth.

Blow out all passages and jets with compressed air and be sure that there are no restrictions or blockages. Never use wire or similar tools to clean jets, fuel passages, or air bleeds. Clean all jets and valves separately to avoid accidental interchange.

Check all parts for wear or damage. If wear or damage is found, replace the defective parts. Especially check the following:

1. Check the float needle and seat for wear. If wear is found, replace the complete assembly.

2. Check the float hinge pin for wear and the float(s) for dents or distortion. Replace the float if fuel has leaked into it.

3. Check the throttle and choke shaft bores for wear or an out-of-round condition. Damage or wear to the throttle arm, shaft, or shaft bore will often require replacement of the throttle body. These parts require a close tolerance of fit; wear may allow air leakage, which could affect starting and idling.

NOTE: *Throttle shafts and bushings are not included in overhaul kits. They can be purchased separately.*

4. Inspect the idle mixture adjusting needles for burrs or grooves. Any such condition requires replacement of the needle, since you will not be able to obtain a satisfactory idle.

5. Test the accelerator pump check valves. They should pass air one way but not the other. Test for proper seating by blowing and sucking on the valve. Replace the valve as necessary. If the valve is satisfactory, wash the valve again to remove breath moisture.

6. Check the bowl cover for warped surfaces with a straightedge.

7. Closely inspect the valves and seats for wear and damage, replacing as necessary.

8. After the carburetor is assembled, check the choke valve for freedom of operation.

Carburetor overhaul kits are recommended for each overhaul. These kits contain all gaskets and new parts to replace those that deteriorate most rapidly. Failure to replace all parts supplied with the kit (especially gaskets) can result in poor performance later.

Some carburetor manufacturers supply overhaul kits of three basic types: minor repair; major repair; and gasket kits. Basically, they contain the following:

Minor Repair Kits:
  All gaskets
  Float needle valve
  All diaphragms
  Spring for the pump diaphragm

Major Repair Kits:
  All jets and gaskets
  All diaphragms
  Float needle valve
  Idle mixture screw
  Pump ball valve
  Float
  Complete intermediate rod
  Intermediate pump lever
  Complete injector tube
  Some cover hold-down screws and washers

Gasket Kits:
  All gaskets

After cleaning and checking all components, reassemble the carburetor, using new parts and referring to the exploded view. When reassembling, make sure that all screws and jets are tight in their seats, but do not overtighten, as the tips will be distorted. Tighten all screws gradually, in rotation. Do not tighten needle valves into their seats; uneven jetting will result. Always use new gaskets. Be sure to adjust the float level when reassembling.

ROCHESTER BV—ONE-BARREL CARBURETOR

This carburetor is used on the 1967 six-cylinder engine.

Automatic Choke Adjustment

1. Disconnect the choke rod from the choke lever at the carburetor.

2. While holding the choke valve shut, pull the choke rod up against the stop in the thermostat housing.

3. Adjust the length of the choke rod so that the bottom edge of the choke rod is even with the top edge of the hole in the choke lever.

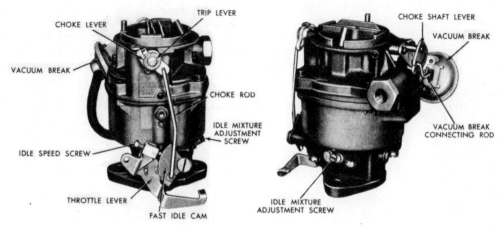

BV components

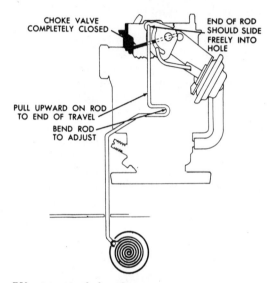

BV automatic choke adjustment

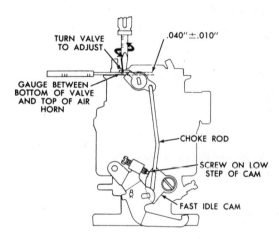

BV idle vent adjustment

4. Check the linkage for freedom of operation.

Idle Vent Adjustment

1. Position the carburetor lever on the low step of the fast idle cam.
2. The distance between the choke valve and the body casting should be 0.050 in.
3. If an adjustment is necessary, turn the valve with a screwdriver.

Fast Idle and Choke Valve Adjustment

1. Position the end of the idle adjusting screw on the next to highest step of the fast idle cam.
2. A 0.050 in. feeler gauge should slide

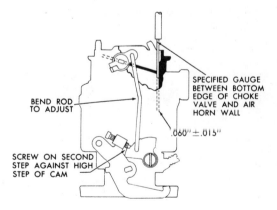

BV choke rod adjustment

easily between the lower edge of the choke valve and the carburetor bore.
3. As necessary, bend the choke rod until the correct clearance is obtained.

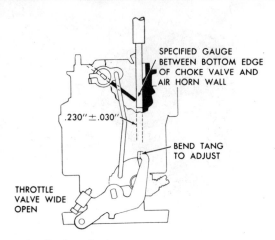

BV unloader adjustment

Unloader Adjustment

1. Open the throttle to the wide-open position.

2. A 0.230/0.270 gauge should slide freely between the lower edge of the choke valve and the bore of the carburetor.

3. As necessary, bend the throttle tang to obtain the proper clearance.

Vacuum Break Adjustment

1. Hold the diaphragm lever against the diaphragm body.

2. The clearance between the lower edge of the choke valve and the air horn wall should be 0.136–0.154 in. on Powerglide cars and 0.154–0.173 in. on manual cars.

3. Bend the diaphragm link, as necessary.

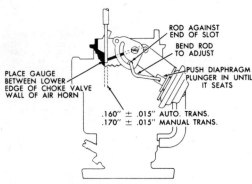

BV vacuum break adjustment

Float Level Adjustment

1. Remove the air cleaner.
2. Disconnect the fuel line, fast idle

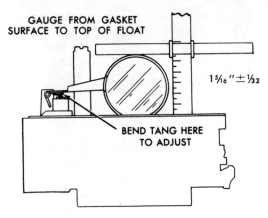

BV float level adjustment

rod, cam-to-choke kick lever, vacuum hose at the diaphragm, and the choke rod at the choke lever.

3. Remove the bowl cover screws and carefully lift the cover off the carburetor.

4. Install a new gasket on the cover before making any adjustments.

5. Invert the cover assembly and measure the float level with a float gauge. It should be $1^5/16$ in.

NOTE: *Rebuilding kits include a float level gauge.*

6. Check float centering while holding the cover sideways. Use the same gauge as in Step 5. The floats should not touch the gauge.

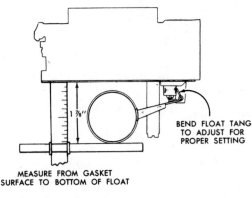

BV float drop adjustment

7. Hold the cover upright and measure the float drop. If the drop is more or less than $1^7/8$ in., bend the stop tang until the drop is correct.

8. Install the cover and reconnect the lines and linkage in the reverse order of removal.

ROCHESTER MV—ONE-BARREL CARBURETOR

The model MV carburetor is a single-bore, downdraft carburetor with an aluminum throttle body, automatic choke, internally balanced venting, and a hot idle compensating system for cars equipped with automatic transmissions. Newer models are also equipped with Combination Emission Control valves (C.E.C.) and an Exhaust Gas Recirculation (EGR) system. An electrically operated idle stop solenoid replaces the idle stop screw of older models.

The MV carburetor is used on six-cylinder cars from 1968 and service procedures apply to all MV carburetors.

Fast Idle Adjustment

NOTE: *The fast idle adjustment must be made with the transmission in Neutral.*

1. Position the fast idle lever on the high step of the fast idle cam.
2. Be sure that the choke is properly adjusted and in the wide-open position with the engine warm.
3. Bend the fast idle lever until the specified speed is obtained.

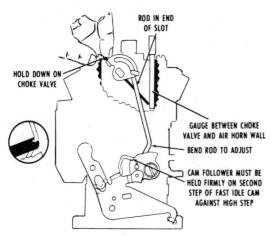

MV fast idle adjustment

Choke Rod (fast idle cam) Adjustment

NOTE: *Adjust the fast idle before making choke rod adjustments.*

1. Place the fast idle cam follower on the second step of the fast idle cam and hold it firmly against the rise to the high step.

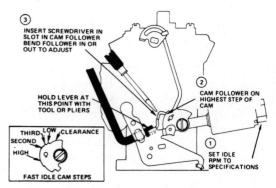

MV choke rod adjustment

2. Rotate the choke valve in the direction of a closed choke by applying force to the choke coil lever.
3. Bend the choke rod, at the point shown in the illustration, to give the specified opening between the lower edge of the choke valve and the inside air horn wall.

NOTE: *Measurement must be made at the center of the choke valve.*

Choke Vacuum Break Adjustments

The adjustment of the vacuum break diaphragm unit insures correct choke valve opening after engine starting.

1. Remove the air cleaner on vehicles with Therm AC air cleaner; plug the sensor's vacuum take off port.
2. Using an external vacuum source, apply vacuum to the vacuum break diaphragm until the plunger is fully seated.
3. When the plunger is seated, push the choke valve toward the closed position.
4. Holding the choke valve in this position, place the specified gauge between the lower edge of the choke valve and the air horn wall.

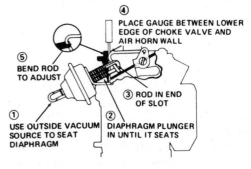

MV choke vacuum break adjustment

5. If the measurement is not correct, bend the vacuum break rod at the point shown in the illustration.

Choke Unloader Adjustment

1. Apply pressure to the choke valve and hold it in the closed position.
2. Open the throttle valve to the wide-open position.
3. Check the dimension between the lower edge of the choke plate and the air horn wall; if adjustment is needed, bend the unloader tang on the throttle lever to adjust to specification.

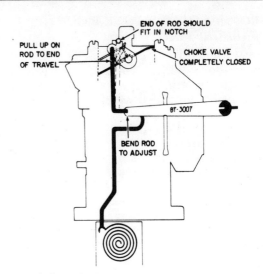

MV choke coil adjustment

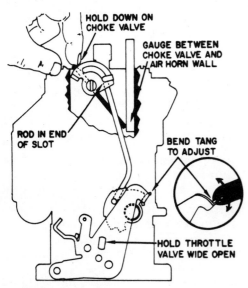

MV choke unloader adjustment

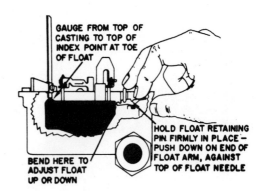

MV float adjustment

Choke Coil Rod Adjustment

1. Disconnect the coil rod from the upper choke lever and hold the choke valve closed.
2. Push down on the coil rod to the end of its travel.
3. The top of the rod should be even with the bottom hole in the choke lever.
4. To make adjustments, bend the rod at the point shown in the illustration.

Float Adjustment

1. Hold the float retainer in place and the float arm against the top of the float needle by pushing down on the float arm at the outer end toward the float bowl casting.
2. Using an adjustable T scale, measure the distance from the toe of the float to the float bowl gasket surface.

NOTE: *The float bowl gasket should be removed and the gauge held on the index point on the float for accurate measurement.*

3. Adjust the float level by bending the float arm up or down at the float arm junction.

Metering Rod Adjustments

1. Hold the throttle valve wide-open and push down on the metering rod against spring tension, then remove the rod from the main metering jet.
2. In order to check adjustment, the slow idle screw must be backed out and the fast idle cam rotated so that the fast idle cam follower does not contact the steps on the cam.
3. With the throttle valve closed, push

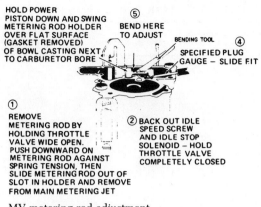

HOLD POWER PISTON DOWN AND SWING METERING ROD HOLDER OVER FLAT SURFACE (GASKET REMOVED) OF BOWL CASTING NEXT TO CARBURETOR BORE

⑤ BEND HERE TO ADJUST

BENDING TOOL

④ SPECIFIED PLUG GAUGE – SLIDE FIT

① REMOVE METERING ROD BY HOLDING THROTTLE VALVE WIDE OPEN. PUSH DOWNWARD ON METERING ROD AGAINST SPRING TENSION, THEN SLIDE METERING ROD OUT OF SLOT IN HOLDER AND REMOVE FROM MAIN METERING JET

② BACK OUT IDLE SPEED SCREW AND IDLE STOP SOLENOID – HOLD THROTTLE VALVE COMPLETELY CLOSED

MV metering rod adjustment

down on the power piston until it contacts its stop.

4. With the power piston depressed, swing the metering rod holder over the flat surface of the bowl casting next to the carburetor bore.

5. Insert a specified size drill between the bowl casting sealing bead and the lower surface of the metering rod holder. The drill should slide smoothly between both surfaces.

6. If adjustment is needed, carefully bend the metering rod holder up or down

at the point shown. After adjustment, reinstall the metering rod.

Idle Vent Adjustment

1. The engine idle must be set at the specified rpm and the choke valve held wide-open so that the fast idle cam follower is not contacting the cam.

NOTE: *If the carburetor is off the car a preliminary idle setting can be made by turning the idle speed screw in 1½ turns from the closed throttle valve position.*

2. With the throttle stop screw held against the idle stop screw, the idle vent valve should be open to specification. To check, a drill of specified size may be inserted between the top of the air horn casting and the bottom surface of the valve.

3. If adjustment is necessary, turn the slotted vent valve head with a screwdriver. Turning the head clockwise *increases* the clearance.

NOTE: *On models equipped with an idle stop solenoid, the solenoid must be activated when checking and adjusting the valve.*

MV Carburetor Specifications

Year	Carburetor Identification①	Float Level (in.)	Metering Rod (in.)	Idle Vent (in.)	Vacuum Break (in.)	Fast Idle Off Car (in.)	Choke Rod (in.)	Choke Unloader (in.)	Fast Idle Speed (rpm)
1968	7028067	5/16	0.085	0.040	0.300	0.090	0.200	0.245	2400②
	7028075	5/16	0.085	0.040	0.290	——	0.200	0.245	2400②
	7028065	5/16	0.075	0.040	0.300	0.090	0.200	0.245	2400②
1969	7029165	9/32	0.085	0.040	0.275	0.120	0.200	0.450	2400②
	7029166	9/32	0.085	0.040	0.260	0.130	0.180	0.450	2800②
	7029167	9/32	0.085	0.040	0.275	0.120	0.200	0.450	2600②
	7029168	9/32	0.085	0.040	0.260	0.130	0.180	0.450	2800②
1970	7040014	1/4	0.100	——	0.200	——	0.170	0.350	——
	7040017	1/4	0.100	——	0.230	——	0.190	0.350	——
1971	7041014	1/4	0.080	——	0.200	——	0.160	0.350	——

MV Carburetor Specifications (cont.)

Year	Carburetor Identification①	Float Level (in.)	Metering Rod (in.)	Idle Vent (in.)	Vacuum Break (in.)	Fast Idle Off Car (in.)	Choke Rod (in.)	Choke Unloader (in.)	Fast Idle Speed (rpm)
1971	7041017	¼	0.078	——	0.225	——	0.180	0.350	——
1972	7042014	¼	0.080	——	0.200	——	0.160	0.500	2400②
	7042017	¼	0.080	——	0.230	——	0.180	0.500	2400②
	7042984	¼	0.080	——	0.200	——	0.160	0.500	2400②
	7042987	¼	0.080	——	0.230	——	0.180	0.500	2400②
1973–74	7043014	¼	0.080	——	0.300	——	0.245	0.500	2400②
	7043017	¾	0.080	——	0.350	——	0.275	0.500	2400②

① The carburetor identification tag is located at the rear of the carburetor on one of the air horn screws
② High step of cam

ROCHESTER 2GC, 2GV—TWO-BARREL CARBURETOR

This two-barrel downdraft carburetor comes in two bore sizes to provide a wide variety of usage. The newer carburetors use a plastic float and a longer needle and seat to provide better fuel control.

Fast Idle Adjustment

On 2GC and 2GV models, the fast idle is set automatically when the curb idle and mixture is set.

Choke Rod (Fast Idle Cam)

1. Turn in the idle cam stop screw until it just contacts the bottom step of the fast idle cam. Then turn the screw one full turn.
2. Place the idle screw on the second step of the fast idle cam against the shoulder of the high step.
3. Hold the choke valve closed and check the clearance between the upper edge of the choke valve and the air horn wall.
4. Adjust the clearance by bending the tang on the choke lever.

Vacuum Break Adjustment

1. Remove the air cleaner. Vehicles with a Therm AC air cleaner should have

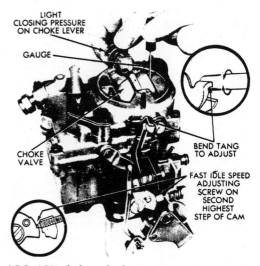

2GC, 2GV choke rod adjustment

the sensor's vacuum take-off port plugged.
2. Using an external vacuum source, apply vacuum to the vacuum break diaphragm until the plunger is fully seated.
3. When the plunger is seated, push the choke valve toward the closed position.
4. Holding the choke valve in this position, place the specified size gauge be-

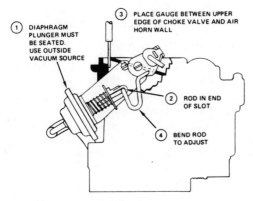

2GC, 2GV vacuum break adjustment

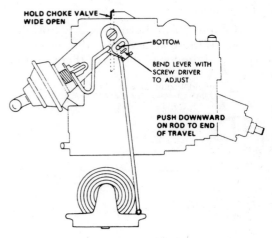

2GC, 2GV choke coil rod adjustment

tween the lower edge of the choke valve and the air horn wall.

5. If the measurement is not correct, bend the vacuum break rod at the point shown in the illustration.

Choke Unloader Adjustment

1. Hold the throttle valves wide-open.
2. Close the choke valve.
3. Bend the unloader tang to obtain the proper clearance between the upper edge of the choke valve and air horn wall.

4. Adjust by bending the lever at the point shown in the illustration.

Float Level

With the air horn assembly upside down, measure the distance from the air horn gasket to the lip at the toe of the float. Bend the float arm to adjust to specifications.

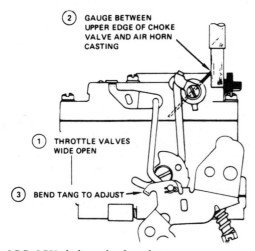

2GC, 2GV choke unloader adjustment

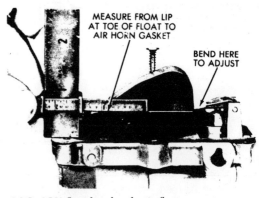

2GC, 2GV float level—plastic float

Choke Coil Rod Adjustment

1. Hold the choke valve completely open.
2. Disconnect the coil rod from the upper lever and push down on the rod to the end of its travel.
3. When the rod is all the way down, it should line up with the bottom of the slotted hole on the choke valve linkage.

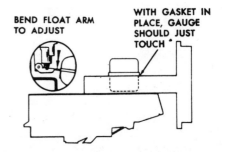

2GC, 2GV float level—metal float

Float Drop

Holding the air horn assembly upright, measure the distance from the gasket to the lip at the toe of the float. If correction

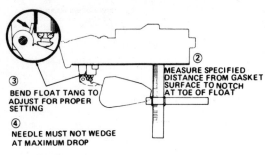

① AIR HORN RIGHT SIDE UP TO ALLOW FLOAT TO HANG FREE (GASKET IN PLACE)

③ BEND FLOAT TANG TO ADJUST FOR PROPER SETTING

② MEASURE SPECIFIED DISTANCE FROM GASKET SURFACE TO NOTCH AT TOE OF FLOAT

④ NEEDLE MUST NOT WEDGE AT MAXIMUM DROP

2GC, 2GV float drop—plastic float

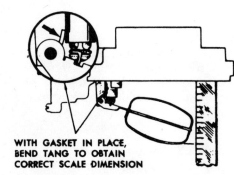

WITH GASKET IN PLACE, BEND TANG TO OBTAIN CORRECT SCALE DIMENSION

2GC, 2GV float drop—metal float

is necessary, bend the float tang at the rear, next to the needle and seat.

Accelerator Pump Rod

1. Back out the idle speed screw and completely close the throttle valves.
2. Place the pump gauge across the air cleaner mounting surface.
3. With the T-scale set to the specified height, the lower leg of the gauge should just touch the top of the accelerator pump rod.
4. Bend the pump rod to adjust.

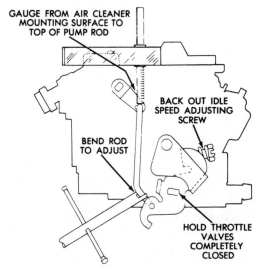

GAUGE FROM AIR CLEANER MOUNTING SURFACE TO TOP OF PUMP ROD

BACK OUT IDLE SPEED ADJUSTING SCREW

BEND ROD TO ADJUST

HOLD THROTTLE VALVES COMPLETELY CLOSED

2GC, 2GV accelerator pump rod adjustment

2GC, 2GV Carburetor Specifications

Year	Carburetor Identification①	Float Level (in.)	Float Drop (in.)	Pump Rod (in.)	Idle Vent (in.)	Vacuum Break (in.)	Automatic Choke	Choke Rod (in.)	Choke Unloader (in.)
1967	7027060	9/16	1 9/16	1 11/32	1 9/16	——	Index	0.085	0.160
	7027061	9/16	1 9/16	1 11/32	1 9/32	——	Index	0.085	0.160
	7027062	9/16	1 9/16	1 11/32	1 9/32	——	Index	0.085	0.160
	7027066	9/16	1 9/16	1 11/32	1 9/32	——	Index	0.085	0.160
	7027071	9/16	1 9/16	1 11/32	1 9/32	——	Index	0.085	0.160
	7037061	9/16	1 9/16	1 11/32	1 9/32	——	Index	0.085	0.160
	7037062	9/16	1 9/16	1 11/32	1 9/32	——	Index	0.085	0.160

2GC, 2GV Carburetor Specifications (cont.)

Year	Carburetor Identification①	Float Level (in.)	Float Drop (in.)	Pump Rod (in.)	Idle Vent (in.)	Vacuum Break (in.)	Automatic Choke	Choke Rod (in.)	Choke Unloader (in.)
1967	7037066	9/16	1 9/16	1 11/32	1 9/32	——	Index	0.085	0.160
	7037071	9/16	1 9/16	1 11/32	1 9/32	——	Index	0.085	0.160
	7037162	9/16	1 9/16	1 11/32	1 9/32	——	Index	0.085	0.160
1968	7028060	9/16	1 3/4	1 11/32	——	0.150	——	0.085	0.180
	7028062	9/16	1 3/4	1 11/32	——	0.150	——	0.085	0.180
	7028066	9/16	1 3/4	1 11/32	——	0.170	——	0.085	0.180
	7028071	9/16	1 3/4	1 11/32	——	0.160	——	0.085	0.180
1969	7028066	9/16	1 3/4	1 11/32	——	0.170	——	0.085	0.180
	7028071	9/16	1 3/4	1 11/32	——	0.160	——	0.085	0.180
	7029060	9/16	1 3/4	1 11/32	——	0.150	——	0.085	0.180
	7029062	9/16	1 3/4	1 11/32	——	0.150	——	0.085	0.180
1970	7040060	11/16	1 3/4	1 11/32	——	0.180	——	0.085	0.180
	7040062	9/16	1 3/4	1 11/32	——	0.150	——	0.085	0.180
	7040064	11/16	1 3/4	1 11/32	——	0.150	——	0.085	0.180
	7040066	11/16	1 3/4	1 11/32	——	0.170	——	0.085	0.180
	7040071	9/16	1 3/4	1 11/32	——	0.160	——	0.085	0.180
	7040072	9/16	1 3/4	1 11/32	——	0.150	——	0.085	0.180
	7040460	11/16	1 3/4	1 11/32	——	0.150	——	0.085	0.180
	7040461	11/16	1 3/4	1 11/32	——	0.150	——	0.085	0.180
	7040462	9/16	1 3/4	1 11/32	——	0.150	——	0.085	0.180
	7040463	9/16	1 3/4	1 11/32	——	0.150	——	0.085	0.180
	7040466	11/16	1 3/4	1 11/32	——	0.170	——	0.085	0.180
	7040471	9/16	1 3/4	1 11/32	——	0.160	——	0.085	0.180
1971	7041060	11/16	1 3/4	1 11/32	——	0.125	——	0.085	0.180

2GC, 2GV Carburetor Specifications (cont.)

Year	Carburetor Identification①	Float Level (in.)	Float Drop (in.)	Pump Rod (in.)	Idle Vent (in.)	Vacuum Break (in.)	Automatic Choke	Choke Rod (in.)	Choke Unloader (in.)
1971	7041061	$^{11}/_{16}$	$1\frac{3}{4}$	$1^{11}/_{32}$	——	0.125	——	0.085	0.180
	7041062	$^{9}/_{16}$	$1\frac{3}{4}$	$1^{11}/_{32}$	——	0.105	——	0.085	0.180
	7041063	$^{9}/_{16}$	$1\frac{3}{4}$	$1^{11}/_{32}$	——	0.105	——	0.085	0.180
	7041064	$^{11}/_{16}$	$1\frac{3}{4}$	$1^{11}/_{32}$	——	0.130	——	0.085	0.180
	7041070	$^{11}/_{16}$	$1\frac{3}{4}$	$1^{11}/_{32}$	——	0.125	——	0.085	0.180
	7041072	$^{9}/_{16}$	$1\frac{3}{4}$	$1^{11}/_{32}$	——	0.105	——	0.085	0.180
	7041074	$^{11}/_{16}$	$1\frac{3}{4}$	$1^{11}/_{32}$	——	0.130	——	0.085	0.180
	7041171	$^{9}/_{16}$	$1\frac{3}{4}$	$1^{11}/_{32}$	——	0.140	——	0.085	0.180
1972	7042060	$\frac{5}{8}$	$1^{9}/_{32}$	$1^{11}/_{32}$	——	0.122	——	0.085	0.180
	7042061	$\frac{5}{8}$	$1^{9}/_{32}$	$1^{11}/_{32}$	——	0.122	——	0.085	0.180
	7042062	$^{9}/_{16}$	$1^{9}/_{32}$	$1^{11}/_{32}$	·——	0.105	——	0.085	0.180
	7042064	$\frac{5}{8}$	$1^{9}/_{32}$	$1^{11}/_{32}$	——	0.150	——	0.085	0.180
	7042100	$^{25}/_{32}$	$1^{31}/_{32}$	$1^{5}/_{16}$	——	0.080	——	0.040	0.215
	7042101	$^{25}/_{32}$	$1^{31}/_{32}$	$1^{5}/_{16}$	——	0.100	——	0.075	0.215
1973–74	7043062	$^{21}/_{32}$	$1^{9}/_{32}$	$1^{5}/_{16}$	——	0.167	——	0.085	0.180
	7043063	$^{21}/_{32}$	$1^{9}/_{32}$	$1^{5}/_{16}$	——	0.167	——	0.085	0.180
	7043071	$^{23}/_{32}$	$1^{9}/_{32}$	$1^{5}/_{16}$	——	0.195	——	0.085	0.180
	7043072	$^{23}/_{32}$	$1^{9}/_{32}$	$1^{5}/_{16}$	——	0.167	——	0.085	0.180
	7043060	$^{21}/_{32}$	$1^{9}/_{32}$	$1^{5}/_{16}$	——	0.157	——	0.085	0.180
	7043061	$^{21}/_{32}$	$1^{9}/_{32}$	$1^{5}/_{16}$	——	0.157	——	0.085	0.180
	7043066	$^{21}/_{32}$	$1^{9}/_{32}$	$1^{5}/_{16}$	——	0.180	——	0.085	0.180
	7043067	$^{21}/_{32}$	$1^{9}/_{32}$	$1^{5}/_{16}$	——	0.180	——	0.085	0.180
	7043070	$^{23}/_{32}$	$1^{9}/_{32}$	$1^{5}/_{16}$	——	0.157	——	0.085	0.180

① The carburetor identification tag is located at the rear of the carburetor on one of the air horn screws.

CARTER WCD—TWO-BARREL CARBURETOR

This is a two-barrel carburetor using a single needle valve even though two floats are provided. On several of these units, the floats operate independently of each other so that the highest float always controls the fuel level. This is necessary when the carburetor is mounted with the float centerline parallel to the centerline of the engine.

Float Adjustment

LATERAL

1. Invert the bowl cover.
2. Remove the bowl cover gasket.
3. Place the float gauge directly under the floats with the notched portions of the gauge fitted over the edges of the casting.

Gauge Point

WCD float level adjustment

4. The sides of the float should barely touch the vertical uprights of the float gauge. A gauge is normally included in a rebuilding kit.
5. Adjustment is made by bending the arms of the floats.

VERTICAL

1. With the float gauge in the same position as for the lateral adjustment, the floats should just clear the horizontal portion of the gauge.
2. The vertical distance between the top center of the float and the machined surface of the casting must be $7/32$ in.
3. Adjust by bending the float arms as required.
4. To install the bowl cover gasket, remove the floats, install the gasket, and reinstall the floats.

Pump Adjustment

1. Install the pump connector link in the outer hole (long stroke) of the pump

WCD pump adjustment

arm with the ends extending away from the countershaft arm.
2. Back out the throttle lever set screw until the throttle valves seat in the carburetor bores.
3. Be sure that the fast idle adjustment screw does not hold the throttle open.
4. Hold a straightedge across the top of the dust cover boss at the pump arm.
5. The flat on top of the pump arm should be parallel to the straightedge.
6. Adjust by bending the throttle connector rod to the upper angle.

Metering Rod Adjustment

1. Complete the pump adjustment.
2. Back out the throttle lever set screw to allow the valves (throttle) to seat in the bores of the carburetor.
3. Loosen the metering rod clamp screw.
4. With the metering rod in place, press down on the vacumeter link until the metering rods bottom in the carburetor body casting.
5. While holding the rods in a down-

WCD metering rod adjustment

ward position, revolve the metering rod arm until the finger on the arm contacts the lip of the vacumeter link.

6. Hold in place and carefully tighten the clamp screw.

Fast Idle Cam Adjustment

1. Loosen the choke lever clamp screw on the choke shaft.

2. Insert a 0.010 in. feeler gauge between the lip of the fast idle cam and the boss of the flange casting.

3. Hold the choke valve tightly closed and take the slack out of the linkage by pressing the choke lever toward the closed position.

4. With the choke valve in the closed position, tighten the fast idle adjusting screw to obtain the specified clearance.

5. Be sure that the fast idle adjusting screw is on the high step of the cam or index mark while making this adjustment.

WCD fast idle cam adjustment

Automatic Choke Adjustment

1. Loosen the choke cover retaining screws.

2. Turn the cover so that the index mark on the cover lines up with the specified mark on the choke housing.

3. See the Specifications Chart for the proper mark alignment.

Choke Unloader Adjustment

1. With the throttle valves wide-open, there should be clearance between the

WCD Automatic Choke Specifications

Year	Model①	Choke
1967	3888S	Index
	4365S	2 Rich
1968	4410S	Index
	4537S	Index
1969	4667S	Index
	4668S	Index
1970	4816S	Index
	4817S	Index
	4950S	Index

① Model numbers located on the tag or the casting

WCD choke unloader

upper edge of the choke valve and the inner wall of the air horn.

2. Adjust by bending the unloader lip on the throttle shaft lever.

3. Adjustment is ³/₁₆ in.

ROCHESTER WGD—TWO-BARREL CARBURETOR

The WGD carburetor is the same basic carburetor as the WCD, the only difference being that the WGD has only one float. The choke is operated by a thermostatic coil. This carburetor is used mainly on 1972 models. It carries model number 6311S.

Float Adjustment

1. With the air horn inverted, check to see that the float is parallel with the outer edge of the air horn casting.

GAUGE FROM **CENTER** —
OF FLOAT TO GASKET SURFACE

5/16" GAUGE

WGD float level adjustment

2. Adjust by bending the float arm. Next, place the gauge between the air horn and the center of the float. The distance should be 5/16 in.

3. Adjust the float level by bending the float arm until the float touches the gauge. The float should not have excessive clearance at the hinge pin and must operate freely.

NOTE: *When adjusting the float, care must be exercised to avoid pressing the flared tip needle into the needle seats as a false setting will result. Allow only the float weight to seat the needle when gauging.*

Pump Adjustment

1. Back out the throttle stop screw.

2. Turn the fast idle cam to "hot" position and fully close the throttle valves.

3. Place a ¼ in. gauge or a similar straightedge across the dust cover boss. The dust cover boss should be parallel with the top surface of the pump arm.

4. Adjust by bending the pump rod at the offset.

NOTE: *This adjustment should be made after the pump adjustment. No metering rod gauges are necessary.*

STRAIGHT EDGE
PUMP ARM

BEND TO ADJUST

WGD pump adjustment

1. Back out the throttle screw and fully close the throttle valves. Press down on the vacuum piston link until the metering rods bottom.

2. While holding the rods down and the metering arm tongue against the lip of the vacuum piston link, carefully tighten the metering arm set screw.

Fast Idle Cam Adjustment

1. Open the throttle to clear the fast idle cam and close the choke valve.

2. With the choke valve held fully closed and the stop on the fast idle cam against the casting, there should be 0.005 in. minimium clearance between the inner and outer choke levers.

3. Adjust by bending the outer lever lug as required.

NOTE: *With the choke fully closed, the tang on the fast idle cam must clear the stop on the throttle body flange.*

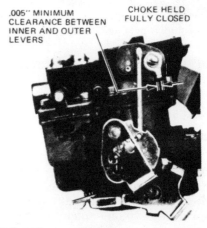

.005" MINIMUM CLEARANCE BETWEEN INNER AND OUTER LEVERS

CHOKE HELD FULLY CLOSED

WGD fast idle cam adjustment

Unloader Adjustment

1. Hold the choke closed lightly.

2. Fully open the throttle, forcing the choke valve open.

3/16" GAUGE

BEND UNLOADER ARM

UNLOADER ARM

WGD choke unloader adjustment

3. Check the clearance between the upper edge of the choke valve and the wall of the air horn. The clearance should be ³/₁₆ in.

4. Adjust by bending the unloader arm as required.

Fast Idle Speed Adjustment

1. With the carburetor on the engine, rotate the fast idle cam until the fast idle tang contacts the cam's high step.

2. With the engine at normal operating temperature, adjust the fast idle tang to obtain an engine speed of 1500 rpm.

WGD fast idle speed adjustment

CARTER AFB—FOUR-BARREL CARBURETOR

This carburetor is used on some 400 cu in. and 326 cu in. engines.

Automatic Choke Adjustment

The automatic choke is correctly adjusted when the scribe mark on the coil housing is aligned with the center notch in the choke housing for automatic transmission cars and one notch lean for manual transmission cars.

Float Adjustment

Remove the metering rods and the bowl cover. Align the float by sighting

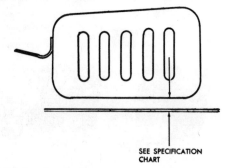

AFB float level adjustment

down its side to determine if it is parallel with the outer edge of the air horn. Bend the float to adjust. Float level is adjusted with the air horn inverted and the air horn gasket in place. Clearance between each float (at the outer end) and the air horn gasket should be ⁵/₁₆ in. Bend to adjust.

Float Drop Adjustment

Float drop is adjusted by holding the air horn in an upright position and bending the float arm until the vertical distance from the air horn gasket to the outer end of each float measures ¾ in.

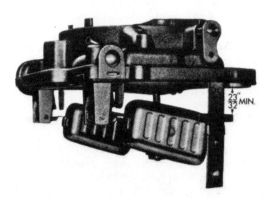

AFB float drop adjustment

Intermediate Choke Rod Adjustment

Remove the choke coil housing assembly, gasket, and baffle plate. Position a 0.026 in. wire gauge between the bottom of the slot in the piston and the top of the slot in the choke piston housing. Close the choke piston against the gauge and secure it with a rubber band. Bend the intermediate choke rod so that the distance between the top edge of the choke valve and the air horn divider measures 0.070 in.

Accelerator Pump Adjustment

The first step in adjusting the accelerator pump is to push aside the fast-idle cam and firmly seat the throttle valves. Bend the pump rod at the lower angle to obtain a 0.375 in. clearance between the air horn and the top of the plunger shaft.

Unloader, Closing Shoe, and Secondary Throttle Adjustment

To adjust the unloader, hold the throttle wide-open and bend the unloader

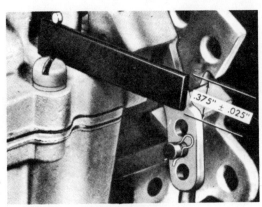

AFB accelerator pump adjustment

tang to obtain a $3/16$ in. clearance between the upper edge of the choke valve and the inner wall of the air horn.

The clearance between the positive closing shoes on the primary and secondary throttle valves is checked with the valves closed. Bend the secondary closing shoe as required to obtain a clearance of 0.020 in.

The secondary throttle opening is governed by the pick-up lever on the primary throttle shaft. It has two points of contact with the loose lever on the primary shaft. If the contact points do not simultaneously engage, bend the pick-up lever to obtain proper engagement. The primary and secondary throttle valve opening must be synchronized.

ROCHESTER MC, MV—FOUR-BARREL CARBURETOR

The Rochester Quadrajet carburetor is a two stage, four-barrel downdraft carburetor. The designation MC or MV refers to the type of choke system the carburetor is designed for. The MV model is equipped with a manifold mounted thermostatic choke coil. The MC model has a choke housing and coil mounted on the side of the float bowl.

The primary side of the carburetor is equipped with 1⅜ in. diameter bores and a triple venturi with plain tube nozzles. During off idle and part throttle operation, the fuel is metered through tapered metering rods operating in specially designed jets positioned by a manifold vacuum responsive piston.

The secondary side of the carburetor contains two 2¼ in. bores. An air valve is used on the secondary side for metering

control and supplements the primary bores.

The secondary air valve operates tapered metering rods which regulate the fuel in constant proportion to the air being supplied.

Fast Idle

1. Position the fast idle lever on the high step of the fast idle cam.
2. Be sure that the choke is wide-open and the engine warm.
3. Turn the fast idle screw to gain the proper fast idle rpm.

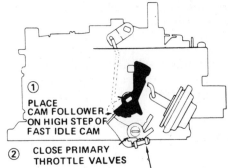

4MC, 4MV fast idle adjustment

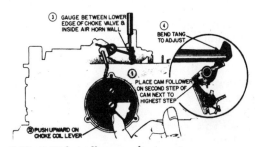

4MC, 4MV fast idle cam adjustment

Choke Rod (Fast Idle Cam)

1. Place the cam follower on the second step of the fast idle cam.
2. Close the choke valve by exerting counterclockwise pressure on the external choke lever.
3. Insert a gauge of the proper size between the lower edge of the choke valve and the inside air horn wall.
4. To adjust, bend the choke rod.

Vacuum Break

1. Fully seat the vacuum break diaphragm using an outside vacuum source.

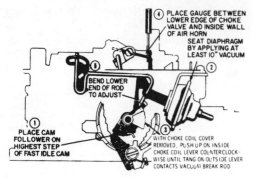

4MC, 4MV vacuum break adjustment

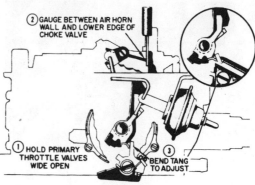

4MC, 4MV choke unloader

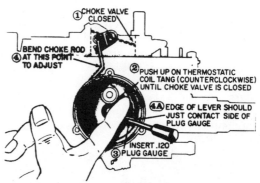

4MC, 4MV choke coil rod adjustment

2. Open the throttle valve enough to allow the fast idle cam follower to clear the fast idle cam.

3. The end of the vacuum break rod should be at the outer end of the slot in the vacuum break diaphragm plunger.

4. The specified clearance should register from the lower end of the choke valve to the inside air horn wall.

5. If the clearance is not correct, bend the vacuum break link at the point shown in the illustration.

Secondary Vacuum Break

1. Using an outside vacuum source, seat the auxiliary vacuum break diaphragm plunger.

2. Rotate the choke lever in the closed position until the spring loaded diaphragm plunger is fully extended.

3. Holding the choke valve closed, check the distance between the lower edge of the choke valve and the air horn wall.

4. To adjust to specifications, bend the vacuum break link.

Choke Unloader

1. Push up on the vacuum break lever and fully open the throttle valves.

2. Measure the distance from the lower edge of the choke valve to the air horn wall.

3. To adjust, bend the tang on the fast idle lever.

Choke Coil Rod

1. Close the choke valve by rotating the choke coil lever counterclockwise.

2. Disconnect the thermostatic coil rod from the upper lever.

3. Push down on the rod until it contacts the bracket of the coil.

4. The rod must fit in the notch of the upper lever.

5. If it does not, it must be bent on the curved portion just below the upper lever.

Secondary Closing Adjustment

This adjustment assures proper closing of the secondary throttle plates.

1. Set the slow idle as per instructions in the appropriate car section. Make sure that the fast idle cam follower is not resting on the fast idle cam.

2. There should be 0.020 in. clearance between the secondary throttle actuating rod and the front of the slot on the secondary throttle lever with the closing tang on the throttle lever resting against the actuating lever.

3. Bend the tang on the primary throttle actuating rod to adjust.

Secondary Opening Adjustment

1. Open the primary throttle valves until the actuating link contacts the upper tang on the secondary lever.

2. With two point linkage, the bottom

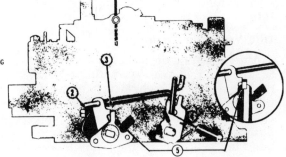

1. CHOKE FULLY OPEN AND FAST IDLE CAM FOLLOWER OFF STEPS OF FAST IDLE CAM.
2. SLOW IDLE PROPERLY SET.
3. MAKE SURE THROTTLE LEVER TANG IS AGAINST SECONDARY THROTTLE ROD OPERATING LEVER AS SHOWN IN 3.
4. GAUGE BETWEEN ROD AND END OF SLOT AS SHOWN IN 4.
5. TO ADJUST, OPEN THROTTLE SLIGHTLY AND BEND TANG

4MC, 4MV secondary closing adjustment

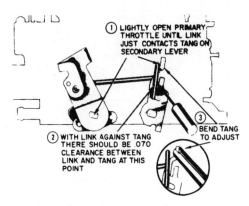

4MC, 4MV secondary opening adjustment

of the link should be in the center of the secondary lever slot.

3. With three point linkage, there should be 0.070 in. clearance between the link and the middle tang.

4. Bend the upper tang on the secondary lever to adjust as necessary.

Float Level

With the air horn assembly upside down, measure the distance from the air horn gasket surface (gasket removed) to the top of the float at the toe.

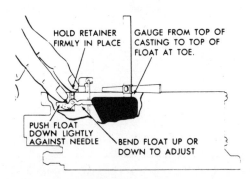

4MC, 4MV float level adjustment

NOTE: *Make sure that the retaining pin is firmly held in place and that the tang of the float is firmly against the needle and seat assembly.*

Secondary Metering Rod Adjustment

1. Measure from the top of each metering rod to the top of the air horn casting.

2. The measurement should be $53/64$ in.; if not, correct by bending the metering rod hanger. Make sure that both rods are adjusted correctly.

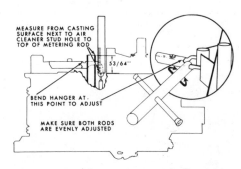

4MC, 4MV secondary metering rod adjustment

Accelerator Pump

1. Close the primary throttle valves by backing out the slow idle screw and making sure that the fast idle cam follower is off the steps of the fast idle cam.

2. Bend the secondary throttle closing tang away from the primary throttle lever.

3. With the pump in the appropriate hole in the pump lever, measure from the top of the choke valve wall to the top of the pump stem.

4. To adjust, bend the pump lever.

5. After adjusting, readjust the secon-

dary throttle tang and the slow idle screw.

Idle Vent Adjustment

After adjusting the acclerator pump rod as specified above, open the primary throttle valve enough to just close the idle vent. Measure from the top of the choke valve wall to the top of the pump plunger stem. If adjustment is necessary, bend the wire tang on the pump lever.

Air Valve Spring Adjustment

To adjust the air valve spring windup, loosen the allen head lockscrew and turn the adjusting screw counterclockwise to remove all spring tension. With the air valve closed, turn the adjusting screw clockwise the specified number of turns after the torsion spring contacts the pin on the shaft. Hold the adjusting screw in this position and tighten the lockscrew.

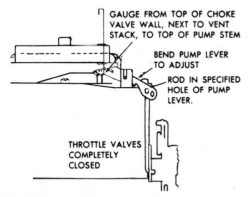

4MC, 4MV accelerator pump adjustment

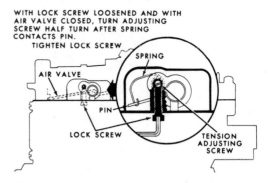

4MC, 4MV air valve spring adjustment

4MC, 4MV Carburetor Specifications

Year	Carburetor Identification ①	Float Level (in.)	Air Valve Spring	Pump Rod (in.)	Idle Vent (in.)	Vacuum Break (in.)	Choke Rod (in.)	Choke Unloader (in.)
1967	7027260	$7/32$	½ turn	$9/32$	$3/8$	0.130	0.085	0.325
	7027261	$7/32$	½ turn	$9/32$	$3/8$	0.130	0.085	0.325
	7027262	$3/16$	½ turn	$9/32$	$3/8$	0.180	0.040	0.325
	7027263	$3/16$	½ turn	$9/32$	$3/8$	0.230	0.090	0.325
	7037260	$7/32$	½ turn	$9/32$	$3/8$	0.130	0.085	0.325
	7037261	$7/32$	½ turn	$9/32$	$3/8$	0.130	0.085	0.325
	7037262	$3/16$	½ turn	$9/32$	$3/8$	0.180	0.040	0.325
	7037263	$3/16$	½ turn	$9/32$	$3/8$	0.230	0.090	0.325
1968	7028260	$5/16$	½ turn	$9/32$	$3/8$	0.245	0.085	0.300
	7028261	$5/16$	½ turn	$9/32$	$3/8$	0.245	0.085	0.300
	7028262	$1/4$	½ turn	$9/32$	$3/8$	0.230	0.100	0.300

4MC, 4MV Carburetor Specifications (cont.)

Year	Carburetor Identification①	Float Level (in.)	Air Valve Spring	Pump Rod (in.)	Idle Vent (in.)	Vacuum Break (in.)	Choke Rod (in.)	Choke Unloader (in.)
1968	7028263	¼	½ turn	9/32	3/8	0.245	0.100	0.300
	7028264	¼	½ turn	9/32	3/8	0.230	0.100	0.300
	7028265	¼	½ turn	9/32	3/8	0.245	0.100	0.300
	7028266	¼	½ turn	9/32	3/8	0.230	0.100	0.300
	7028267	¼	½ turn	9/32	3/8	0.245	0.100	0.300
	7028268	¼	½ turn	9/32	3/8	0.230	0.100	0.300
	7028269	¼	½ turn	9/32	3/8	0.245	0.100	0.300
	7028271	¼	½ turn	9/32	3/8	0.245	0.100	0.300
	7028274	¼	½ turn	9/32	3/8	0.230	0.100	0.300
	7028275	¼	½ turn	9/32	3/8	0.245	0.100	0.300
	7028276	¼	½ turn	9/32	3/8	0.230	0.100	0.300
	7028277	¼	½ turn	9/32	3/8	0.245	0.100	0.300
1969	7029260	3/16	½ turn	9/32	3/8	0.150	0.100	0.300
	7029261	3/16	½ turn	9/32	3/8	0.180	0.100	0.300
	7029262	9/32	½ turn	9/32	3/8	0.245	0.100	0.300
	7029263	9/32	½ turn	9/32	3/8	0.245	0.100	0.300
	7029268	9/32	½ turn	9/32	3/8	0.245	0.100	0.300
	7029270	9/32	½ turn	¼	3/8	0.245	0.100	0.300
	7029273	9/32	½ turn	¼	3/8	0.245	0.100	0.300
	7028270	¼	½ turn	9/32	3/8	0.245	0.100	0.300
1970	7040262	9/32	7/16 turn	——	——	0.400	0.100	——
	7040263	9/32	7/16 turn	——	——	0.400	0.100	——
	7040264	9/32	7/16 turn	——	——	0.400	0.100	——
	7040267	9/32	7/16 turn	——	——	0.400	0.100	——

4MC, 4MV Carburetor Specifications (cont.)

Year	Carburetor Identification①	Float Level (in.)	Air Valve Spring	Pump Rod (in.)	Idle Vent (in.)	Vacuum Break (in.)	Choke Rod (in.)	Choke Unloader (in.)
1970	7040268	$\frac{9}{32}$	$\frac{7}{16}$ turn	——	——	0.400	0.100	——
	7040270	$\frac{9}{32}$	$\frac{7}{16}$ turn	——	——	0.245	0.100	——
	7040273	$\frac{9}{32}$	$\frac{7}{16}$ turn	——	——	0.245	0.100	——
	7040274	$\frac{9}{32}$	$\frac{7}{16}$ turn	——	——	0.400	0.100	——
1971	7041262	$\frac{9}{32}$	$\frac{7}{16}$ turn	——	——	0.240	0.100	——
	7041263	$\frac{9}{32}$	$\frac{7}{16}$ turn	——	——	0.240	0.100	——
	7041264	$\frac{9}{32}$	$\frac{7}{16}$ turn	——	——	0.240	0.100	——
	7041267	$\frac{9}{32}$	$\frac{1}{2}$ turn	——	——	0.370	0.100	——
	7041268	$\frac{9}{32}$	$\frac{1}{2}$ turn	——	——	0.430	0.100	——
	7041270	$\frac{9}{32}$	$\frac{1}{2}$ turn	——	——	0.430	0.100	——
	7041271	$\frac{9}{32}$	$\frac{7}{16}$ turn	——	——	0.240	0.100	——
	7041273	$\frac{9}{32}$	$\frac{1}{2}$ turn	——	——	0.370	0.100	——
1972	7042262	$\frac{1}{4}$	$\frac{7}{16}$ turn	$\frac{13}{32}$	——	0.290	0.100	——
	7042263	$\frac{1}{4}$	$\frac{11}{16}$ turn	$\frac{13}{32}$	——	0.290	0.100	——
	7042264	$\frac{1}{4}$	$\frac{5}{8}$ turn	$\frac{13}{32}$	——	0.290	0.100	——
	7042270	$\frac{1}{4}$	$\frac{7}{16}$ turn	$\frac{7}{16}$	——	0.290	0.100	——
	7042273	$\frac{1}{4}$	$\frac{7}{16}$ turn	$\frac{7}{16}$	——	0.290	0.100	——
1973–74	7043263	$\frac{13}{32}$	$\frac{5}{8}$ turn	$\frac{13}{32}$	——	0.290	0.100	——
	7043264	$\frac{13}{32}$	$\frac{1}{2}$ turn	$\frac{13}{32}$	——	0.290	0.100	——
	7043274	$\frac{13}{32}$	$\frac{9}{16}$ turn	$\frac{13}{32}$	——	0.290	0.100	——
	7043262	$\frac{13}{32}$	$\frac{3}{8}$ turn	$\frac{13}{32}$	——	0.290	0.100	——
	7043265	$\frac{13}{32}$	$\frac{9}{16}$ turn	$\frac{13}{32}$	——	0.290	0.100	——
	7043272	$\frac{13}{32}$	$\frac{3}{8}$ turn	$\frac{13}{32}$	——	0.290	0.100	——

① Model number is located on a tag or on the casting.

5 · Chassis Electrical

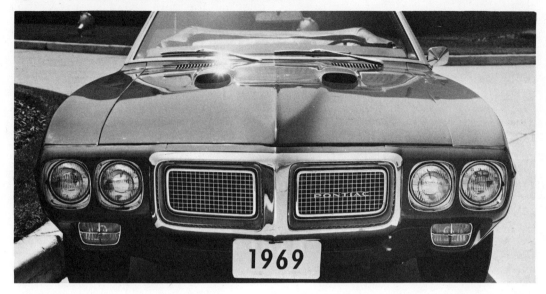

1969

Understanding and Troubleshooting Electrical Systems

For any electrical system to operate it must make a complete circuit; that is, the power flow from the battery must make a complete circle. When an electrical component is operating, power flows from the battery to the component. It passes through the component causing the component to perform its function (lighting a light bulb), and returns to the battery through the ground of the circuit. This ground is usually (but not always) the metal part of the car the electrical component is mounted on.

Perhaps the easiest way to visualize this is to think of connecting a light bulb with two wires attached to it to your car battery. The battery in your car has two posts—negative and positive. If one of the two wires attached to the light bulb were attached to the negative post of the battery and the other wire were attached to the positive post, there would be a complete circuit. Current from the battery would flow out one post, through the wire attached to it and then to the light bulb, making it light. It would then leave

the light bulb, travel through the other wire, and return to the other post of the battery. The typical automotive circuit differs from this simple circuit in two ways. First, instead of having a return wire from the bulb to the battery, the current returns to the battery through the chassis of the vehicle. Since the negative battery cable is attached to the chassis and the chassis is made of electrically conductive metal, the chassis can serve as a ground wire to complete the circuit. Secondly, most automotive circuits contain switches to turn components on and off as required.

There are many types of switches, but the most common simply serves to prevent the passage of current when it is turned off. Since the switch is part of the circle necessary for a complete circuit, turning off the switch leaves an opening in the circle, creating an incomplete circuit.

Some electrical components which require a large amount of current to operate also have a relay in their circuit. A relay is an electrically operated switch. The horn circuit is one which uses a relay.

Did you ever notice that instrument panel lights get brighter with increased engine speed? That happens because your alternator (which supplies the battery) puts out more current at speeds above idle. This is a normal occurrence; however, it is possible for larger surges of current to pass through the electrical system of your car. If such a surge of current were to reach an electrical component it could burn it out. To prevent this from happening, fuses are used in the current supply wires of most of the major electrical units of your car. When an electrical current of excessive power passes through a component's fuse, the fuse blows out (melts) and breaks the circuit to the component, saving it from destruction.

The fuse also protects the component from damage if the power supply wire to the component is grounded before the current reaches the component. Remember, every complete circuit from a power source must include a component designed to use this electrical power. Let's return for a moment to our earlier example. If you were to disconnect the light bulb from the wires and touch the two wires together (don't try it) the result would be a display of sparks. A similar thing happens (on a smaller scale) when the power supply wire to a component, or the electrical component itself, becomes grounded before the normal ground connection for the circuit. To prevent damage to the system, the fuse for the circuit blows to interrupt the circuit and protect the component from damage. Grounding a wire from a power source makes a complete circuit, but taking away the component required to use the power creates a short circuit. Short circuits are usually caused by a shorted switch or broken wiring insulation, allowing the bare wire to contact a metal part of the car and grounding the current before it reaches the component.

Some electrical systems on the car are protected by a circuit breaker (basically a self-repairing fuse). When a short occurs in a system protected by a circuit breaker, the circuit breaker opens the circuit in the same way that a fuse does. When the short is removed from the circuit or the surge subsides, the circuit breaker resets itself and does not have to be replaced as a fuse does.

The final protective device in the chassis electrical system is a fuse link. A fuse link is a wire that acts as a fuse. It is usually connected between the starter relay and the main wiring harness for the car.

Electrical problems generally fall into one of three areas:

1. The component that is not functioning is not receiving current;

2. The component itself is not functioning;

3. The component is not properly grounded.

Problems that fall into the first category are by far the most complicated. It is the current supply system to the component which contains all the switches, relays, fuses, etc.

The electrical system can be checked with a test light and a jumper wire. A test light is a device that looks like a pointed screwdriver with a wire attached to it. It also contains a light bulb in its handle. A jumper wire is a piece of wire with an alligator clip attached to each end. To check the system you must follow the wiring diagrams found in this chapter. A wiring diagram is a road map of the car's electrical system.

If a unit is not working, you must follow a systematic plan to determine which of the three causes is the villain.

1. Locate the switch that controls the faulty unit and turn it on.

2. Disconnect the power supply wire.

3. Attach the ground wire on the test light to a good metal ground.

4. Touch the probe end of the test light to the end of the power supply wire. If the unit is receiving current, the test light will go on.

NOTE: *If the unit is one which works only when the ignition key is turned on (turn signal) make sure the key is turned on.*

If the bulb does not go on, the problem is in the circuit between the battery and the unit. As mentioned earlier, this includes all the switches, fuses, and relays in the system. Turn to the wiring diagram and find the unit on the diagram. Now follow the wire that runs from the unit back to the battery. The problem is an open cirucit between the battery and the unit.

If the fuse is blown and, when replaced, immediately blows again, there is a short circuit in the system which must be located and repaired. If there is a switch in the system, by-pass it with a jumper wire. This is done by connecting one end of the jumper wire to the power supply wire into the switch and the other end of the jumper wire to the wire coming out of the switch. Consult the wiring diagram again. If the test light lights with the jumper wire installed, the switch or whatever was by-passed is defective.

NOTE: *Never substitute the jumper wire for the unit; this could result in a short circuit.*

5. If the test light goes on, current is getting to the unit that is not working. This eliminates the first of the three possible causes. Connect the power supply wire to the unit. Connect a jumper wire from the unit to a good metal ground. Do this with the switch turned on and, also, the ignition switch turned on if it is required. If the unit works with the jumper wire installed, there is a bad ground. This is usually caused by the metal area where the unit mounts to the car being coated with foreign matter.

6. If neither of the above tests locates the source of the trouble, the unit itself is defective.

The above test procedure can be applied to any of the components of the chassis electrical system. For any electrical system to work, all connections must be clean and tight.

Heater

BLOWER

Removal and Installation

1967–69

1. Disconnect the battery ground cable.
2. Disconnect the hoses and wiring from the fender skirt.
3. Remove the wheel opening trim.
4. Remove the rocker panel molding.
5. Loosen the rear lower fender-to-body bolt.
6. Remove the 9 rearmost fender skirt attaching screws.
7. Pull the lower rear edge of the fender out. Pull the skirt down. Place a

block of wood between the fender and the skirt.

8. Remove the blower-to-case attaching screws. Remove the blower assembly.
9. Remove the blower wheel retaining nut. Separate the blower and motor.
10. Reverse the procedure to install. The open end of the blower should be away from the motor.

1970–74

1. Jack up the front of the car and remove the right front wheel.
2. Cut an access hole about ¾ of the way around the stamped outline on the right fender skirt. An air chisel is the preferred method, but you could also drill holes around the perimeter and then chisel it by hand.
3. Bend the sheet metal out so that you have access to the blower motor.
4. Disconnect the blower wiring.
5. Remove the blower motor.
6. Reverse the removal procedure to install the blower.
7. Bend the cut portion back into place. Use sheet metal screws to retain it to the panel. Coat the cut seam with undercoating or sealer.

HEATER CORE

Removal and Installation

1967 EXCEPT AIR-CONDITIONED CARS

1. Disconnect the battery ground cable and drain the radiator.
2. Remove the heater hoses from the core. The top hose connects to the water pump and the lower hose goes to the thermostat housing.
3. Remove the cables and all electrical connections from the heater and defroster assembly.
4. Remove the nuts from the core case studs located on the firewall.
5. From inside the car, remove the case-to-firewall mounting screws and also the heater and defroster assembly.
6. Remove the retaining springs and core.
7. Install the core and retaining springs, making sure the core-to-case sealer is in good shape.
8. Complete the installation by reversing the removal procedure.

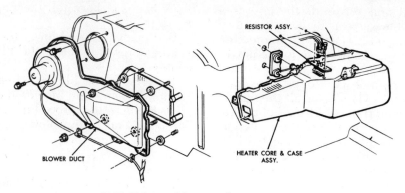

1967–69 heater blower and core mounting

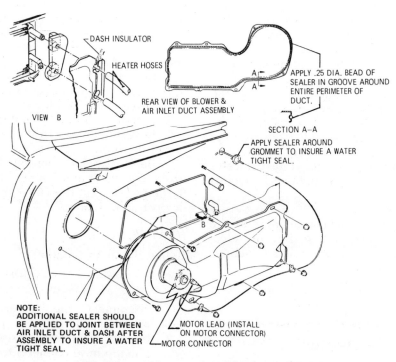

1970–74 heater blower and air inlet duct mounting

1968–74 EXCEPT AIR-CONDITIONED CARS

1. Disconnect the battery ground cable.

2. Drain the radiator.

3. Disconnect the heater hoses. Plug the core inlet and outlet.

4. Remove the nuts from the air distributor duct studs on the firewall.

5. From beneath the dash, drill out the lower, right-hand distributor duct stud with a ¼ in. drill.

6. On 1970 and later models remove the glove box and radio, then the defroster duct-to-distributor duct screw.

7. Pull the distributor duct from the firewall mounting. Remove the resistor wires. Lay the duct on the floor.

8. Remove the core assembly from the distributor duct.

9. Reverse the procedure to install.

1967–69 WITH AIR CONDITIONING

1. Remove the glove box.

2. Remove the lower instrument panel air-conditioning duct and outlet as-

sembly by removing the 5 attaching screws and retainer.

3. Lower the duct and outlet assembly after disconnecting the right and left-side nozzle connections.

4. Disconnect the temperature control cable and vacuum hose.

5. Drain the cooling system and remove the two water hoses attached to the heater core.

6. Remove the six heater core-to-cowl attaching nuts. It is necessary to cut a 1 in. diameter hole in the right-hand fender skirt to remove the lower nut.

7. Remove two screws from the heater core and case evaporator housing seal and remove the seal and retainer.

8. Remove the core and case assembly.

9. Mark the heater cam and bracket assembly to ensure proper reinstallation and remove the heater cam and bracket.

10. Remove the front case-to-rear case attaching screws and separate the cases.

11. Remove the heater core retaining screws and core.

12. Reverse the above steps for installation.

1970–74 WITH AIR CONDITIONING

1. Drain the coolant.

2. Remove the glove box and door.

3. Remove the cold air duct on the lower right-hand side.

4. Remove the left and center lower A/C ducts.

5. Raise the car and remove the rocker panel trim on the right-side and remove the screws holding the forward trim brackets.

6. Remove the 3 lower fender bolts at rear of the fender.

7. Remove the 4 fender-to-skirt bolts at the rear of the wheel opening.

8. Remove the two fender skirt bolts near the blower motor area.

9. Pry the rear portion of the fender out at the bottom to gain access to the hose clamp on the water valve-to-core hose and disconnect the hose at the heater core.

10. Disconnect the water pump hose at the heater core.

11. Remove the two heater case retaining nuts under the hood at the dash.

12. Remove the two heater case retaining bolts inside the car.

13. Remove the console and tape player if equipped.

14. Disconnect the temperature cable at the heater case.

15. Remove the heater outlet duct.

16. Remove the lower defroster duct screw.

17. Remove the right kick panel, and the heater core and case as an assembly.

18. Disconnect the vacuum hoses from the heater case and remove the core from the case.

19. Reverse the above steps for installation.

Radio

Removal and Installation

1. Disconnect the battery ground cable.

2. Remove the glove compartment, and ash tray housing as necessary.

3. Remove the knobs, controls, washers, trim plate, and nuts from the radio.

4. Remove the hoses from the center air-conditioning duct as necessary.

5. Disconnect all wiring leads.

6. Remove the screw from the radio rear mounting bracket and lower the radio.

7. To install, reverse the above procedure.

Windshield Wipers

MOTOR

Removal and Installation

1967

1. Make certain that the wiper motor is in the park position.

2. Disconnect the washer hoses and electrical connectors.

3. Remove the 3 motor bolts. Pull the wiper motor assembly from the cowl opening and loosen the nuts retaining the drive rod ball stud to the crank arm.

4. Reverse the procedure to install, checking the sealing gaskets at the motor.

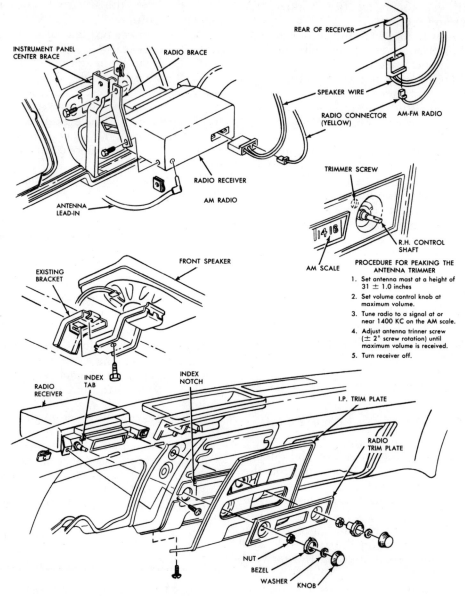

REAR OF RECEIVER

INSTRUMENT PANEL
CENTER BRACE

RADIO BRACE

SPEAKER WIRE

RADIO CONNECTOR   AM-FM RADIO
(YELLOW)

TRIMMER SCREW

RADIO RECEIVER

AM RADIO

ANTENNA
LEAD-IN

R.H. CONTROL
SHAFT

FRONT SPEAKER

EXISTING
BRACKET

AM SCALE

PROCEDURE FOR PEAKING THE
ANTENNA TRIMMER

1. Set antenna mast at a height of
   31 ± 1.0 inches

2. Set volume control knob at
   maximum volume.

3. Tune radio to a signal at or
   near 1400 KC on the AM scale.

4. Adjust antenna trimmer screw
   (± 2° screw rotation) until
   maximum volume is received.

5. Turn receiver off.

INDEX
TAB

INDEX
NOTCH

RADIO
RECEIVER

I.P. TRIM PLATE

RADIO
TRIM PLATE

NUT

BEZEL

WASHER   KNOB

1967–68 radio mounting

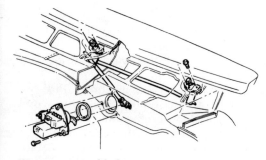

Wiper motor and linkage

Make sure that the motor is in the park position before installation.

1968–74

1. Make sure that the wiper motor is in the park position.

2. Disconnect the washer hoses and electrical connectors.

3. Remove the plenum chamber grille or access cover. Remove the nut retaining the crank arm to the motor assembly.

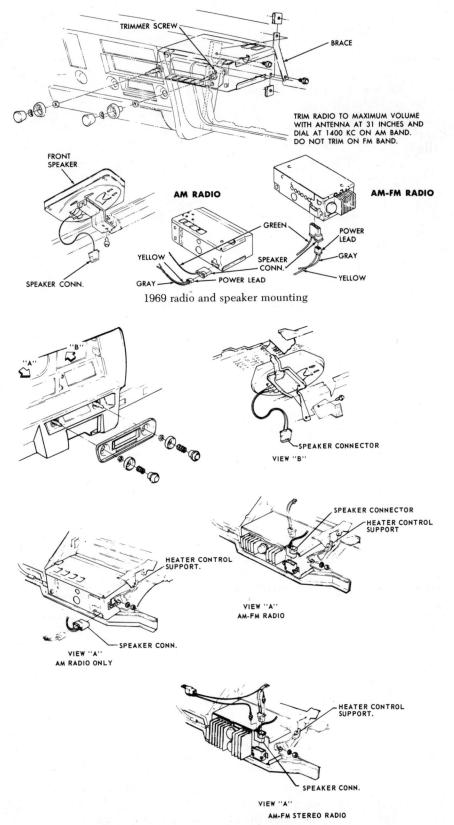

TRIM RADIO TO MAXIMUM VOLUME
WITH ANTENNA AT 31 INCHES AND
DIAL AT 1400 KC ON AM BAND.
DO NOT TRIM ON FM BAND.

1969 radio and speaker mounting

1970–74 radio and speaker mounting

4. Remove the retaining screws or nuts and remove the motor. Do not allow the motor to hang by the drive link.

5. Reverse the procedure to install, checking the sealing gaskets at the motor. Make sure that the motor is in the park position before installation.

WIPER TRANSMISSION

Removal and Installation

1. Make sure that the wiper motor is in the park position.
2. Disconnect the battery ground cable.
3. Remove the wiper arm and blade assemblies from the transmission. On the articulated left arm assemblies, remove the carburetor type clip retaining the pinned arm to the blade arm.
4. Remove the plenum chamber air intake grille or screen.
5. Loosen the nuts retaining the drive rod ball stud to the crank arm and detach the drive rod from the crank arm.
6. Remove the transmission retaining screws. Lower the transmission and drive rod assemblies into the plenum chamber.
7. Remove the transmission and linkage from the plenum chamber through the cowl opening.
8. Reverse the procedure to install, making sure that the wiper blade assemblies are installed in the park position. On recessed wiper arms, this occurs at ⅜ in. from the top of the reveal molding.

Instrument Cluster

Removal and Installation

1967–69

1. Disconnect battery.
2. Remove lower instrument panel cover.
3. Remove ashtray bracket screws, radio retaining nuts, and glove compartment.
4. Disconnect heater control cables and wires.
5. Disconnect speedometer cable, then remove upper left-hand vent duct connector.

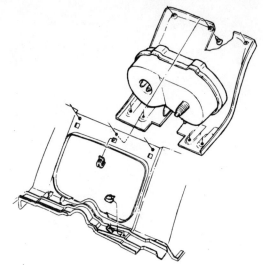

1967–68 instrument cluster mounting

6. Disconnect headlight switch shaft.
7. Remove screws across top and bottom of instrument panel and the nut on the right-hand side (stud through dash).
8. Loosen toe plate screws, remove lower column support nuts, and drop steering column.

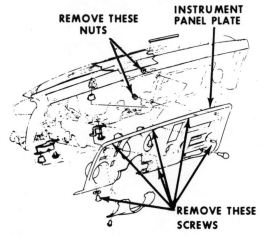

1969 instrument cluster mounting

9. Pull panel out far enough to reach behind it, then disconnect printed circuit board, windshield wipers, and cigarette lighter.
10. Remove ground straps and cluster retaining screws.
11. Carefully remove cluster.
12. To install, reverse removal procedure, making sure steering column is properly aligned.

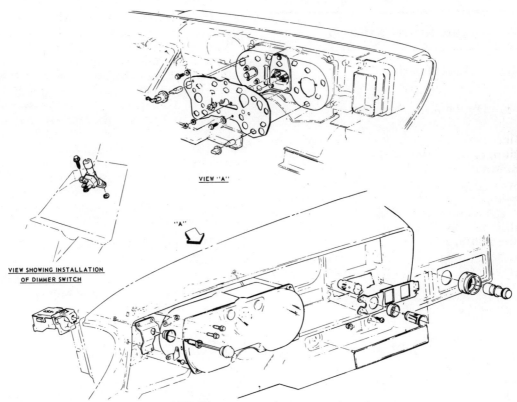

VIEW "A"

"A"

VIEW SHOWING INSTALLATION
OF DIMMER SWITCH

1970–74 instrument cluster mounting

1970

1. Disconnect the battery and remove the fuse block from the firewall.

2. Remove the upper and lower left-side instrument panel trim plates and the lower A/C duct extensions, if so equipped.

3. Remove the left-side garnish molding and the left lower instrument panel brace, under the steering column, and the toe plate.

4. Remove the left-side pad bolts and fuse block screws.

5. Disconnect the body connectors, dimmer, brake, left-side door jamb switches, and the speedometer cable.

6. Drop the steering column and disconnect the ignition, neutral, turn signal, and back-up switches.

7. Remove the glove box and door, right-side garnish molding, and right lower A/C duct at the case, if so equipped.

8. Remove the right-side lower instrument bolts and the upper instrument nuts, and disconnect the right-side door jamb switch connector and temperature cable.

9. Pad the steering column and remove the instrument cluster.

1971–74

1. Disconnect the battery ground cable.

2. Remove the upper instrument panel trim plate.

3. Remove the lower instrument panel trim and bracket at the steering column.

4. Loosen the two steering column nuts and carefully lower the column.

5. Remove the cluster screws, pull out the cluster and disconnect the speedometer and wiring for the printed circuit.

6. Remove the cluster. To install, reverse the removal procedure.

Turn Signal Flasher Location

The turn signal flasher is located under the dash to the right of the steering column.

Ignition Switch

Removal and Installation
1967–68

1. Disconnect the battery ground cable.

2. Remove the lock cylinder by positioning the switch in the Accessory position and inserting a piece of wire in the hole in the cylinder face. Push in on the wire and turn the key counterclockwise to remove the cylinder.

3. Remove the bezel nut and pull out the ignition switch.

4. Unsnap the locking tangs on the connector with a screwdriver. Unplug the connector.

5. Reverse the removal procedure to install the switch.

1969–74

See "Lock Cylinder Replacement" in Chapter 8 for these models.

Seat Belts

BUZZER SYSTEM–1973

The front seat belt warning system consists of a switch in each belt retractor, a sensor switch in the seat cushion on the passenger side, a reminder light, and a warning buzzer. The circuit wiring is routed through the ignition switch and parking brake warning switch on manual transmission models or through the ignition switch and transmission switch on models equipped with automatic transmissions.

With the ignition switch on and the parking brake released on cars equipped with manual transmissions, or with the shift selector in a forward position on automatic transmission models, the warning circuit (light and buzzer) is closed (activated) until the driver's seat belt is extended to open (de-activate) the circuit. The seat sensor on the passenger side will react to weights in excess of 47 lbs. on the seat cushion and close the warning circuit. Extending the passenger belt will open the circuit.

SEAT BELT/STARTER INTERLOCK—1974

All 1974 Firebirds are equipped with the sequential interlock seat belt system. The sequential interlock system requires the driver and right front seat occupant to first sit in their seats, then fasten their seat belts before the engine can be started. The middle seat position, on cars equipped with a front bench seat, is not included in the interlock system, but the belt must be buckled if this seat is occupied to avoid activating the familiar buzzer and warning light system. The seat sensors are similar to those found in the 1973 buzzer systems.

Engine restarting is possible without interference from the interlock system if the driver has not left his seat. In the event of system malfunction, an emergency by-pass switch under the hood permits starting when the ignition key is in the ON position.

The buzzer/warning light system will be activated if a front seat belt is not fastened at an occupied front seat after the engine is started and the transmission is shifted from Park or Neutral to a forward gear.

Wiring Diagrams

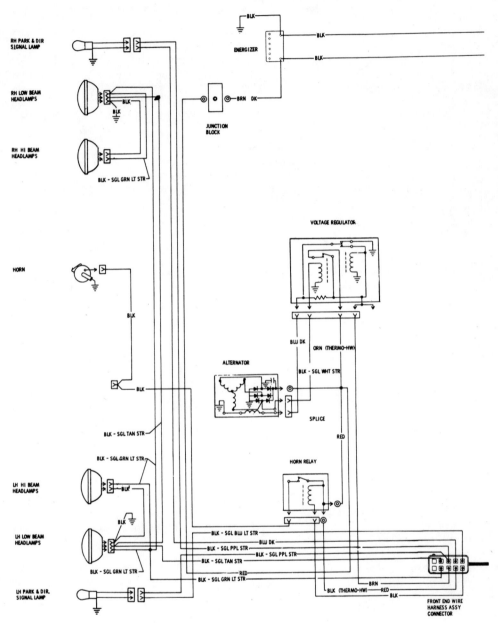

1967 front

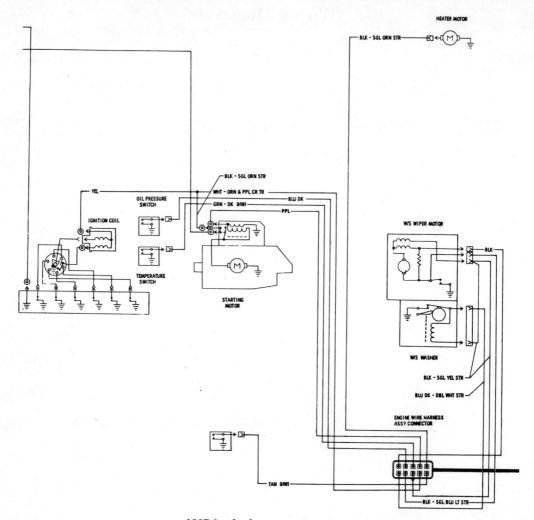

HEATER MOTOR

BLK - SGL ORN STR

BLK - SGL ORN STR
WHT - ORN & PPL CR TR
BLU DK
GRN - DK (HW)
PPL

YEL

OIL PRESSURE SWITCH

IGNITION COIL

TEMPERATURE SWITCH

STARTING MOTOR

W/S WIPER MOTOR

BLK

W/S WASHER

BLK - SGL YEL STR

BLU DK - DBL WHT STR

ENGINE WIRE HARNESS ASSY CONNECTOR

TAN (HW)

BLK - SGL BLU LT STR

1967 6 cylinder engine harness

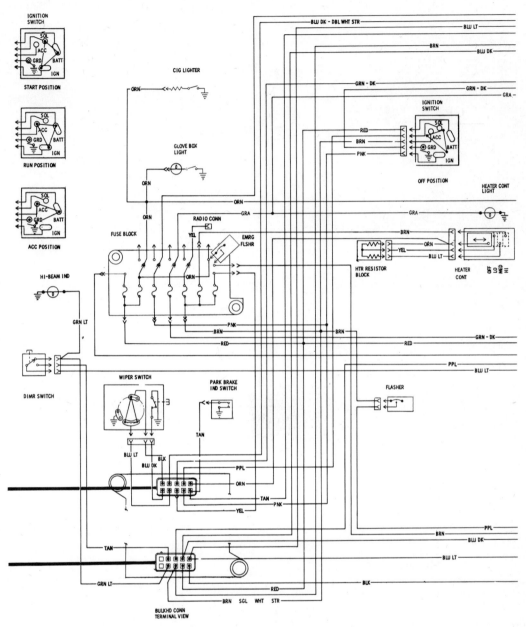

1967 instrument panel

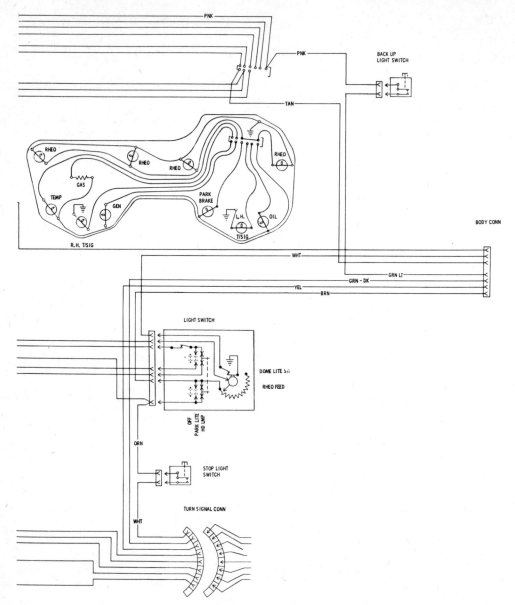

1967 instrument panel

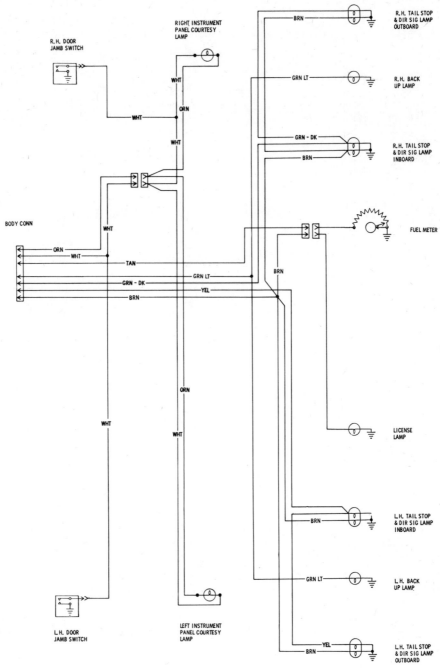

1967 rear

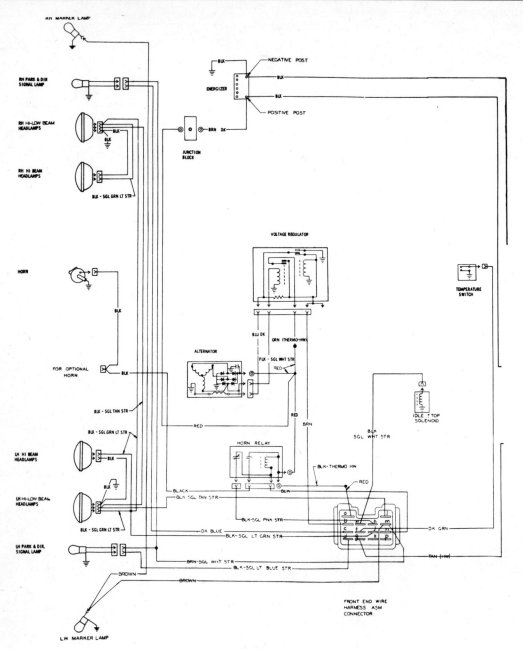

1968 front

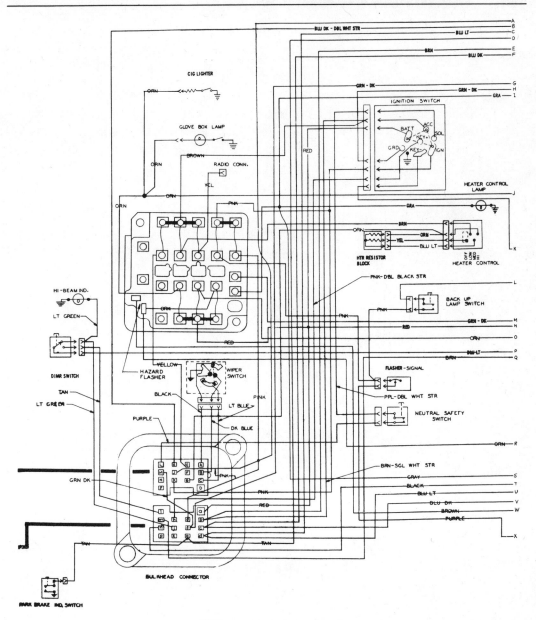

1968 passenger compartment

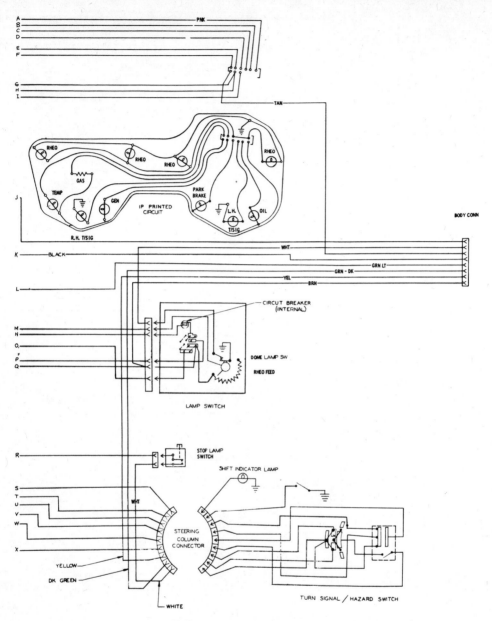

1968 passenger compartment

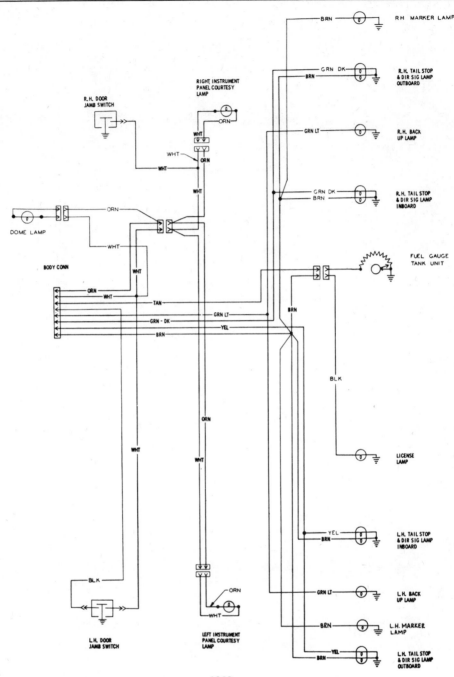

1968 rear

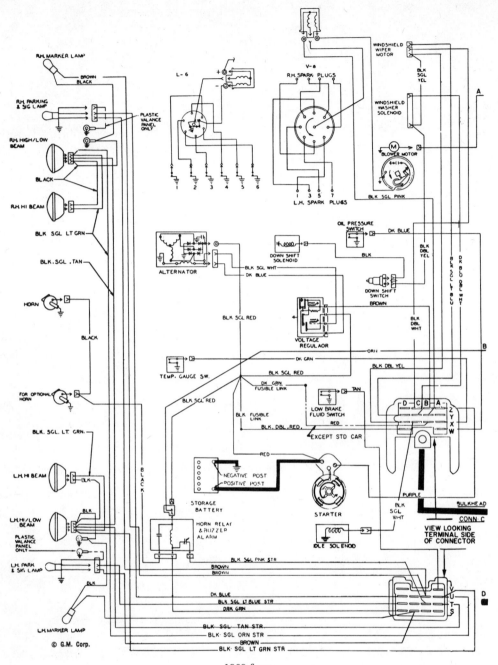

1969 front

1969 passenger compartment

© G.M. Corp.

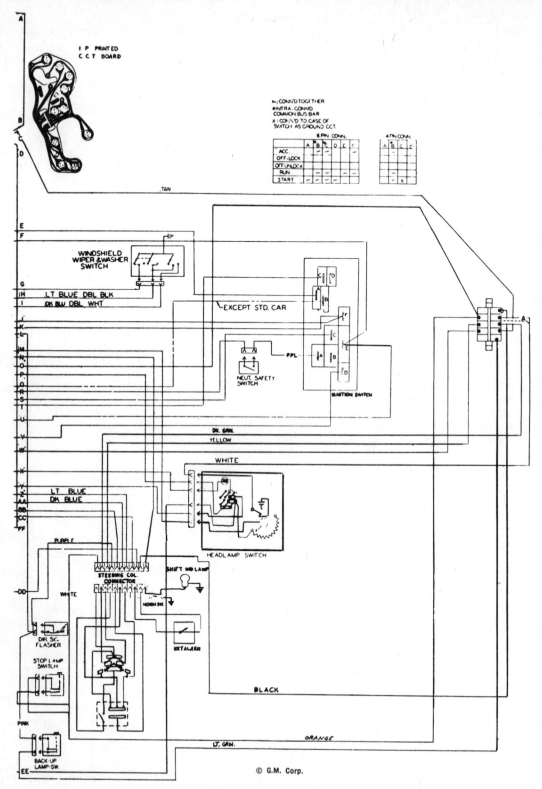

I P PRINTED
C C T BOARD

← : CONN'D TOGETHER
● INTRA - CONN'D
   COMMON BUS BAR
X : CONN'D TO CASE OF
   SWITCH AS GROUND CCT

	6 PIN CONN.						**4 PIN CONN.**			
	A	B	C	D	E	F	A	B	C	C
ACC.		–		–				–		
OFF-LOCK										
OFF-UNLOCK								–		
RUN		–		–				–		
START	–	–	–	–						X

TAN

WINDSHIELD
WIPER & WASHER
SWITCH

EXCEPT STD. CAR

LT BLUE DBL BLK

DK BLU DBL WHT

NEUT. SAFETY
SWITCH

PPL

IGNITION SWITCH

DK. GRN.

YELLOW

WHITE

LT BLUE
DK BLUE

HEADLAMP SWITCH

PURPLE

STEERING COL.
CONNECTOR

SHIFT IND LAMP

WHITE

HORN SW.

DIR. SIG.
FLASHER

STOP LAMP
SWITCH

KEY ALARM

BLACK

PINK

ORANGE

LT. GRN.

BACK-UP
LAMP-SW.

© G.M. Corp.

1969 passenger compartment

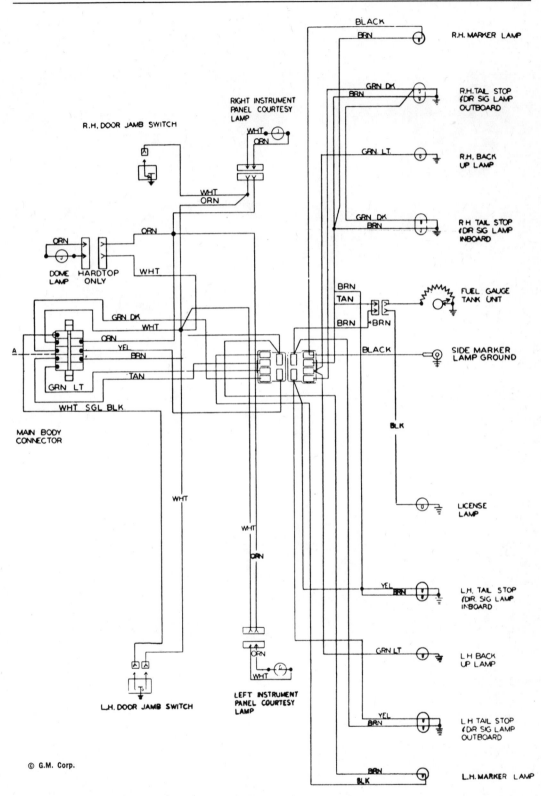

BLACK

BRN ⊤ R.H. MARKER LAMP

GRN DK
BRN R.H. TAIL STOP
(DIR SIG LAMP
OUTBOARD

GRN LT. R.H. BACK
UP LAMP

GRN DK
BRN R.H. TAIL STOP
(DIR SIG LAMP
INBOARD

RIGHT INSTRUMENT
PANEL COURTESY
LAMP

WHT
ORN

R.H. DOOR JAMB SWITCH

WHT
ORN

ORN

ORN
DOME HARDTOP
LAMP ONLY

WHT

BRN
TAN FUEL GAUGE
TANK UNIT
BRN ⊦BRN

GRN DK
WHT
A
ORN
YEL BLACK SIDE MARKER
BRN LAMP GROUND
TAN
GRN LT

WHT SGL BLK

MAIN BODY
CONNECTOR

BLK

WHT

LICENSE
LAMP

WHT

ORN

YEL
BRN L.H. TAIL STOP
(DIR SIG LAMP
INBOARD

ORN

GRN LT L.H BACK
UP LAMP
WHT

LEFT INSTRUMENT
PANEL COURTESY
LAMP

L.H. DOOR JAMB SWITCH

YEL
BRN L H TAIL STOP
(DIR SIG LAMP
OUTBOARD

© G.M. Corp.

BRN
BLK L.H. MARKER LAMP

1969 rear

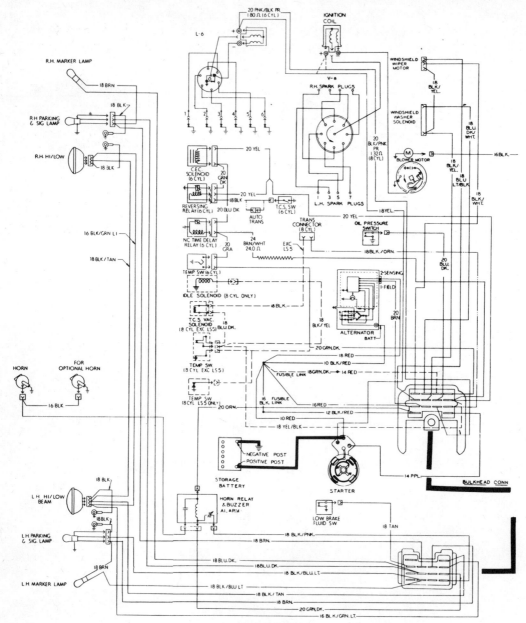

1970–71 front

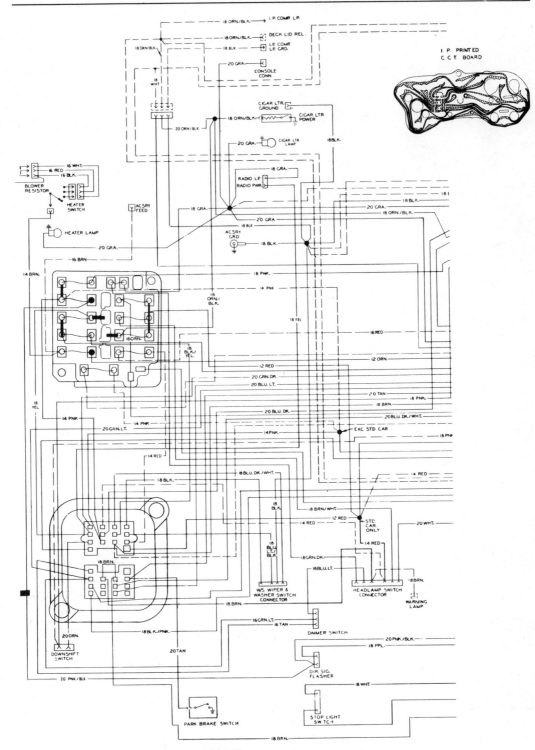

1970–71 passenger compartment

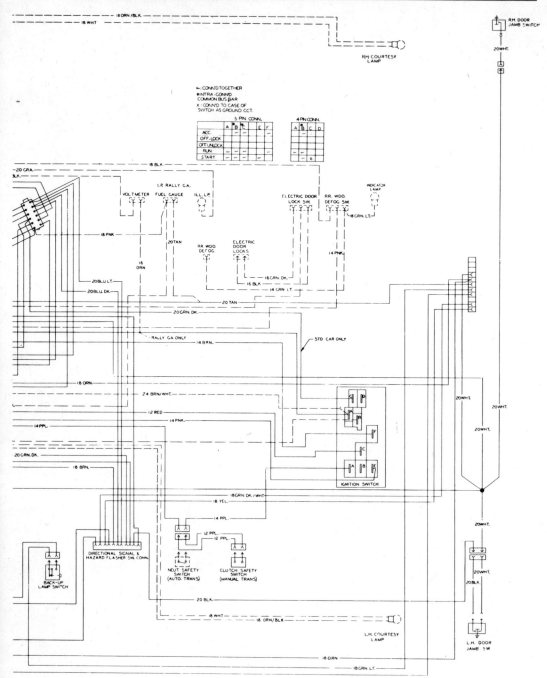

1970–71 passenger compartment

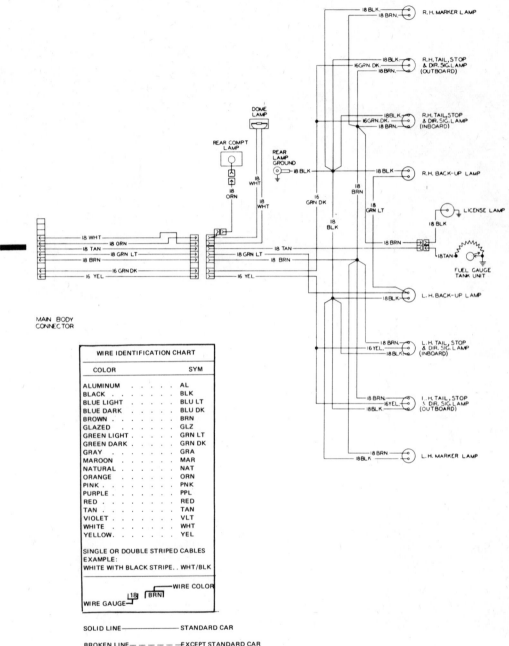

MAIN BODY
CONNECTOR

WIRE IDENTIFICATION CHART	
COLOR	SYM
ALUMINUM	AL
BLACK	BLK
BLUE LIGHT	BLU LT
BLUE DARK	BLU DK
BROWN	BRN
GLAZED	GLZ
GREEN LIGHT	GRN LT
GREEN DARK	GRN DK
GRAY	GRA
MAROON	MAR
NATURAL	NAT
ORANGE	ORN
PINK	PNK
PURPLE	PPL
RED	RED
TAN	TAN
VIOLET	VLT
WHITE	WHT
YELLOW.	YEL

SINGLE OR DOUBLE STRIPED CABLES
EXAMPLE:
WHITE WITH BLACK STRIPE . . WHT/BLK

WIRE COLOR
WIRE GAUGE — 18 BRN

SOLID LINE ———————— STANDARD CAR

BROKEN LINE — — — — —EXCEPT STANDARD CAR

HYPHENATED LINE — — – —AUTOMATIC TRANSMISSION

1970–71 rear

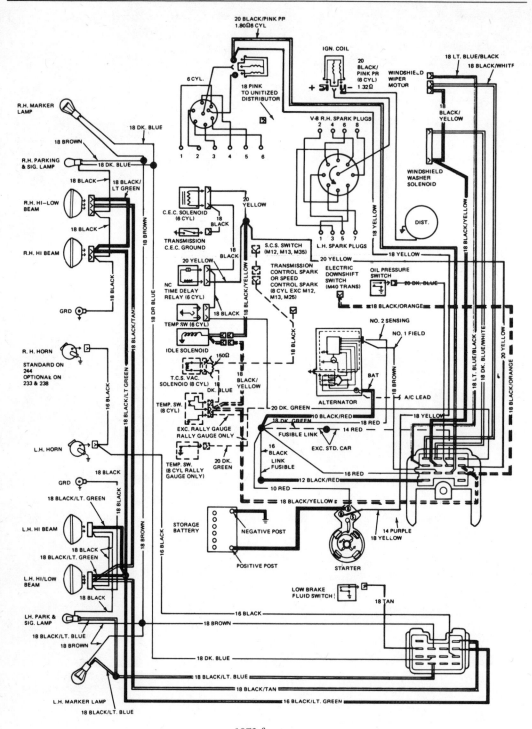

1972 front

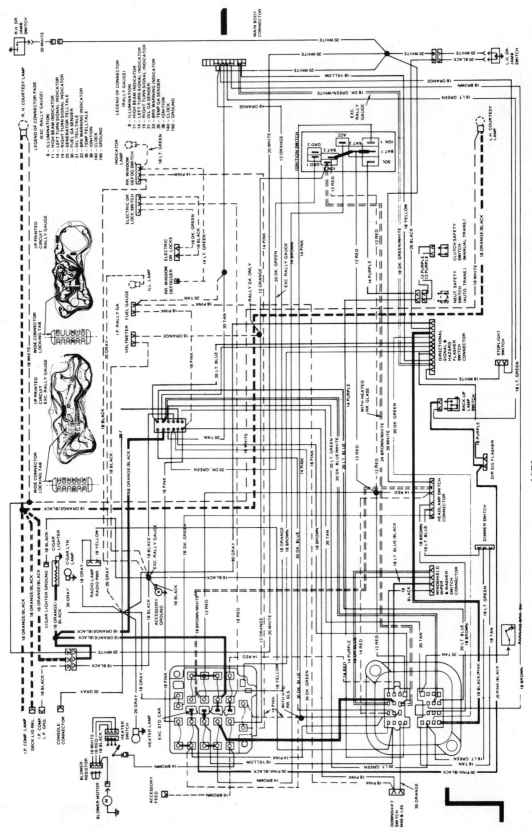

1972 passenger compartment

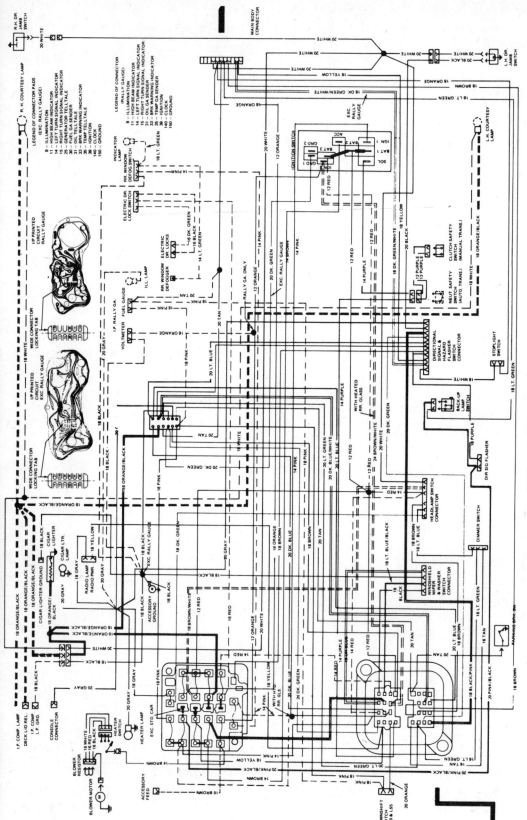

1972 passenger compartment

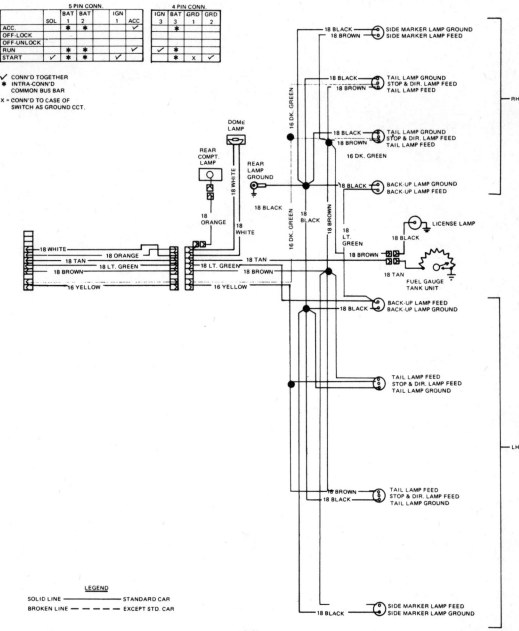

		BAT 1	BAT 2	IGN 1	ACC
	SOL				
ACC.		∗	∗		✓
OFF-LOCK					
OFF-UNLOCK					
RUN		∗	∗		✓
START	✓	∗	∗	✓	

5 PIN CONN.

	IGN 3	BAT 3	GRD 1	GRD 2
		∗		
	✓	∗		
		∗	x	✓

4 PIN CONN.

✓ CONN'D TOGETHER
∗ INTRA-CONN'D COMMON BUS BAR
x = CONN'D TO CASE OF SWITCH AS GROUND CCT.

LEGEND

SOLID LINE ———————— STANDARD CAR
BROKEN LINE — — — — — EXCEPT STD. CAR

1972 rear

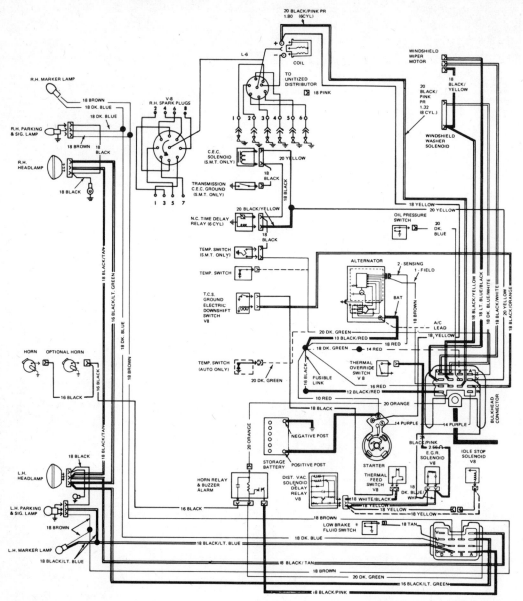

1973 front

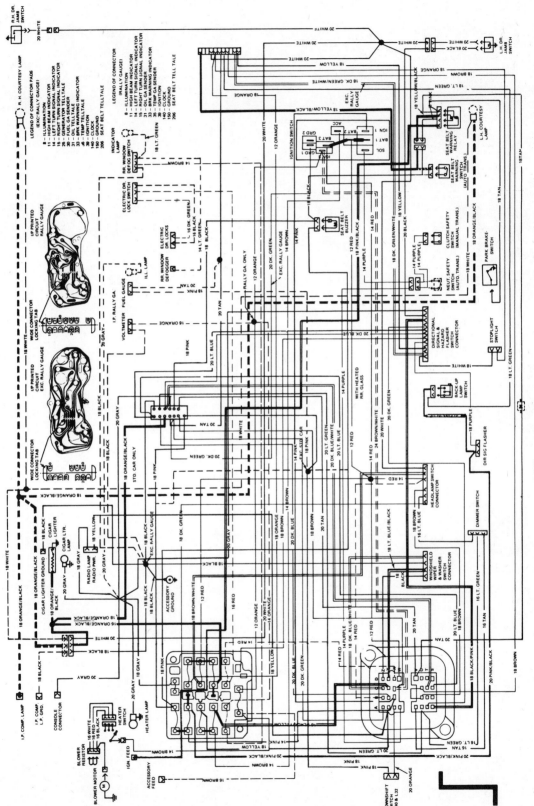

1973 passenger compartment

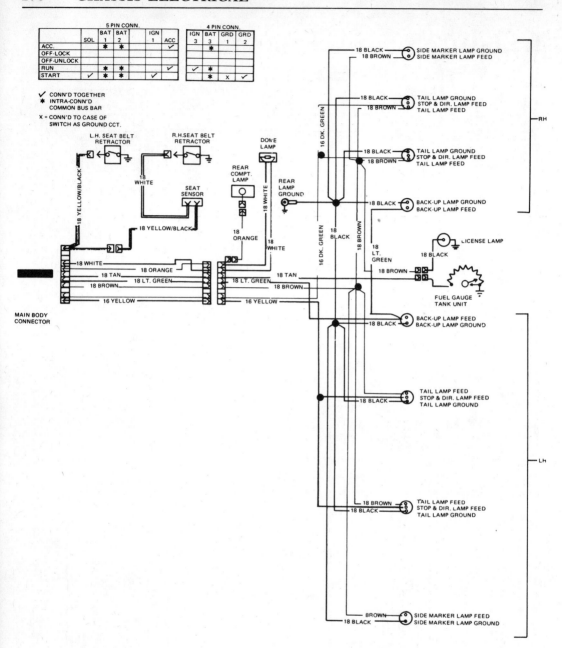

1973 rear

6 · Clutch and Transmission

1974

The purpose of the clutch is to disconnect and connect engine power from the transmission. A car at rest requires a lot of engine torque to get all that weight moving. An internal-combustion engine does not develop a high starting torque (unlike steam engines), so it must be allowed to operate without any load until it builds up enough torque to move the car. Torque increases with engine rpm. The clutch allows the engine to build up torque by physically disconnecting the engine from the transmission, relieving the engine of any load or resistance. The transfer of engine power to the transmission (the load) must be smooth and gradual; if it weren't, driveline components would wear out or break quickly. This gradual power transfer is made possible by gradually releasing the clutch pedal. The clutch disc and pressure plate are the connecting link between the engine and transmission. When the clutch pedal is released, the disc and plate contact each other (clutch engagement), physically joining the engine and transmission. When the pedal is pushed in, the disc and plate separate (the clutch is disengaged), disconnecting the engine from the transmission.

The clutch assembly consists of the flywheel, the clutch disc, the clutch pressure plate, the throwout bearing and fork, the actuating linkage and the pedal. The

flywheel and clutch pressure plate (driving members) are connected to the engine crankshaft and rotate with it. The clutch disc is located between the flywheel and pressure plate, and splined to the transmission shaft. A driving member is one that is attached to the engine and transfers engine power to a driven member (clutch disc) on the transmission shaft. A driving member (pressure plate) rotates (drives) a driven member (clutch disc) on contact and, in so doing, turns the transmission shaft. There is a circular diaphragm spring within the pressure plate cover (transmission side). In a relaxed state (when the clutch pedal is fully released), this spring is convex; that is, it is dished outward toward the transmission. Pushing in the clutch pedal actuates an attached linkage rod. Connected to the other end of this rod is the throwout bearing fork. The throwout bearing is attached to the fork. When the clutch pedal is depressed, the clutch linkage pushes the fork and bearing forward to contact the diaphragm spring of the pressure plate. The outer edges of the spring are secured to the pressure plate and are pivoted on rings so that when the center of the spring is compressed by the throwout bearing, the outer edges bow outward and, by so doing, pull the pressure plate in the same direction—away from the clutch disc. This action separates the disc

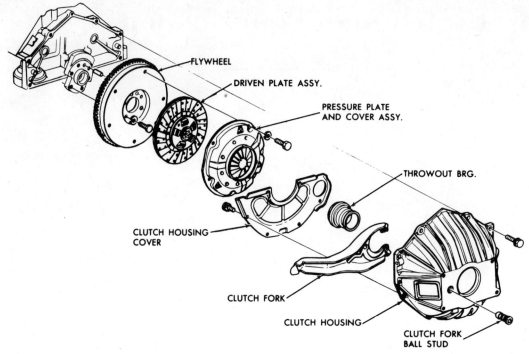

FLYWHEEL

DRIVEN PLATE ASSY.

PRESSURE PLATE
AND COVER ASSY.

THROWOUT BRG.

CLUTCH HOUSING
COVER

CLUTCH FORK

CLUTCH HOUSING

CLUTCH FORK
BALL STUD

Exploded view of the clutch and flywheel assembly

from the plate, disengaging the clutch and allowing the transmission to be shifted into another gear. A coil type clutch return spring attached to the clutch pedal arm permits full release of the pedal. Releasing the pedal pulls the throwout bearing away from the diaphragm spring resulting in a reversal of spring position. As bearing pressure is gradually released from the spring center, the outer edges of the spring bow inward, pushing the pressure plate into closer contact with the clutch disc. As the disc and plate move closer together, friction between the two increases and slippage is reduced until, when full spring pressure is applied (by fully releasing the pedal), the speed of the disc and plate are the same. This stops all slipping, creating a direct connection between the plate and disc which results in the transfer of power from the engine to the transmission. The clutch disc is now rotating with the pressure plate at engine speed and, because it is splined to the transmission shaft, the shaft now turns at the same engine speed. Understanding clutch operation can be rather difficult at first; if you're still confused after reading this, consider the following analogy. The action of the diaphragm spring can be com-

pared to that of an oil can bottom. The bottom of an oil can is shaped very much like the clutch diaphragm spring and pushing in on the can bottom and then releasing it produces a similar effect. As mentioned earlier, the clutch pedal return spring permits full release of the pedal and reduces linkage slack due to wear. As the linkage wears, clutch free-pedal travel will increase and free-travel will decrease as the clutch wears. Free-travel is actually throwout bearing lash.

The diaphragm spring type clutches used in Firebirds are available in two different designs: flat diaphragm springs or bent springs. The bent fingers are bent back to create a centrifugal boost ensuring quick re-engagement at higher engine speeds. This design enables pressure plate load to increase as the clutch disc wears and makes low pedal effort possible even with a heavy-duty clutch. The throwout bearing used with the bent finger design is 1¼ in. long and is shorter than the bearing used with the flat finger design. These bearings are not interchangeable. If the longer bearing is used with the bent finger clutch, free-pedal travel will not exist. This results in clutch slippage and rapid wear.

The transmission varies the gear ratio

between the engine and rear wheels. It can be shifted to change engine speed as driving conditions and loads change. The transmission allows disengaging and reversing power from the engine to the wheels.

Manual Transmission

Removal and Installation

3-SPEED AND 4-SPEED—1967–69

1. Raise the car and remove the driveshaft. On floor-shift models, remove the trim plate and shifter boot.

2. On 1968–69 models, it may be necessary to disconnect the exhaust pipe at the manifold.

3. Disconnect the speedometer cable and, on floor-shift models, disconnect the back-up light switch.

4. Remove the crossmember-to-frame bolts. On floor-shift models, remove the bolts holding the control lever support to the crossmember.

5. Remove the transmission mount bolts.

6. Using a suitable jack and a block of wood (to be placed between the jack and the engine), raise the engine slightly and remove or relocate the crossmember.

7. Remove the shift levers from the transmission side cover.

8. On floor-shift models, remove the stabilizer rod (if so equipped) situated between the shift lever assembly and the transmission.

9. Remove the transmission-to-bell-housing bolts. Remove the top bolts first and insert guide pins into the holes, then remove the bottom bolts.

10. Remove the transmission.

11. Lift the transmission into position and insert the mainshaft into the bell-housing.

12. Install the transmission-to-bell-housing bolts and lockwashers, and torque them to 50 ft lbs.

13. Install the transmission shift levers to the side cover. On floor-shift models, install the stabilizer rod (if so equipped).

14. Raise the engine slightly, position the crossmember, and install the bolts.

15. Install the transmission mount bolts. On floor-shift models, install the bolts holding the shift lever support to the crossmember.

CAUTION: *Lubricate the tailshaft bushing before the driveshafts are installed.*

16. Install the driveshaft and, if removed, install the exhaust pipe to manifold.

17. Connect the speedometer cable and, on floor-shift cars, connect the back-up light.

18. Fill the transmission with lubricant.

3-SPEED AND 4-SPEED—1970–74

1. On floor-shift models, remove the shift knob and console trim plate.

2. Raise the car and support it with floor stands.

3. Disconnect the speedometer cable and the TCS switch wiring.

4. Remove the driveshaft as outlined in the next Chapter.

5. Remove the bolts securing the transmission mounts to the crossmember and also those bolts securing the crossmember to the frame. Remove the crossmember.

6. Remove the shift levers from the side of the transmission.

7. Disconnect the back drive rod from the bellcrank.

8. Remove the bolts from the shift control assembly and carefully lower the assembly until the shift lever clears the rubber shift boot. Remove the assembly from the car.

9. Remove the transmission-to-bell-housing bolts and lift the transmission from the car.

10. Lift the transmission and insert the mainshaft into the bellhousing.

11. Install and torque the transmission-to-clutch housing bolts and lockwashers.

12. Install the shift lever.

13. Install the shift levers to the transmission side cover.

14. Connect the back drive rod to the bellcrank.

15. Raise the engine high enough to position the crossmember. Install and tighten the crossmember-to-frame bolts and transmission mounts to crossmember bolts.

16. Install the driveshaft.

17. Connect the speedometer cable and TCS wiring.

18. Fill the transmission with the specified lubricant. If applicable, install the console trim plate and shift knob. Adjust the linkage.

Linkage Adjustment

1967–68 COLUMN SHIFT

1. Located on the left-side of the transmission case are two levers. Manipulate these levers until the transmission is in Neutral. Depress the clutch pedal, start the engine, and release the pedal slowly. If the car fails to move and engine is still running with pedal fully released, the transmission is in Neutral. If the car moves, the transmission is in gear and the levers should be repositioned until Neutral is found. Loosen the swivel nuts on both shift rods.

2. Move the shift lever (on the column) to the Neutral position. Raise the hood and locate the shifter tube levers on the steering column. Align the First and Reverse lever with the Second and Third lever. Using a pin (use a large L-shaped allen wrench), hold these levers in alignment (most cars have alignment holes in the levers and an alignment plate) until the linkage is connected.

3. Make the final adjustments to align the shift rods and levers at the transmission into the Neutral position. Road-test the car and check the shifting operation. If the adjustment is correct, the alignment pin should pass freely through all alignment holes. If not, readjustment is necessary.

1969 COLUMN SHIFT

1. Turn the ignition switch to the "Off" position.

2. Loosen the swivel nuts on both shift rods.

3. Place the column-mounted shift lever in the Reverse position. There are

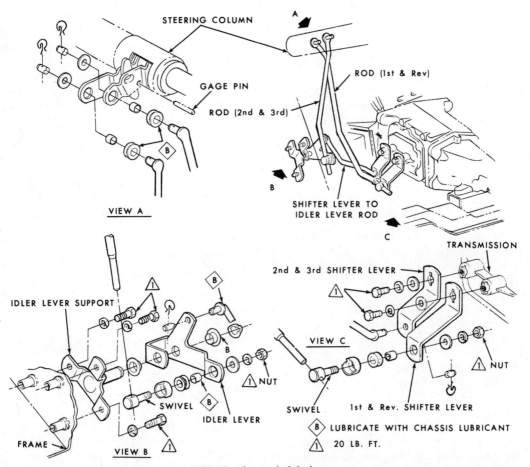

1967–68 column shift linkage

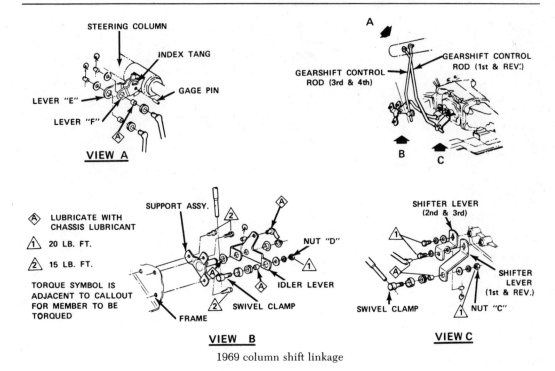

STEERING COLUMN

INDEX TANG

GAGE PIN

LEVER "E"

LEVER "F"

VIEW A

A

GEARSHIFT CONTROL
ROD (3rd & 4th)

GEARSHIFT CONTROL
ROD (1st & REV.)

B   C

Ⓐ LUBRICATE WITH
     CHASSIS LUBRICANT

△1 20 LB. FT.

△2 15 LB. FT.

TORQUE SYMBOL IS
ADJACENT TO CALLOUT
FOR MEMBER TO BE
TORQUED

SUPPORT ASSY.

NUT "D"

IDLER LEVER

SWIVEL CLAMP

FRAME

VIEW B

SHIFTER LEVER
(2nd & 3rd)

SHIFTER
LEVER
(1st & REV.)

SWIVEL CLAMP   NUT "C"

VIEW C

1969 column shift linkage

two levers located on the side of the transmission case. The lever to the front of the transmission controls Second and Third gears while the other lever controls First and Reverse. Place this First and Reverse lever into the Reverse position. Push up on the First/Reverse shift rod until the column lever is in the Reverse detent position. Tighten the swivel nut.

4. Place the column lever and the transmission levers (located on the side of the case) in Neutral. (To determine Neutral, see Step 1 for 1967–68 cars.) The shift tube levers are located on the steering column mast jacket. Make sure that the column lever is in Neutral and hold it in this position by inserting a pin through the alignment holes in the shift tube levers.

5. Hold the Second/Third shift rod steady (to prevent a change in adjustment) and tighten the swivel locknut.

6. Remove the alignment pin from the shift tube levers and shift the column shift lever to the Reverse position. Turn the ignition key to "Lock" and check the ignition interlock control. If it binds, leave the control in "Lock" and readjust the First-Reverse rod at the swivel.

7. Move the column lever through the gear positions and return it to Neutral. The alignment pin should pass freely

through the alignment holes of the shift tube levers. If it doesn't, loosen the swivel nuts and readjust.

1970–74 Column Shift

1. Place the shift lever (on the column) in Reverse and the ignition switch in "Off."

2. Raise the car and support it with floor stands.

3. Loosen the locknuts on the shift rod swivels. Pull down slightly on the First/Reverse control rod on the lower steering column to remove any slack. Tighten the locknut at the transmission lever.

4. Unlock the ignition switch and shift the column lever into Neutral. Position the shift tube levers (located on the lower steering column) in Neutral by aligning the lever alignment holes. Hold them in this position by inserting a $3/16$ in. pin through the alignment holes.

5. Hold the Second/Third shift rod steady and tighten the rod locknut.

6. Remove the alignment tool from the shift tube levers and check the shifting operation.

7. Place the column lever in Reverse and check the movement of the ignition key. In Reverse and only Reverse, the key must turn freely in and out of "Lock."

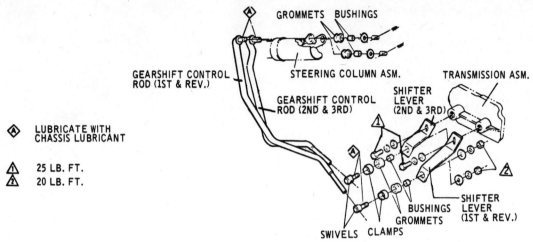

1970–74 column shift linkage

1967–Saginaw 3-Speed and Muncie 4-Speed Floor Shift

1. Place the transmission levers (located on the side plate of the transmission) in Neutral. The lever closest to the bellhousing operates Second and Third gears while the other lever controls First and Reverse. Check for Neutral in the manner described in Step 1 of "Linkage Adjustment—Column Shift."

2. Place the floor-mounted shift lever in Neutral and insert the locating pin into the notch of the shift lever and bracket assembly. On the four-speed, connect the reverse rod to the lever and secure with a retainer.

3. Loosely install the nut and clevis on the end of the shift rod and attach the other end of the rod to the lever located

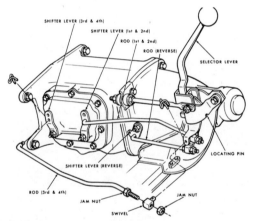

1967 Muncie 4-speed linkage

beneath the shift lever bracket. Secure the assembly with a retainer.

4. After attaching the rod to the lever, move the lever against the locating pin and adjust the clevis (U-shaped shackle) to the transmission lever until the clevis pin passes freely through the holes. Place a washer on the pin and secure it with a cotter pin. Prevent the clevis from turning by tightening the nut.

5. Install a nut, a swivel, and another nut on the other shift rod. Attach the other end of this rod to the other transmission lever and secure it with a retainer.

6. Located beneath the floor-mounted shift lever are two levers (three on a four-speed); each connected to a shift rod. The first lever and rod were connected in Step 3. Move the second lever against the locating pin and attach the swivel to this

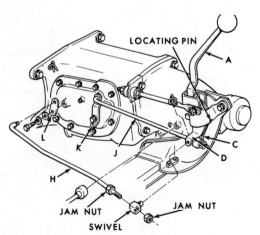

1967 Saginaw 3-speed linkage

lever, then secure it with a retainer. Tighten both nuts against the swivel.

7. Remove the locating pin and check the shift operation. Adjust the clevis and swivel if readjustment is necessary.

1967—WARNER T-16 3-SPEED FLOOR SHIFT

1. Place the transmission levers in Neutral. Verfiy the Neutral setting in the manner described in Step 1 of "Linkage Adjustment—Column Shift."

2. Place the floor-mounted shift lever in Neutral along with the two levers di-

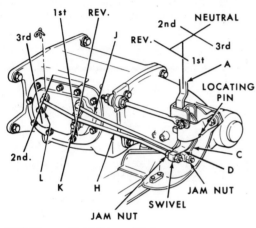

1967 Warner T–16 3-speed linkage

rectly below it. Hold the levers in Neutral by inserting a locating pin into the lever bracket assembly.

3. Insert the longer rod into the transmission lever and secure it with a retainer. Attach the swivel end of the rod to the other lever and secure it with a retainer. Repeat this procedure for the shorter rod.

4. Remove the locating pin and check the shift operation.

1968–69—3-SPEED AND 4-SPEED FLOOR SHIFT

1. On 1969 models, turn the ignition key to the "Off" position.

2. Loosen the swivel locknuts on the shift rods. On 1969 models, it will be necessary to loosen the locknut on the back drive rod.

3. Place the shift levers on the side of the transmission and the shift lever in the car in Neutral. Lock the car shift lever in Neutral by placing a pin in the notch of the lever and bracket assembly directly below the shift lever.

4. Move the shift rod nut against the swivel on each rod, then tighten the locknut against the other side of the swivel. Remove the locating pin and check the shifting operation.

5. On 1968 and 1969 models with a

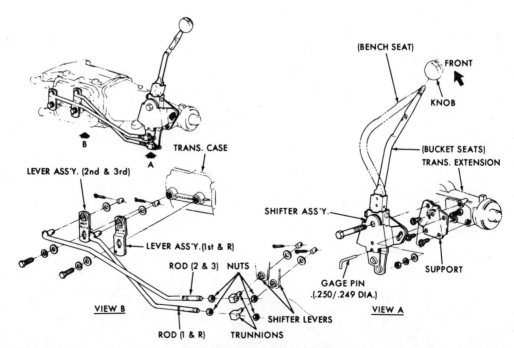

1968–69 Saginaw 3-speed linkage

Muncie four-speed, readjust the reverse rod by shortening it 3 turns of the jam nut. On 1969 models, shift into Reverse. Push up on the back drive control rod in order to place the column mechanism in the Reverse position. Pull down slightly on the rod to remove any slack and tighten the jam nut. Place the ignition switch in "Lock." The switch should not bind when moved in and out of "Lock"; if it does, readjust the back control rod. Check the shifting operation and correct it as necessary.

1970–74—3-Speed and 4-Speed Floor Shift

1. Turn the ignition switch "Off" ("Lock" for 1970 cars), raise the car, and support it on jackstands.
2. Loosen the swivel locknuts on all shift rods and on the back drive control rod.
3. Place the transmission shift levers (on the side of the transmission) in Neutral.
4. Place the floor shift lever in Neutral and lock it in this position by installing a ¼ in. pin into the lever bracket assembly directly below the shift lever.

5. Move the shift rod nut up against the swivel on each shift rod and hold it in place by tightening the locknuts.
6. Remove the locating pin from the control bracket assembly and shift the transmission into Reverse. On 1971 and 1972 models, place the ignition key in "Lock." To remove any slack in the steering column mechanism, pull down on the back drive rod and tighten the nut. When in Reverse, it must be possible to easily turn the ignition key in and out of the "Lock" position. If any binding exists, leave the key in "Lock" and readjust the back drive control rod.
7. Check the shifting operation and readjust as necessary.

Clutch

TROUBLESHOOTING

There is no substitute for careful examination and experience when attempting a diagnosis. The following are some

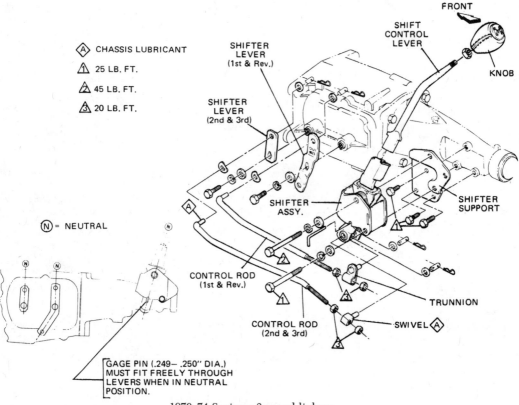

1970–74 Saginaw 3-speed linkage

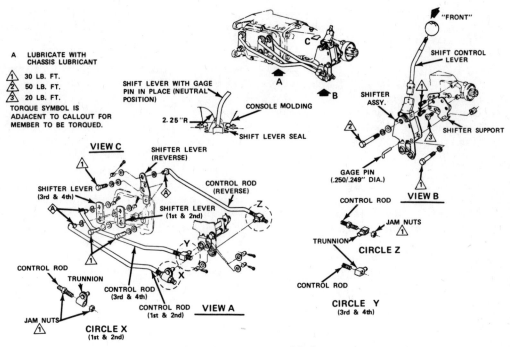

1970–74 Saginaw 4-speed linkage

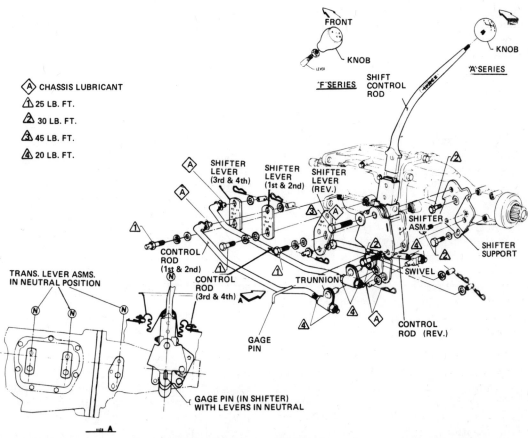

1970–74 Muncie 4-speed linkage

symptoms that may accompany clutch troubles.

1. Excessive noise.
2. Clutch chatter or grab.
3. Clutch slip.
4. Clutch drag or failure to release.
5. Pedal pulsation.
6. Low clutch facing life.
7. Gear lock-up or hard shifting.
8. Hard pedal.

Excessive Noise

There are five common sources of clutch noise:

1. Release bearing.
2. Clutch shaft pilot bearing.
3. Transmission pinion shaft bearing.
4. Transmitted engine noises.
5. Clutch linkage noises.

RELEASE BEARING

Release bearing noises vary with the degree of bearing failure. A dry or damaged bearing usually makes a shrill or scraping sound when depressing the clutch pedal to the point of release finger-to-bearing contact. This means that the noise should be audible at the lower end of clutch pedal free-play. Continued use of a car, with the release bearing in this condition, is damaging to the clutch release fingers.

The usual cause of release bearing failure is overwork—caused by riding the clutch. Other causes are not enough pedal free-play, lack of lubricant in the bearing, or clutch release fingers that are worn or out of true.

PILOT BEARING

Clutch shaft pilot bearing noises can be heard only when the bearing is in operation. This is at any time crankshaft speed is different from that of the clutch shaft, (clutch disengaged with transmission in gear).

This is a high-pitched squeal, caused by a dry bearing and requires replacement.

TRANSMISSION PINION SHAFT BEARING

A rough, or otherwise damaged, transmission pinion (input) shaft bearing noise can be heard only when the clutch is engaged, with the transmission in any shift position. The noise is usually quite noticeable with the gears in Neutral. This noise should diminish and completely disappear as the transmission pinion gear slows down and stops after clutch release. This noise is easily distinguished from release bearing noise because of the opposite conditions of encounter.

TRANSMITTED ENGINE NOISES

Assuming that the clutch pedal has the required amount of free-play, there should be no objectionable amount of engine noise transmitted to the passenger area via the clutch. Some engine noises are transmitted through the positive pressure of the clutch release bearing and fingers to the clutch housing. Here they are amplified by the shape of the clutch housing and heard in the passenger compartment in the guise of clutch or transmission trouble. Engine noise transmission can usually be modified through clutch pedal manipulation.

CLUTCH LINKAGE NOISE

Clutch linkage noise is usually a clicking or snapping sound that can be heard or felt in the pedal itself when moving it completely up or down. Locating the cause of trouble and correcting it is a matter of repositioning and lubrication. The trouble may be in the clutch assist spring, the retract spring, the release bearing lever, or even at the release bearing.

Clutch Chatter or Grab

The cause of clutch chatter or grab can usually be located within the clutch assembly. To correct the trouble the clutch must be removed. Symptoms resembling clutch trouble may be misleading and originate in other areas.

In order to isolate the cause of the problem, it is suggested that the following items be checked in this order.

1. Be sure that the clutch linkage is in adjustment and not binding. If necessary, lubricate, align, and adjust the linkage.
2. Check for worn or loose engine or transmission mounts. If necessary, tighten or replace mounts.
3. Check for wear, looseness, or misalignment of the universal joints. Check the attaching bolts on the clutch pressure plate, transmission, and clutch housing. Tighten, align, or replace as necessary.
4. Check the freedom of movement of

CLUTCH AND TRANSMISSION   189

the clutch release bearing on its sleeve. Free up or replace as necessary.

5. Check for oil or grease on the flywheel, friction disc, or pressure plate.

6. Make sure that the friction disc is true and that the disc hub is not binding on the splines of the transmission input shaft (clutch shaft).

7. Be sure that the disc or the pressure plate is not broken.

8. Examine the clutch pressure plate and cover plate assembly for cracks or heat discoloration.

Clutch Slip

Clutch slippage is usually most noticeable when pulling away, and during acceleration from a standing start. A severe, but positive, test for slippage is to start the engine, set the parking brake and apply the service brakes; shift the transmission into High gear and release the clutch pedal while accelerating the engine. A clutch in good condition should hold and stall the engine. If the clutch slips, the cause may be one or more of the following:

1. Improper linkage adjustment (not enough free-play).

2. Broken or disconnected parts.

3. Clutch linkage or lever mechanism binding or broken, not allowing full pressure plate application.

4. Friction disc oil-saturated or excessively worn.

5. Pressure plate worn, springs weak from temper loss or failure (damaging heat will usually cause parts to appear blue).

Clutch Drag or Failure to Release

There are many reasons for clutch drag (spin) or failure to release. The following conditions, therefore, apply to unmodified versions of standard vehicles. Changing the driven plate mass (replacing the standard driven plate with a heavy-duty unit), changing transmission oil viscosity, etc., may influence clutch spin-time. Three seconds is a good, typical, spin-time for the standard transmission and clutch, driven under normal conditions, in average temperate zone climates.

The friction disc and some of the transmission gears spin briefly after clutch disengagement, so normal clutch action should not be confused with a dragging clutch.

Clutch drag, failure to release, or abnormal spin-time may be caused by one or more of the following:

1. Improper clutch linkage adjustment.

2. Clutch plate hub binding on the transmission input (pinion) shaft.

3. A warped or bent friction disc or pressure plate; or loose friction material on the driven disc.

4. The transmission input shaft may be binding or sticking in the pilot bearing.

5. Misalignment of transmission to the engine.

6. Transmission lubricant low or not heavy enough.

Pedal Pulsation

This condition can be felt by applying light foot pressure to the clutch pedal with the engine idling. It may be caused by any of the following:

1. Bent or uneven clutch release finger adjustment.

2. Excessive flywheel run-out due to bent wheel or crankshaft flange; or the flywheel may not be properly seated on the crankshaft flange.

3. Release bearing cocked on transmission bearing retainer.

4. Poor alignment of transmission with the engine.

Low Clutch Facing Life

This sort of complaint warrants a close study of the operator's driving habits. Poor clutch facing wear may be caused by any of the following:

1. Riding the clutch.

2. Drag strip type operation.

3. Continuous overloading, or the hauling of heavy trailers or other equipment.

4. Holding the car from drifting backward on a grade by slipping the clutch instead of using the brakes.

5. Improper pedal linkage adjustment (free-play and pedal height).

6. Rough surface on flywheel or pressure plate.

7. Presence of oil or water on clutch facing.

8. Weak pressure plate springs, causing clutch creep or slip.

Gear Lock Up or Hard Shifting

This trouble is so closely related to "Clutch Drag or Failure to Release" that diagnosis should be conducted in the same way as given under that heading. If, after checking the items listed and finding that the transmission still locks up or is hard to shift, the trouble probably lies in the transmission cover or shifter assembly, or in the transmission proper. In that case, transmission work is needed.

Hard Pedal

A stiff clutch pedal or a clutch release that requires abnormal pedal pressure may result from one or more of the following:

1. Dry and binding clutch linkage and levers.
2. Linkage out of alignment.
3. Improper (heavy) retracting spring.
4. Dry or binding release bearing sleeve or transmission bearing retainer.
5. Assist spring missing or improperly adjusted.
6. Wrong type clutch assembly (heavy-duty) being used.

CLUTCH SERVICE

Removal and Installation

1. Support engine and remove the transmission.
2. Disconnect the clutch fork pushrod and spring.
3. Remove the flywheel housing.
4. Slide the clutch fork from the ball stud and remove the fork from the dust boot. The ball stud is threaded into the clutch housing and may be replaced, if necessary.
5. Install an alignment tool to support the clutch assembly during removal. Mark the flywheel and clutch cover for reinstallation, if they do not already have "X" marks.
6. Loosen the clutch-to-flywheel attaching bolts evenly, one turn at a time, until spring pressure is released. Remove the bolts and clutch assembly.
7. Clean the pressure plate and flywheel face.
8. Support the clutch disc and pressure plate with an alignment tool. The driven disc is installed with the damper springs on the transmission side. On some 1967 6 cylinder engines, the clutch disc is installed in a reverse manner with the damper springs to the flywheel side.

9. Turn the clutch assembly until the mark on the cover lines up with the mark on the flywheel, then install the bolts. Tighten down evenly and gradually to avoid distortion.
10. Remove the alignment tool.
11. Lubricate the ball socket and fork fingers at the release bearing end with high melting-point grease. Lubricate the recess on the inside of the throwout bearing and throwout fork groove with a light coat of graphite grease.
12. Install the clutch fork and dust boot into the housing. Install the throwout bearing to the throwout fork. Install the flywheel housing. Install the transmission.
13. Connect the fork pushrod and spring. Lubricate the spring and pushrod ends.
14. Adjust the shift linkage and clutch pedal free-play.

Linkage Inspection

A clutch may have all the symptoms of going bad when the real trouble lies in the linkage. To avoid the unnecessary replacement of a clutch, make the following linkage checks:

a. Start the engine and depress the clutch pedal until it is about ½ in. from the floor mat and move the shift lever between First and Reverse (First and Second on a four-speed) several times. If this can be done smoothly without any grinding, the clutch is releasing fully. If the shifting is not smooth, the clutch is not releasing fully and adjustment is necessary.

b. Check the condition of the clutch pedal bushings for signs of sticking or excessive wear.

c. Check the throwout bearing fork for proper installation on the ball stud. The fork could possibly be pulled off the ball if not properly lubricated.

d. Check the cross-shaft levers for distortion or damage.

e. Check the car for loose or damaged motor mounts. Bad motor mounts can cause the engine to shift under acceleration and bind the clutch linkage at the cross-shaft. There must be some

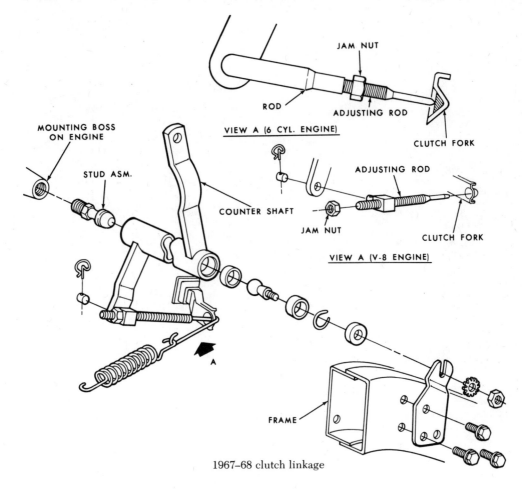

JAM NUT

ROD

ADJUSTING ROD

VIEW A (6 CYL. ENGINE)

CLUTCH FORK

MOUNTING BOSS
ON ENGINE

STUD ASM.

ADJUSTING ROD

COUNTER SHAFT

JAM NUT

CLUTCH FORK

VIEW A (V-8 ENGINE)

A

FRAME

1967–68 clutch linkage

clearance between the cross-shaft and motor mount.

f. Check the throwout bearing clearance between the clutch spring fingers and the front bearing retainer on the transmission. If there is no clearance, the fork may be improperly installed on the ball stud or the clutch disc may be worn out.

Linkage Adjustment

Only one adjustment is necessary to compensate for all normal clutch wear. Depress the clutch pedal and slowly release it. If adjusted correctly, the throwout bearing should begin to disengage the clutch diaphragm spring levers when the top of the pedal pad is 1–1⅛ in. from the floor mat. The car should begin to move forward. If clutch engagement begins at a point noticeably greater than 1⅛ in. from the floor mat or less than 1 in. from the floor mat, this free-play measurement must be adjusted as follows:

1967–69

a. Disconnect the pedal return spring at the fork.

b. Hold the clutch pedal against the rubber stop and loosen the locknut.

c. Turn the adjusting rod out and against clutch fork until the throwout bearing lightly contacts the pressure plate fingers.

d. Turn the rod into the swivel 3 times and tighten the locknut.

e. Install the clutch spring and check pedal free-play (1–1⅛ in.).

1970–74

The clutch on these models can be adjusted as outlined above or by the alternate procedure below.

a. Disconnect the return spring at the clutch fork.

b. Hold the pedal against the rubber bumper on the dash brace.

c. Push the clutch fork so that the

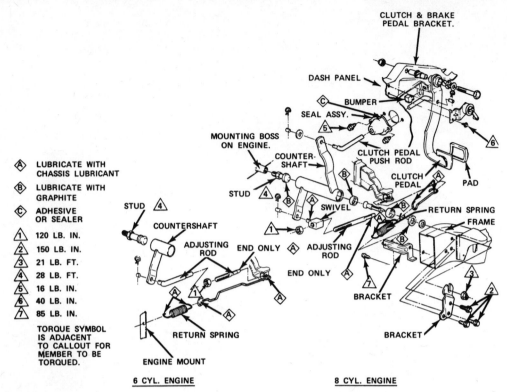

1969 clutch linkage

(A) LUBRICATE WITH CHASSIS LUBRICANT
(B) LUBRICATE WITH GRAPHITE
(C) ADHESIVE OR SEALER
(1) 120 LB. IN.
(2) 150 LB. IN.
(3) 21 LB. FT.
(4) 28 LB. FT.
(5) 16 LB. IN.
(6) 40 LB. IN.
(7) 85 LB. IN.

TORQUE SYMBOL IS ADJACENT TO CALLOUT FOR MEMBER TO BE TORQUED.

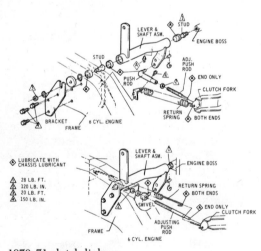

1970–71 clutch linkage

throwout bearing lightly contacts the pressure plate fingers.

d. Loosen the locknut and adjust the length of the rod so that the swivel or rod can slip freely into the gauge hole in the lever. Increase the length of the rod until all free-play is removed.

e. Remove the rod or swivel from the gauge hole and insert it in the lower hole on the lever. Install the re-

tainer and tighten the locknut to 10 ft lbs.

f. Install the return spring and check free-play measurement from the floor mat to top of the pedal pad. It should measure 1–1½ in.

Neutral Safety Switch

A clutch-operated neutral safety switch was used beginning in 1970. The ignition switch must be in the "Start" position and the clutch must be fully depressed before the car will start. The switch mounts to the clutch pedal arm. Removal of this switch is obvious and simple. This switch cannot be adjusted.

Automatic Transmission

TWO-SPEED—1967–72

Filter Service

The Powerglide has a strainer in the oil pan. If the fluid is dirty, remove the oil

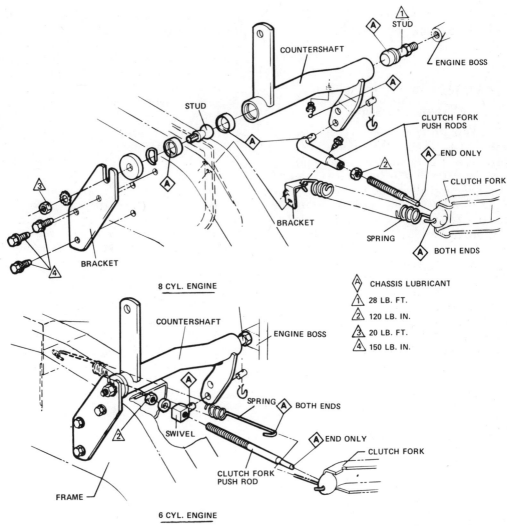

STUD

COUNTERSHAFT

ENGINE BOSS

STUD

CLUTCH FORK
PUSH RODS

END ONLY

CLUTCH FORK

BRACKET

SPRING

BOTH ENDS

BRACKET

8 CYL. ENGINE

CHASSIS LUBRICANT
1 28 LB. FT.
2 120 LB. IN.
3 20 LB. FT.
4 150 LB. IN.

COUNTERSHAFT

ENGINE BOSS

SPRING BOTH ENDS

END ONLY

SWIVEL

CLUTCH FORK

FRAME

CLUTCH FORK
PUSH ROD

6 CYL. ENGINE

1972–74 clutch linkage

pan and clean the pan and strainer with solvent.

Low Band Adjustment

The low band should be adjusted at least once every 12,000 miles, or sooner if low band slippage is apparent.

1. Raise the car and place the transmission lever in Neutral.

2. Remove the cap from the adjusting screw and loosen the screw locknut ¼ turn.

3. Hold the locknut in place with a wrench and, using a small torque wrench, torque the screw to 70 in. lbs then back off the screw exactly 4 turns—if the transmission has 6,000 or more miles on it—or exactly 3 turns—for a transmission with less than 6,000 miles. These

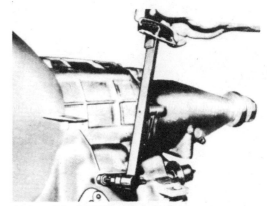

Powerglide (M-35) low band adjustment

turns must be exact since anything less than 4 turns (6,000 miles or more) would cause the band to be too tight, resulting in a drag and band damage; anything more than 4 turns would be too loose, resulting in band slippage. Tighten the locknut.

Shift Linkage Adjustment

COLUMN SHIFT

1. The shift tube and levers located in the mast jacket of the steering column must move freely and must not bind.

2. Pull the shift lever toward the steering wheel and allow the lever to be positioned in Drive by the transmission detent. The pointer may be out of adjustment, so don't use the pointer on the column as a reference for positioning the lever. The pointer must be adjusted last.

3. Release the selector lever. The lever should not go into Low unless the lever is lifted.

4. Lift the lever toward the steering wheel and permit the lever to be placed in Neutral by the transmission detent.

5. Release the lever; it should not go into Reverse unless the lever is lifted.

6. If the linkage is adjusted correctly, the shift lever will not move past the Neutral detent and the Drive detent unless the lever is lifted so that it can pass over the mechanical stop in the steering column.

7. If adjustment is necessary, place the lever in the Drive or High detent position. If the indicator pointer is out of alignment, you must rely upon the detent position to determine what gear you are in (see Steps 2 and 3).

8. Loosen the adjustment swivel or clamp at the cross-shaft and move the shift lever so that it contacts the drive stop in the column.

9. Tighten the swivel and recheck the adjustment. See Steps 2 and 6.

10. If the indicator pointer fails to line up properly with the gear symbol (P, R, N, D, L) or aligns with a wrong symbol (being in Reverse when the pointer indicates Neutral, etc.), the cause may be a bent indicator wire. Inspect it and repair.

11. If necessary, readjust the neutral safety switch to agree with the detent positions. The ignition key should move

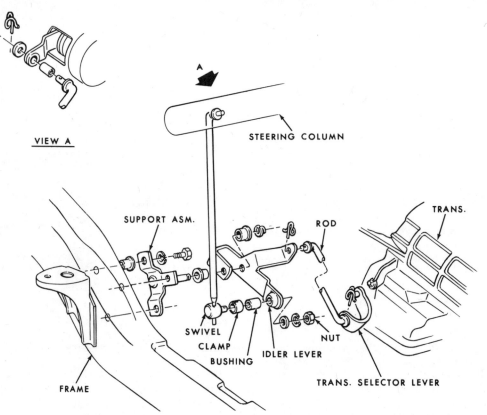

1967–68 column shift linkage—Powerglide (M-35) and Turbo Hydra-Matic

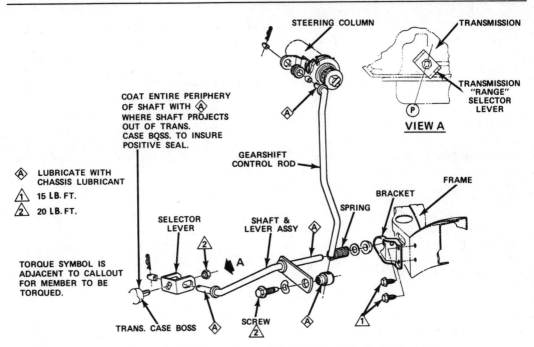

1969 column shift linkage—Powerglide (M-35) and Turbo Hydra-Matic

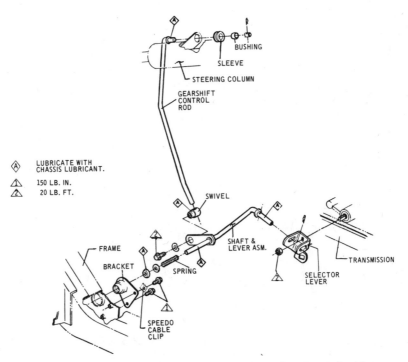

1970–74 column shift linkage—Powerglide (M-35) and Turbo Hydra-Matic

into "Lock" only when the shift lever is in Park.

CAUTION: *The above adjustments must be made correctly to prevent early transmission failure caused by* controls not being fully engaged with the detent. This results in a situation in which fluid pressure is reduced causing only partial engagement of the clutches. It may appear to run well but *the pressure reduction may be just enough to cause clutch failure after only a few miles of operation.*

FLOOR SHIFT

1967

1. Loosen the nuts on either side of the swivel located on the lower rod.

2. Move the transmission lever (on the side of the transmission) counter-clockwise until it stops. This is the Low detent. From Low, move it one detent clockwise to the Drive detent.

3. Position the floor-shift lever in the Neutral or Drive detent notch.

4. An actuating lever is located directly below the floor-shift lever and is connected to the lower rod. Pull this lever toward the rear of the car until the pawl rod moves to the rear (the small rod on the side of the floor-shift lever) and

comes in contact with the last detent (closest to the seats).

5. Place a 0.094 in. spacer between the rod swivel and the rear mounted nut. Do not tighten this nut; merely move it up so that it contacts the spacer. Located on the front side of the swivel is another nut. Tighten this nut against the swivel, then remove the spacer and tighten the rear nut so that the swivel is locked between both nuts.

1968–74

These models use a cable-operated linkage.

1. Place the shift lever in Drive.

2. Disconnect the cable from the transmission lever. Place the transmission lever in Drive by rotating the lever counterclockwise to the Low detent, then clockwise one detent to Drive.

3. Measure the distance from the rear-

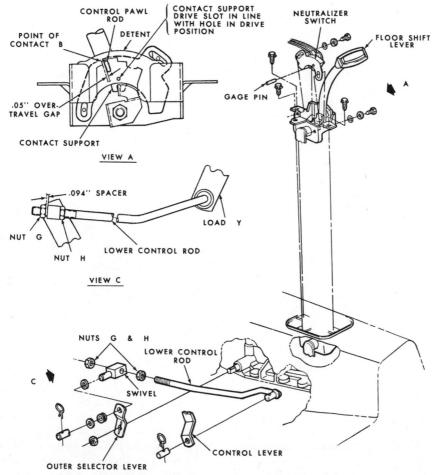

1967 floor shift linkage—Powerglide (M-35) and Turbo Hydra-Matic

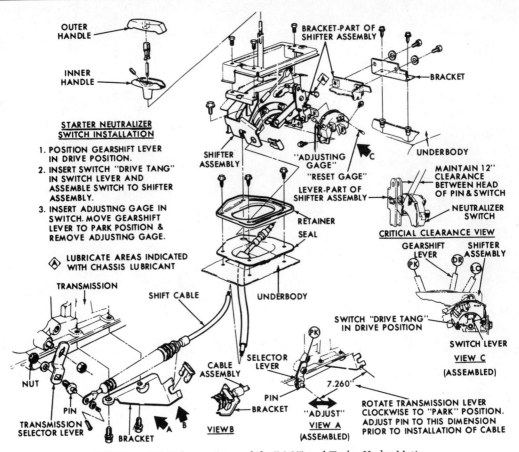

1968 floor shift linkage—Powerglide (M-35) and Turbo Hydra-Matic

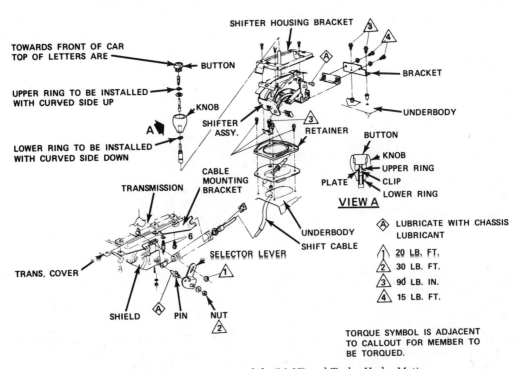

1969 floor shift linkage—Powerglide (M-35) and Turbo Hydra-Matic

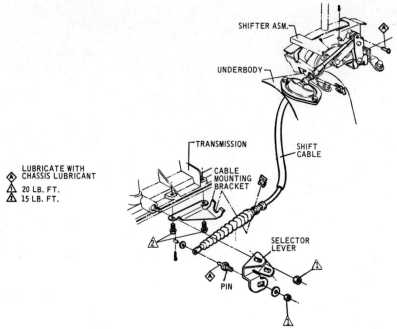

1970–74 Turbo Hydra-Matic floor shift linkage

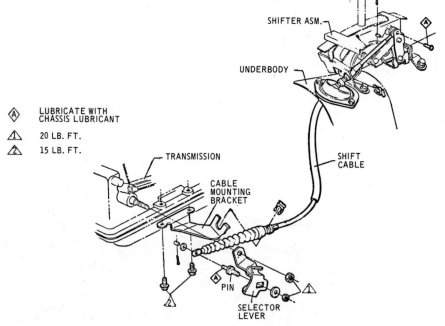

1970–74 Powerglide (M-35) floor shift linkage

ward face of the attachment bracket to the center of the cable attachment pin. Adjust this dimension to 5.5 in. by loosening and moving cable end stud nut.

For 1969–74 models:

4. Place the shift lever in Park and the ignition switch in "Lock."

5. Loosen and adjust the column (back drive) rod.

6. With the selector lever in Park, the ignition key should move freely to "Lock." "Lock" should not be obtainable in any transmission position other than Park.

Throttle Valve (Downshift)
Linkage Adjustment

6 CYLINDER

1. Depress the accelerator pedal.
2. The bellcrank on inline engines must be at wide-open throttle.
3. The dash lever at the firewall must be 1/64–1/16 in. off the lever stop.
4. The transmission lever must be against the transmission internal stop.
5. Adjust the linkage to simultaneously obtain the conditions in Steps 1–4, above.

V8

1. Remove the air cleaner.
2. Disconnect the accelerator linkage at the carburetor.
3. Disconnect both return springs.
4. Pull the throttle valve upper rod forward until the transmission is through the detent.
5. Open the carburetor to the wide-open throttle position. Adjust the swivel on the end of the upper throttle valve rod so that the carburetor reaches the wide-open throttle position at the same time that the ball stud contacts the end of the slot in the upper throttle valve rod. A tolerance of 1/32 in. is allowable.

Neutral Safety Switch Replacement
1967–74

The neutral safety switch prevents the engine from being started in any transmission position other than Park or Neutral. The switch is located under the instrument panel on the upper side of the steering column on column-shift cars or inside the console on floor-shift models.

1. Remove the console if equipped with a floor shift.
2. Disconnect the electrical connectors.
3. Remove the neutral safety switch.
4. Place all 1967–70 column shift models in Drive and all 1971 and later models in Neutral. On floor-shift models, from 1967 to early 1972, place the shift lever in Drive. On those models produced since mid-1972, place the lever in Park.
5. Align the slot in the contact support with the hole in the switch and insert a 3/8 in. diameter pin (a drill bit of the same size is suitable) to hold them in place. The switch is now in a drive position.

6. Place the contact support drive slot over the drive tang. Install and tighten the mounting screws.
7. Remove the aligning pin. Connect the electrical wiring and replace the console.
8. Set the parking brake and hold your foot on the service brake pedal. Check to see that the engine will start only in Park or Neutral.

TURBO HYDRA-MATIC
(350 AND 400)

Filter Service

The 350 transmission has a strainer in the oil pan. If the fluid appears unusually dirty, remove the oil pan and clean the pan and strainer thoroughly with solvent. The Turbo Hydra-Matic 400 also has a filter in the oil pan. To replace it, remove the pan, unbolt the filter, and install a new one. Drain the fluid every 24,000 miles (or sooner if used for trailer pulling or heavy operation) and replace the filter or strainer. See Chapter 1 for additional information.

Front and Rear Band Adjustment

Band adjustment on the Turbo Hydra-Matic cannot be made externally; it can only be made during an overhaul.

Neutral Safety Switch Adjustment

The switch adjustment for the Turbo Hydra-Matic is the same as for Powerglide. For the adjustment procedure, see the "Powerglide" Section, above.

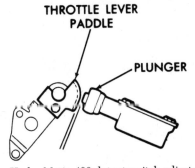

Turbo Hydra-Matic 400 detent switch adjustment

Shift Linkage Adjustment

The Turbo Hydra-Matic linkages are the same as those used on the Powerglide models. Adjustments are the same except that the transmission lever is adjusted to Drive by moving the lever clockwise to the Low detent and then counterclockwise two detent positions to Drive.

Detent Cable (Downshift) Adjustment—350

Instead of using a linkage as does the Powerglide, the Turbo Hydra-Matic 350 uses a cable (between the carburetor and transmission) to effect a downshift into a lower gear.

1. Pry up on each side of the detent cable snap-lock with a screwdriver to release the lock. On cars with a retaining screw, loosen the detent cable screw.

2. Squeeze the locking tabs and disconnect the snap-lock assembly from the throttle bracket.

3. Place the carburetor lever in the wide-open throttle position. Make sure that the lever is against the wide-open stop. On cars with Quadrajet carburetors, disengage the secondary lockout before placing the lever in the wide-open position.

NOTE: *The detent cable must be pulled through the detent position.*

4. With the carburetor lever in the wide-open position, push the snap-lock on the cable, or tighten the retaining screw.

NOTE: *Do not lubricate the detent cable.*

Detent Switch Adjustment—400

Turbo Hydra-Matic 400 transmissions are equipped with an electrical detent (downshift) switch operated by the throttle linkage.

1968–74

1. Place the carburetor lever in the wide-open position and place the automatic choke in the "Off" position.

2. Fully depress the switch plunger.

3. Adjust the switch mounting to create a distance of 0.20 in. (1968) or 0.22–0.24 in. for 1969–74 models.

7 · Drive Train

Driveshaft and U-Joints

The driveshaft (propeller shaft) is a long steel tube that transmits engine power from the transmission to the rear axle assembly. It is connected to, and revolves with, the transmission output shaft (remember, the transmission shaft is connected to and revolves with the engine crankshaft) whenever the transmission is put into gear. With the transmission in neutral, the driveshaft does not move. Located at each end of the driveshaft is a flexible joint that rotates with the shaft. These flexible joints, known as U-joints (universal joints) perform an important function. The rear axle assembly moves with the car. It moves up and down with every bump or dip in the road. The driveshaft by itself is a rigid tube incapable of bending. When combined with the flexing capabilities of the U-joints, however, it can do so. A slip joint is coupled to the front of the driveshaft by a universal joint. This U-joint allows the yoke (slip joint) to move up or down with the car. The yoke is a cylinder containing splines that slides over and meshes with the splines on the transmission output shaft. When the rear axle moves up and down, the yoke slides back and forth a small amount on the transmission shaft. Therefore, it combines with the U-joints in allowing the driveshaft to move with the movements of the car. The rear universal joint is secured to a companion flange which is attached to, and revolves with, the rear axle drive pinion.

A U-joint consists of a cross piece (trunnion) and, on each of the four ends, a dust seal and a series of needle bearings that fit into a bearing cup. Each U-joint connects one yoke with another and the bearings allow the joints to revolve within each yoke.

1967–68 Firebird driveshafts use a conventional snap-ring to hold each bearing cup in the yoke. The snap-ring fits into a groove located in each yoke end just on top of each bearing cup. The 1969–74 driveshaft has its U-joints attached differently. Nylon material is injected through a small hole in the yoke and flows along a circular groove between the U-joint and the yoke, creating a synthetic snap-ring. Disassembly of the later model U-joint requires the joint to be pressed from the yoke. This results in damage to the bearing cups and destruction of the nylon rings. Replacement kits include new bearing cups and snap-rings to replace the original nylon rings. These replacement rings must go inboard of the yoke in contrast to outboard mounting of the early models. Previous service to the later U-joints can be recognized by the presence of snap-rings inboard of the yoke.

Bad U-joints, requiring replacement, will produce a clunking sound when the car is put into gear. This is due to worn needle bearings or a scored trunnion end possibly caused by improper lubrication during assembly. Firebird U-joints require no periodic maintenance and therefore have no lubrication fittings. A clunking sound can also be produced by two other components. The Firebird three-speed automatic transmission has a rear seal that prevents the transmission from lubricating the front slip joint. All other transmissions allow a slight lubrication of this slip joint because they contain a different type of rear seal. If a driveline clunk should develop in a Firebird with a three-speed automatic, clean the slip joint and pack it with one tablespooon of chassis lube. A similar clunk can be the result of improper rear end gear lash but, due to its complexity, should be checked only after checking the more probable causes.

Some driveshafts (generally heavy-duty applications) use a damper as part of the slip joint. This vibration damper cannot be serviced separately from the slip joint. If either component goes bad, the two must be replaced as a unit.

DRIVESHAFT

Removal and Installation

1. Raise the vehicle and safely support it on jackstands. Paint a reference line from the rear end of the driveshaft to the companion flange so that they can be re-assembled in the same position.
2. Disconnect the rear universal joint by removing the U-bolts or retaining straps.
3. To prevent loss of the needle bearings, tape the bearing caps to the trunnion.
4. Remove the driveshaft from the transmission by sliding it rearward.
   NOTE: *Do not be alarmed by oil leakage at the transmission output shaft. This oil is there to lubricate the splines of the front yoke.*
5. Check the yoke seal in the transmission case extension and replace it if nec-

essary. See the "Transmission" Section of Chapter 6 for replacement procedures.

6. Position the driveshaft and insert the front yoke into the transmission so that the splines mesh with the splines of the transmission shaft.
7. Using reference marks made during removal, align the driveshaft with the companion flange and secure it with U-bolts or retaining straps.

U-JOINTS

Overhaul

1. Remove the driveshaft as explained above and remove the snap-rings from the ends of the bearing cup.
2. After removing the snap-rings, place the driveshaft on the floor and place a large diameter socket under one of the bearing cups. Tap on the bearing opposite this one with a hammer and a drift. This will push the trunnion through the yoke enough to force the bearing cup out of the yoke and into the socket. Repeat this procedure for the other bearing cups. If a hammer fails to loosen the cups, a press may be necessary.
   NOTE: *A 1969–74 driveshaft secures its U-joints in a different manner than the conventional snap-rings of the 1967–68 designs.*

On the later design, nylon is injected through a small hole in the yoke and flows along a circular groove between the

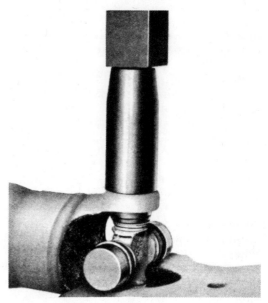

Pressing out the bearing

U-joint and the yoke, thus creating a synthetic snap-ring. Disassembly requires the joint to be pressed from the yoke. If a press is not available, it may be carefully hammered out using the same procedure (Step 2) as the early design, although it may require more force to break the nylon ring. Either method, press or hammer, will damage the bearing cups and destroy the nylon rings. Replacement kits include new bearing cups and metal snap-rings to replace the original nylon rings.

3. Thoroughly clean the entire U-joint assembly with solvent. Inspect for excessive wear in the yoke bores and on the four ends of the trunnion. The needle bearings should not be scored, broken, or loose in their cups. Bearing cups may suffer slight distortion during removal and should be replaced.

4. Pack the bearings with chassis lube (lithium base) and completely fill each trunnion end with the same lubricant.

5. Place new dust seals on the trunnions with the cavity of the seal toward the end of the trunnion. Care must be taken to avoid distortion of the seal. A suitable size socket and a vise can be used to press on the seal.

Installing the snap-ring retainer

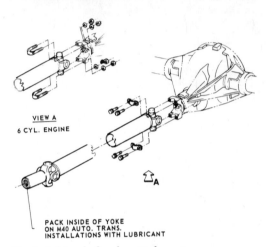

VIEW A
6 CYL. ENGINE

PACK INSIDE OF YOKE
ON M40 AUTO. TRANS.
INSTALLATIONS WITH LUBRICANT

Typical driveshaft yoke attachment

Installing the trunnion into the yoke

6. Insert one bearing cup about a quarter of the way into the yoke and place the trunnion into the yoke and bearing cup. Install another bearing cup, press in both cups, and install the snap-rings. Snap-rings on the 1967–68 shafts must go on the outside of the yoke while the 1969–74 shaft requires that the rings go on the inside of the yoke. The gap in the later model ring must face toward the

yoke. Once installed, the trunnion must move freely in the yoke.

NOTE: *The 1969–74 shaft uses two different sizes of bearing cup at the differential end. The larger cups (the ones with the groove) fit into the driveshaft yoke.*

Rear Axle

AXLE SHAFT

Removal and Installation

Two types of axles are used on these models, the C and the non-C type. Axle shafts in the C type are retained by C-shaped locks, which fit grooves at the inner end of the shaft. Axle shafts in the non-C type are retained by the brake backing plate, which is bolted to the axle housing. Bearings in the C type axle consist of an outer race, bearing rollers, and a roller cage retained by snap-rings. The non-C type axle uses a unit roller bearing (inner race, rollers, and outer race), which is pressed onto the shaft up to a shoulder. When servicing C or non-C type axles, it is imperative to determine the axle type before attempting any service. Before attempting any service to the drive axle or axle shafts, remove the axle carrier cover and visually determine if the axle shafts are retained by C-shaped locks at the inner end, or by the brake backing plate at the outer end. If the shafts are *not* retained by C locks, proceed as follows. Most 1970 and later Firebirds are equipped with the C type axle.

NON-C TYPE

1. Remove the wheel, tire, and brake drum.
2. Remove the nuts which hold the retainer plate to the backing plate. Disconnect the brake line.
3. Remove the retainer and install the nuts fingertight to prevent the brake backing plate from being dislodged.
4. Pull out the axle shaft and bearing assembly, using a slide hammer.

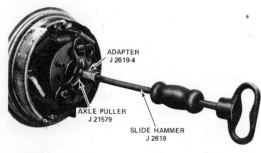

Removing the non-C type axle shaft

5. Install the axle shaft into the housing. Turn it until the grooves mesh.
6. Install the retainer nuts.
7. Connect the brake line.
8. Install the brake drum, wheel, and tire.
9. Bleed the brakes.

C TYPE

1. Raise the vehicle and remove the wheels.
2. The differential cover has already been removed (see NOTE above). Remove the differential pinion shaft lockscrew and the differential pinion shaft.

Removing the pinion shaft on the C type differential

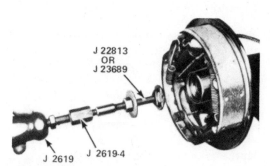

Removing the C type axle shaft

3. Push the flanged end of the axle shaft toward the center of the vehicle and remove the C lock from the end of the shaft.
4. Remove the axle shaft from the housing, being careful not to damage the oil seal.
5. Install the axle into the housing.
6. Install the C lock to the shaft.
7. Install the differential pinion lockscrew.
8. Install the differential cover.
9. Install the wheels and lower the car to the ground.

8 · Suspension and Steering

Rear Suspension

The Firebird was introduced in 1967 with a paired elliptical, single-leaf spring rear suspension. Shock absorbers were mounted on the spring brackets. Models with the more powerful optional engines were additionally equipped with radius rods to increase rear axle control. In 1968, the single-leaf rear springs were replaced with multi-leaf units and the shock absorbers were stagger-mounted, one on either side of the axle. A rear stabilizer also has been installed on the high-performance models such as the Formula and Trans Am.

SPRINGS

Removal and Installation

1. Raise the rear of the car enough for the axle assembly to hang freely. Place jackstands under both frame side rails near the front of the spring.
2. Remove the spring tension by raising the axle assembly.
3. Remove the lower bolt from the shock absorber.
4. Loosen the bolt holding the spring eye to its bracket.

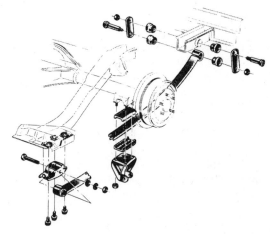

1967 spring mounting

5. Remove the spring retainer bracket.
6. Remove the parking brake cable from the retainer bracket mounted on the spring-mounted plate.
7. Remove the retaining nuts from the lower spring plate to the axle bracket.
8. Remove both upper and lower rubber spring pads and the spring plate.
9. Place a jack under the spring and remove the lower bolt from the rear shackle. Remove the spring from the car. Remove the shackle upper bolt and shackle bushings from the frame.

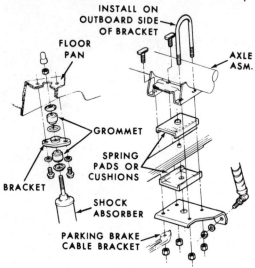

UPPER SHOCK MOUNTING (BOTH SIDES)

LOWER SHOCK MOUNTING (L.H. SHOWN. R.H. OPPOSITE)

INSTALL ON OUTBOARD SIDE OF BRACKET

FLOOR PAN

AXLE ASM.

GROMMET

SPRING PADS OR CUSHIONS

BRACKET

SHOCK ABSORBER

PARKING BRAKE CABLE BRACKET

LEFT SHOCK IS MOUNTED BEHIND AXLE HOUSING AND RIGHT SHOCK IS MOUNTED IN FRONT OF AXLE HOUSING

1968–69 spring and shock absorber mounting

10. Position the front mounting bracket to the front eye of the spring.

11. Install the bolt so that the bolt head is toward the center of the car.

12. Place the shackle upper bushings in the frame and position the shackles up to the bushings and loosely install the bolt and nut.

13. Install the bushing in the rear eye of the spring, lift the spring up the shackles and loosely install the shackle bolt and nut.

IMPORTANT: *The parking brake cable must be on the underside of the spring.*

14. Raise the front of the spring and position the bracket to the underbody, making sure that the tab on the bracket is inserted into the slot on the body.

15. Loosely install the spring-to-underbody bracket.

16. Place the spring upper cushion between the spring and axle bracket aligning the cushion ribs with the bracket ribs.

17. Place the lower spring cushion on the spring locating dowel.

18. Place the lower mounting plate over the dowel on the spring lower pad and loosely install the nuts.

19. Position the shock absorber to the spring plate and loosely install the bolt and nut to the eye of the spring, making sure that the head of the bolt is toward the front of the car.

20. Position and secure the parking brake cable in the cable bracket.

21. Lower the car and tighten the bolts.

SHOCK ABSORBERS

NOTE: *If the ride of your car has become increasingly bouncy and/or fluid leakage can be observed on the shock absorbers, it's time to replace them. Push up and down on the rear bumper several times and then let go. If the car continues to move up and down the shocks aren't doing their job.*

Removal and Installation

1967–69

1. Raise the rear of the car and support the rear axle assembly.

2. Remove the lower mounting bolt.

3. Remove the upper bracket mounting screws and also the shock and bracket.

4. Remove the nut, retainer, grommet, gasket, and bracket from the shock rod.

5. Inspect the grommets and gasket, and replace them if they are worn or rotted.

6. To install, reverse the removal procedures.

1970–74

1. Raise the car and support the rear axle.

2. Remove the lower nut, retainer, and grommet.

3. Remove the upper bolts and lift out the shock. Replace distorted or damaged bushings.

4. To install, reverse the removal procedure.

Front Suspension

Front suspension design from 1967 through 1974 is basically the same. The coil springs ride on the lower control arms and the ball joints (upper and lower,

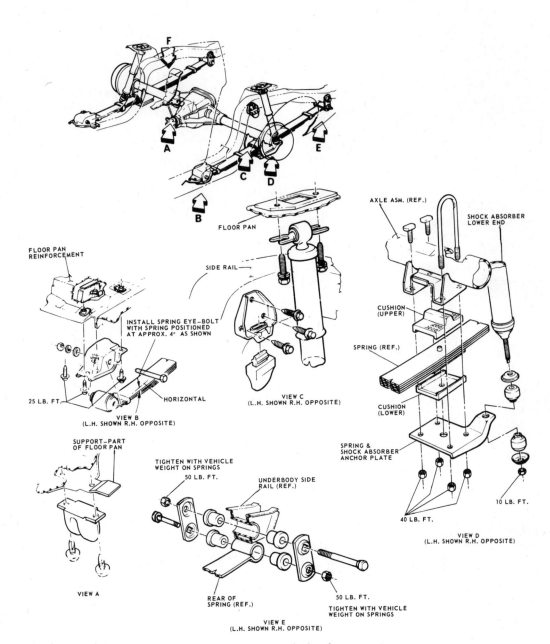

1970-74 spring and shock absorber mounting

each side) connect the upper and lower control arms to the steering knuckle. Camber and caster angle is adjusted by shims located between the upper control arm inner support shaft and the support bracket attached to the frame. Maintenance to the front suspension includes lubrication of the four ball joints (unless they are prelubed replacements), and adjustment and lubrication of front wheel bearings.

SPRINGS

Removal and Installation

1. Hold the shock absorber upper stem to keep it from turning, then disconnect the shock absorber at the top.

2. Support the car by the frame so that the control arms hang free, remove the wheel assembly (replace one wheel nut to hold the brake drum), shock absorber,

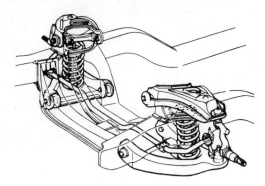

Front suspension

and stabilizer bar-to-lower control arm link.

3. Place a steel bar through the shock absorber mounting hole in the lower control arm so that the notch seats over the bottom spring coil and the bar extends outboard beyond the end of the control arm and slightly toward the front of the car.

4. With a suitable jack, raise the end of the bar.

5. Remove the lower ball stud cotter pin and nut, then remove the ball stud from the knuckle.

NOTE: *Place a chain around the spring and through the lower arm for safety.*

6. Lower the jack supporting the steel bar and control arm until the spring can be removed.

7. Install by reversing the removal procedure. When installing a spring, make sure that the end of the spring is visible through the hole in the lower control arm. That is, looking up from beneath the car, you should see the spring end through this hole.

SHOCK ABSORBERS

NOTE: *Signs of leakage or a particularly bouncy ride indicate the need for new shock absorbers.*

Removal and Installation

1. Raise the car and, with an open-end wrench, hold the upper stem of the shock and prevent it from turning. While holding the stem, remove the nut, retainer, and rubber grommet.

2. Remove the two lower bolts and also the shock absorber.

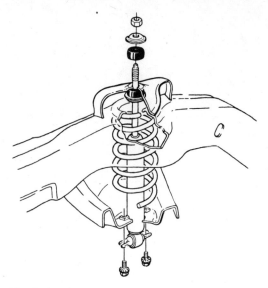

Shock absorber mounting

3. Place the lower retainer and rubber grommet over the upper stem and extend the shock.

4. Insert the upper stem through the mounting hole in the upper control arm bracket.

5. Keep the upper stem from turning with an open-end wrench, and install and tighten the nut.

6. Install the lower mounting bolts and lower car.

BALL JOINTS

Inspection

NOTE: *Before performing this inspection, make sure that the wheel bearings are adjusted correctly and that the control arm bushings are in good condition. 1974 Firebirds feature a visual wear indicator on the lower ball joint. Wear will be indicated by the recession of the grease nipple into the ball joint. The nipple protrudes 0.050 in. If the round part of the nipple is flush or inside the ball joint cover surface, replace the ball joint.*

1. Raise the car by placing the jack under the lower control arm at the spring seat.

2. Raise the car until there is a 1–2 in. clearance under the wheel.

3. Insert a bar under the wheel and pry upward. If the wheel raises more than ⅛

in., the ball joints are worn. Determine whether the upper or lower ball joint is worn by visual inspection while prying on the wheel.

NOTE: *Due to the distribution of forces in the suspension, the lower ball joint is usually the defective joint.*

Upper Ball Joint Replacement

1. Support the car by placing a jack under the outer end of the lower control arm.
2. Remove the wheel and tire assembly.
3. Remove the cotter pin and nut from the stud.

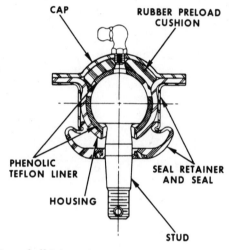

Upper ball joint cutaway

4. Remove the stud from the steering knuckle by prying on the control arm with a large bar and rapping on the steering knuckle with a hammer.
5. Cut off the ball joint rivets with a chisel, or drill them out.
6. It may be necessary to enlarge the stud attaching holes in the control arm to accept the larger 5/16 in. bolts. Inspect and clean the tapered hole in the steering knuckle. If the hole is damaged or deformed, the knuckle *must* be replaced.
7. Install the new joint and connect the stud to the steering knuckle. When installing the stud nut, never back off on the nut to align the cotter pin holes; always tighten the nut to the next hole.
8. Replacement ball joints may not include the lube fitting. If not, install a self-threading fitting into the tapped hole.

Lower Ball Joint Replacement

1. Raise the car and support the lower control arm with a floor jack. Remove the wheel and tire assembly.
2. On cars with disc brakes, it will be necessary to remove the caliper assembly.

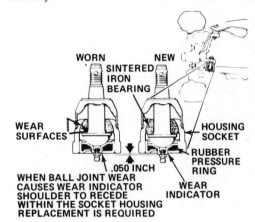

1974 ball joint wear indicator

3. Loosen the lower ball stud nut. Break the ball stud loose. Remove the ball stud nut.
4. Remove the ball stud from the steering knuckle.
5. The ball joint in 1967–70 models is attached with rivets which must be chiseled or ground off. Beginning with 1971 models, the ball joint is pressed in and must be pressed out.
6. Install the new ball joint, using the bolts supplied with the service ball joint (drill out the rivet holes to accommodate the mounting bolts) on 1967–70 models. The thick-headed bolt is installed on the forward side of the control arm. Press in the ball joint on 1971 and later models.
7. Install the ball stud in the steering knuckle boss. This may be done by raising the lower control arm with the jack.
8. Install the nut on the ball stud, tightening to 80–90 ft lbs.
9. Install the lube fitting.

UPPER CONTROL ARM

Removal and Installation

1. Raise the vehicle on a hoist.
2. Support the outer end of the lower control arm with a jack.
3. Remove the wheel.
4. Separate the upper ball joint from

the steering knuckle as described above under "Upper Ball Joint Replacement."

5. Remove the control arm shaft-to-frame nuts.

NOTE: *Tape the shims together and identify them so that they can be installed in the positions from which they were removed.*

6. Remove the bolts which attach the control arm shaft to the frame and remove the control arm. Note the positions of the bolts.

7. Install in the reverse order of removal. Make sure that the shaft-to-frame bolts are installed in the same position they were in before removal and that the shims are in their original positions. Tighten the thinner shim pack first. After the car has been lowered to the ground, bounce the front end to center the bushings and then tighten the bushing collar bolts to 45 ft lbs.

LOWER CONTROL ARM

Removal and Installation

1. Remove the spring as described earlier.

2. Remove the ball stud from the steering knuckle as described earlier.

3. Remove the control arm pivot bolts and the control arm.

4. To install, reverse the above procedure. If any bolts are to be replaced, do so with bolts of equal strength and quality.

Front End Alignment

CASTER, CAMBER, AND TOE-IN

Caster is the angle at which the front steering axis tilts either forward or backward from a vertical position. Positive caster is a backward tilt while a forward tilt is negative caster. Caster angle on the Firebird suspension cannot be seen with the eye, it requires the use of instruments. Caster angle can, however, be visualized. If you look down from the top of the upper control arm to the ground, you notice that the upper and lower ball joints do not line up (unless a 0 degree caster angle existed). With any angle (other than 0 degrees), one ball joint

would be slightly ahead or slightly to the rear of the other. If you had a positive angle, the lower ball joint would be slightly ahead (more to the front of the car) of the upper ball joint.

The front wheels will tilt outward or inward at the top depending on whether the camber is positive or negative. Camber angle then is the amount (in degrees) that a wheel tilts from a perfectly vertical position. When the wheels tilt outward at the top, it has positive camber; camber is negative when the wheel tilts inward at the top.

Toe-in, measured in fractions of an inch, is the turning in of the front of the front wheels. The front wheels must roll parallel to each other; if they don't, uneven tire wear will result.

When performing a front wheel alignment, the mechanic checks all three of these measurements and makes any necessary adjustments. Since one adjustment affects each of the others, they must be adjusted in a specific order: caster, camber, and then toe-in. Proper wheel alignment is necessary for ease and stability of steering and controlling tire wear.

PRELIMINARY CHECKS BEFORE MAKING ADJUSTMENTS

Steering problems and improper tire wear are not always caused by incorrect wheel alignment. To avoid wasting time on any front end adjustments, the following areas should be checked and corrected first:

1. Loose or improperly adjusted steering gear.

2. Steering gear not tightly secured to frame.

3. Excessively worn ball joints.

4. Loose tie-rod or steering connections.

5. Worn springs or improper spring heights.

6. Unbalanced or underinflated tires.

7. Improperly adjusted wheel bearings.

8. Faulty shock absorbers.

CASTER AND CAMBER ADJUSTMENT

Before making these adjustments, lift the front bumper and release it quickly to allow the car to return to its normal height.

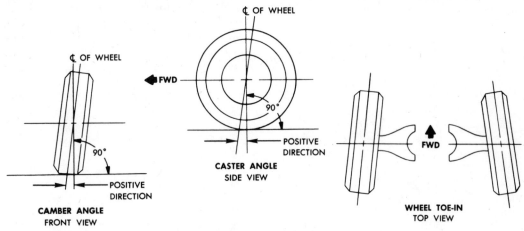

Caster, camber, and toe-in

1. Located between the upper control arm shaft and the frame bracket are two shim packs, one behind each bolt. Shims may be added, subtracted, or transferred from one bolt to the other in order to change caster and camber.

2. Changing caster angle can be done by transferring shims from the front bolt to the rear bolt or from front to rear. Transferring one shim to the front bolt from the rear bolt will decrease positive caster. On 1967 models, one shim ($1/32$ in.) will change caster about ¼ degree, or $1/5$ degree on 1968–70 cars.

3. Changing camber angle is done by changing shims at both the front and rear bolts. Adding an equal number of shims at both the front and rear bolts will decrease positive camber. One shim ($1/32$ in.) at each bolt will move camber about $1/5$ degree.

4. To make this adjustment, merely loosen the upper shaft nuts, add or subtract shims as necessary and tighten the nuts.

NOTE: *Special equipment is required to measure these angles properly.*

TOE-IN ADJUSTMENT

As explained earlier, toe-in is the inward pointing of both front wheels. It is the difference of the distance between the extreme front and the distance between the extreme rear of both front wheels.

1. If the equipment being used measures the toe-in of each individual wheel:

a. Set the steering gear on the high point, mark the 12 o'clock position on the steering shaft, and position the steering wheel for straight-forward driving.

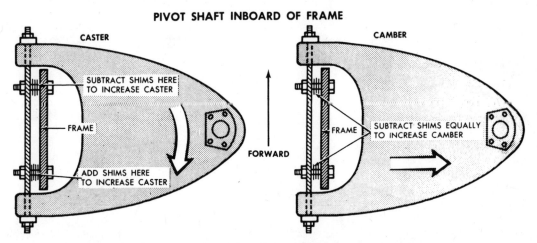

Caster and camber adjustment

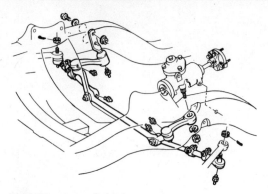

1967–69 steering linkage

rod and adjust to the specified toe-in.

c. Loosen the clamp bolts on the other tie-rod. Turn both rods the same amount and in the same direction. This places the steering gear on its high point.

d. On 1967 and 1968 models, make the above adjustments and position the inner tie-rod clamps making sure that the slot is away from the open end of the clamp. Position the outer clamps with the bolt on top and 30° to either side of the vertical.

e. On 1969 and 1970 models, position the inner tie-rod clamps with the open end of the clamp and the slot in line. The open end of the clamp must be within 15° to either side of the tie-rod sleeve slot. Position the outer clamps with their open ends facing up and the top of the bolt facing the rear. The bolt must be 30° (1969) or 55° (1970) to either side of the horizontal.

b. Loosen the clamp bolt at each end of each tie-rod and adjust to total toe-in as specified. Each wheel is a half of the total toe-in number.

2. If a tram gauge is being used:

a. Set the front wheels in a straight-ahead position.

b. Loosen the clamp bolts on one tie-

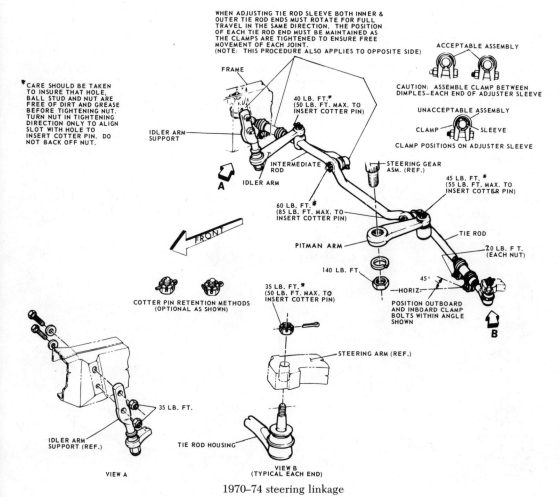

1970–74 steering linkage

Wheel Alignment Specifications

| Year | CASTER | | CAMBER | | | | WHEEL PIVOT RATIO (deg) | |
	Range (deg)	Pref Setting (deg)	Range (deg)	Pref Setting (deg)	Toe-in (in.)	Steering Axis Inclin.	Inner Wheel	Outer Wheel
'67–'69	0 to 1P	½P	¼N to ¾P	¼P	⅛ to ¼	8.25 to 9.25	20	——
'70–'71	½N to 1½N	1N	¼P to 1¼P	¾P	⅛ to ¼	8.25 to 9.25	20	22
'71–'72	½N to ½P	0	½P to 1½P	1P	⅛ to ¼	8.25 to 9.25	20	22
'73–'74	½N to ½P	0	½P to 1½P	1P	⅛ to ¼	10.35	20	22

N Negative   P Positive

f. On 1971 and later models, the clamps must be placed between the locating dimples at each end of the sleeve. The bolts on the outer and inner clamps must be within 45° of the horizontal. The slit in the sleeve may be in any position, but not closer than 0.10 in. to the edge of the clamp opening or within the opening.

Steering

Firebirds have recirculating ball type steering. Forces are transmitted from a worm to a sector gear through ball bearings. Relay type steering linkage is used with a pitman arm connected to one end of the relay rod. The other end of the relay rod is connected to an idler arm which is attached to the frame. The relay rod is connected to the steering arms by two adjustable tie-rods. All Firebirds are equipped with a collapsible steering column designed to collapse on impact, thereby reducing possible chest injuries during accidents. When making any repairs to the steering column or steering wheel, excessive pressure or force capable of collapsing the column must be avoided. Beginning 1969, the ignition lock, ignition switch, and an antitheft system were built into each column. The key cannot be removed unless the transmission is in "Park" (automatic) or "Reverse (manual) with the switch in the "Lock" position. Placing the lock in the "Lock" position activates a rod within

the column which locks the steering wheel and shift lever. On floorshift models, a back drive linkage between the floorshift and the column produces the same effect.

STEERING WHEEL

CAUTION: *Steering columns are collapsible. When replacing the wheel, do not hammer or exert any force against the column.*

Standard Wheel Replacement

1967–69

1. Disconnect the battery ground cable.
2. Disconnect the column wiring harness from the chassis wiring harness.
3. Remove the horn button cap or ornament and retainer.
4. Remove the receiving cup, spring, bushing, and pivot ring.
5. Remove the steering wheel nut and washer.
6. Install a puller and turn the puller bolt clockwise to remove the wheel.
7. Make sure that the turn signal lever is in the neutral position before installing the wheel; otherwise, damage may be done to the control.
8. With the turn signal and horn assemblies in place, position the wheel on the shaft and install the washer and nut.
9. Install the spring (dish side up), pivot ring, bushing, and receiving cup.
10. Install the retainer and horn button cap or ornament.
11. Connect the wiring.

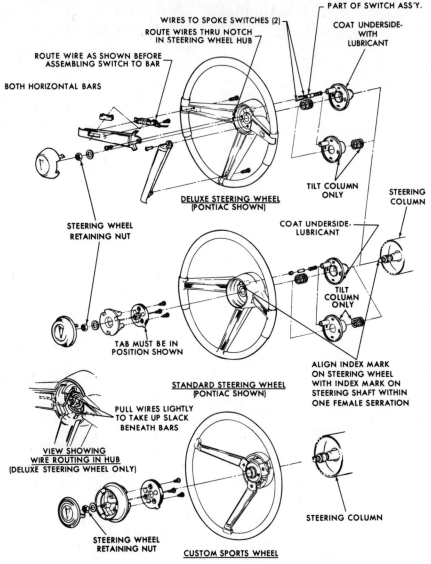

PART OF SWITCH ASS'Y.

WIRES TO SPOKE SWITCHES (2)

COAT UNDERSIDE-
WITH
LUBRICANT

ROUTE WIRES THRU NOTCH
IN STEERING WHEEL HUB

ROUTE WIRE AS SHOWN BEFORE
ASSEMBLING SWITCH TO BAR

BOTH HORIZONTAL BARS

TILT COLUMN
ONLY

STEERING
COLUMN

DELUXE STEERING WHEEL
(PONTIAC SHOWN)

STEERING WHEEL
RETAINING NUT

COAT UNDERSIDE-
LUBRICANT

TILT
COLUMN
ONLY

TAB MUST BE IN
POSITION SHOWN

ALIGN INDEX MARK
ON STEERING WHEEL
WITH INDEX MARK ON
STEERING SHAFT WITHIN
ONE FEMALE SERRATION

STANDARD STEERING WHEEL
(PONTIAC SHOWN)

PULL WIRES LIGHTLY
TO TAKE UP SLACK
BENEATH BARS

VIEW SHOWING
WIRE ROUTING IN HUB
(DELUXE STEERING WHEEL ONLY)

STEERING COLUMN

STEERING WHEEL
RETAINING NUT

CUSTOM SPORTS WHEEL

1967–69 steering wheels

1970

1. Disconnect the battery ground cable.

2. Remove the wheel shroud.

3. Remove the 3 spacer screws and also the spacer, plate, and spring.

4. Remove the shaft nut.

5. Install a wheel puller and turn the puller bolt clockwise to remove the wheel.

6. Position the eylet and insulator in the horn contact tower.

7. Position the wheel on the shaft and align the notch in the wheel hub with the mark on the shaft.

IMPORTANT: *The horn contact tower must engage the hole in the steering wheel.*

8. Install and tighten the wheel nut.

9. Install the belleville spring with the concave side down, followed by the plate and spacer. Install the spacer screws.

10. Install the wheel shroud and secure it with two screws.

11. Connect the battery cable.

1971–74

1. Disconnect the battery ground cable.

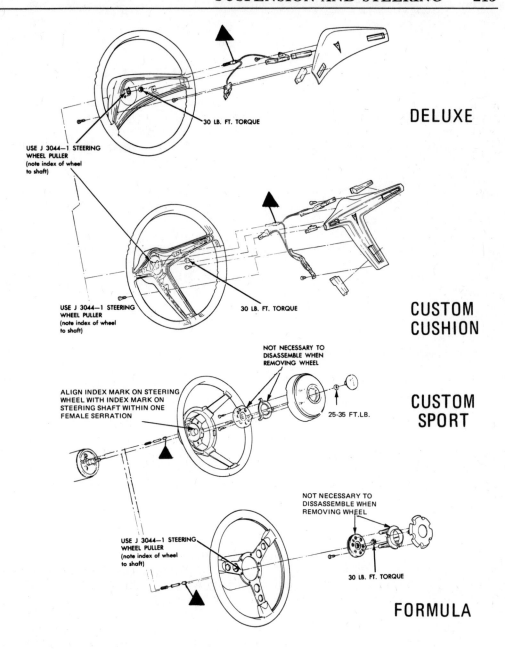

DELUXE

30 LB. FT. TORQUE

USE J 3044—1 STEERING
WHEEL PULLER
(note index of wheel
to shaft)

USE J 3044—1 STEERING
WHEEL PULLER
(note index of wheel
to shaft)

30 LB. FT. TORQUE

CUSTOM
CUSHION

NOT NECESSARY TO
DISASSEMBLE WHEN
REMOVING WHEEL

ALIGN INDEX MARK ON STEERING
WHEEL WITH INDEX MARK ON
STEERING SHAFT WITHIN ONE
FEMALE SERRATION

25-35 FT.LB.

CUSTOM
SPORT

NOT NECESSARY TO
DISASSEMBLE WHEN
REMOVING WHEEL

USE J 3044—1 STEERING
WHEEL PULLER
(note index of wheel
to shaft)

30 LB. FT. TORQUE

FORMULA

PUSH INSULATOR INTO CANCELLING CAM TOWER AND ROTATE
COUNTER—CLOCKWISE TO RELEASE OR CLOCKWISE TO LOCK
IN POSITION.

1970–74 steering wheels

2. Remove the wheel shroud (curved outside cover) and horn contact lead assembly.

3. Remove the steering wheel nut.

4. Install the wheel puller, turn the puller bolt clockwise, and remove the wheel.

5. Set the turn signal lever in the neutral position and tighten the wheel onto the shaft. Overtightening the nut may cause the wheel to rub.

6. Place the shroud onto the wheel while guiding the horn lead into the turn signal tower.

7. Install the shroud screws and connect the battery.

Deluxe Wheel Replacement

1968–69

1. Disconnect the battery ground cable.

2. On 1968 models, disconnect the steering column wiring from the chassis wiring harness.

3. Remove the screws from the underside of the wheel.

4. Lift off the steering wheel shroud and disconnect the horn wires.

5. Remove the nut and washer securing the wheel to the shaft.

6. Install a wheel puller, turn the puller bolt clockwise, and remove the wheel.

7. Position the turn signal cam and horn contact, install the wheel to the shaft, and secure them with a washer and nut.

8. Position the horn wires and, on 1968 models, attach the horn buttons.

9. Install the shroud.

10. Install the screws on the underside of the wheel and, on 1968 models, connect the column wiring.

11. Connect the battery cable.

Cushioned Rim Wheel

1971–74

1. Disconnect the battery ground cable.

2. Remove the horn button cap.

3. Remove the steering wheel nut.

4. Remove the upper horn insulator, receiver, and belleville spring.

5. Install the wheel puller, turn the puller bolt clockwise, and remove the wheel.

6. Place the turn signal lever in the neutral position, position the wheel to the shaft, and tighten the nut.

7. Position the horn lower insulator, eyelet, and spring in the horn contact tower. Install the belleville spring, receiver, and horn upper insulator.

8. Install the horn button cap and connect the battery cable.

TURN SIGNAL SWITCH

Replacement

1967–68

1. Disconnect the battery ground cable.

2. Disconnect the signal switch wiring from the wiring harness under the instrument panel.

3. Remove the steering wheel.

4. If applicable, remove the shift lever.

5. Remove the four-way flasher lever arm.

6. If equipped with an automatic transmission, remove the dial indicator housing and lamp assembly from the column.

7. Remove the mast jacket lower trim cover.

8. Remove the C-ring and washers from the upper steering shaft.

9. Loosen the signal switch screws, move the switch counterclockwise, and remove it from the mast jacket.

10. Remove the upper support bracket assembly.

CAUTION: *Support the column; do not allow it to be suspended by the lower reinforcement only.*

11. Remove the wiring harness protector and clip, and then reinstall the support bracket and finger-tighten the bolts.

12. Remove the shift lever bowl from the mast jacket and disconnect it from the wiring harness.

13. Remove the 3 lockplate screws, being careful not to lose the 3 springs.

14. Disassemble the switch and upper bearing housing from the switch cover.

15. Insert the upper bearing housing assembly and switch assembly into the switch cover.

16. Align the switch and bearing housing with the mounting holes in the cover and install the 3 mounting screws.

17. Slide the springs onto the screws and install the lockplate over the springs. Tighten the screws 3 turns into the lockplate.

18. Position the switch wire through the shift lever bowl and place the upper end assembly on top of the bowl.

19. Place the shift lever bowl and signal switch assembly on top of the jacket, inserting the lockplate tangs into the slots.

20. Push down on the cover assembly and turn clockwise to lock the assembly into position.

21. Tighten the signal mounting screws.

22. Remove the mast jacket support

bracket, then install the wiring, wiring cover, and clip, and install and tighten the support bracket.

23. Install a C-ring onto the shaft.

24. Install the dial indicator and lamp assembly on the column if so equipped.

25. Install the mast jacket lower trim cover if so equipped.

26. Install the four-way flasher knob and the turn signal lever.

27. Install the shift lever.

28. Install the steering wheel.

29. Connect the wiring and battery cable.

1969–74

1. Remove the steering wheel.

2. Remove the trim cover from the column.

3. Remove the cover from the shaft.

4. Using a compressing tool, compress the lockplate. With the plate compressed, pry out the snap-ring from its shaft groove and throw it away.

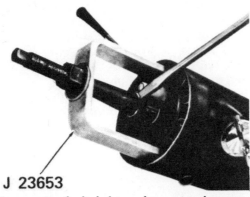

J 23653

Compressing the lockplate and removing the snap-ring

5. Slide the cancelling cam, spring, and washer off the shaft.

6. Remove the turn signal lever.

7. Remove the four-way flasher knob.

8. Pull the switch connector out of the bracket and wrap it with tape to prevent it from snagging.

9. If applicable, place tilt columns in the low position and remove the harness cover.

10. Remove the switch.

11. To install, reverse the removal procedure, being sure to use only the specified nuts and bolts. Using screws that are slightly too long could prevent the column from collapsing during a collision.

12. When installing the cancelling cam, spring, and washer, make sure that the switch is in neutral and that the flasher knob is out.

13. Use a compressing tool to compress the lockplate and install a new snap-ring.

LOCK CYLINDER

Replacement

1969–74

1. Remove the steering wheel and the directional signal switch. See the applicable procedures above.

2. Place the lock cylinder in "Lock" (up to 1970), or "Run" (starting 1971).

3. Insert a small screwdriver into the turn signal housing slot. Keeping the screwdriver to the right-side of the slot, break the housing flash loose and depress the spring latch at the lower end of the lock cylinder. Remove the lock cylinder.

4. To install, hold the lock cylinder sleeve and rotate the knob clockwise against the stop. Insert the cylinder into the housing, aligning the key and keyway. Hold a 0.070 in. drill between the lock bezel and the housing. Rotate the cylinder counterclockwise, maintaining a light pressure until the drive section of the cylinder mates with the sector. Push in until the snap-ring pops into the grooves. Remove the drill. Check the operation of the cylinder.

IGNITION SWITCH

Replacement

1969–74

1. Lower the steering column. The column must be carefully supported to prevent damage.

2. Remove the lock cylinder as above.

NOTE: *Pull the actuating rod for the switch up, until a definite stop is felt, then push it down one detent to "Lock."*

3. Remove the two switch screws and the switch assembly.

4. When replacing the switch, make sure that the switch and lock are in "Lock." Do not use switch screws that are longer than the originals, or the compressibility feature of the column may be lost.

MANUAL STEERING GEAR

Removal and Installation

1. Remove the nuts, lockwashers, and bolts at the steering coupling.

2. Remove the pitman arm nut and washer, and mark the sector shaft and arm so that they can be reassembled in the same position.

3. Remove the pitman arm with a puller type tool.

4. Remove the mounting screws and also the steering gear.

5. To install, reverse the removal procedure making sure that the marks made on the pitman arm and the shaft are aligned.

Adjustments

Before making any adjustments, check front end alignment, shocks, wheel balance, and tire pressure as possible causes of shimmy or hard or loose steering.

1. Remove the pitman arm nut and mark the arm and sector shaft so that they can be reassembled in the same position. Remove the pitman arm with a puller type tool used above in manual steering gear removal.

2. On 1967–70 cars, loosen the locknut and turn the pitman shaft lash adjuster screw counterclockwise a few turns. On 1971–74 models, loosen the steering gear adjuster plug locknut and back off on the plug ¼ turn. This removes load from bearings created by close meshing of the rack and sector teeth. Slowly turn the steering wheel in one direction until stopped and then back away one turn (½ turn on 71–74 cars). Damage may result from turning the wheel hard against the stop when the relay rod is disconnected.

3. Disconnect the battery ground cable and remove any necessary steering wheel parts to get to the steering wheel nut. Place a socket and torque wrench on the nut and measure the torque required to keep the wheel moving. If the torque is not 16 in. lbs, an adjustment is necessary. On those cars with tilt steering, it will be necessary to disconnect the steering coupling to get a torque measurement of the column. After doing this, subtract this torque from any taken on the gear.

4. To adjust worm bearings (1967–70), loosen the locknut and turn the worm bearing adjuster until there is no noticeable end-play in the worm. Adjust the thrust bearing preload (1971–74) by tightening the adjuster plug until the proper preload is obtained and then tighten the locknut. Check torque at the steering wheel and adjust to get the correct torque of 5–8 in. lbs (4–6 in. lbs for 1972–74). Tighten the locknut (1967–74) and check the torque again. If the steering wheel action feels lumpy after adjusting the worm bearings, the worm bearings must be damaged.

5. After adjusting the worm, adjust the lash adjuster screw. Gently turn the steering wheel from one stop to the other and count the number of turns as you go. Turn the wheel back exactly halfway to the center position. Turn the lash adjuster screw clockwise to remove all free-play in the gear, and then tighten the locknut. Check the torque at the steering wheel nut and take the highest reading. Readjust if the reading is not 4–10 in. lbs greater than the worm bearing preload (5–8 in. lbs) made in Step 4. If there is too much torque, turn the lash adjuster screw counterclockwise and then turn it clockwise until the torque is correct.

6. Tighten the lash adjuster locknut and recheck the torque.

7. If the torque is correct, connect the pitman arm to the sector shaft, making sure that the marks are in alignment.

8. Install the steering wheel shroud and connect the battery cable.

POWER STEERING GEAR

Adjustments

1. Disconnect the pitman arm from the relay rod.

2. Loosen the locknut on the pitman arm adjusting screw and turn the screw to the limit through the side cover.

3. Disconnect the column wiring from the chassis wiring harness under the dashboard.

4. Disconnect the battery ground cable.

5. Remove the horn button or shroud.

6. Turn the steering wheel from stop to stop and count the number of turns. Divide that number in half and move the steering wheel to its exact center of travel.

7. Install an in. lbs torque wrench on the steering wheel nut and check the combined ball and thrust bearing preload by turning through the center of travel and observing the highest torque reading.

8. Tighten the pitman shaft adjusting screw and rechek torque until total steering gear preload is 11 in. lbs (1967) or 14 in. lbs (all others).

9. Install the horn button and connect the wiring harness and battery cable.

POWER STEERING PUMP

Removal and Installation

1. Disconnect the hoses from the pump and raise the ends so that fluid will not run out. Tape the ends to keep out dirt.

2. Cap the pump fittings to prevent fluid leakage.

3. Remove the pump belt.

4. Remove the pump.

5. Remove the nut from the drive pulley and then remove the pulley from the shaft. Do not hammer the pulley off the pump.

6. Installation is a reversal of removal. After the hoses are connected, fill the pump reservoir with fluid and bleed the pump by turning the pulley backward or counterclockwise (as viewed from front) until the air bubbles disappear.

7. Bleed the system as follows:

Bleeding Power Steering System

1. Fill the fluid reservoir.

2. Let the fluid stand undisturbed for two minutes, then crank the engine for about two seconds. Refill the reservoir as necessary.

3. Repeat Steps 1 and 2, above, until the fluid level remains constant after cranking the engine.

4. Raise the front of the car until the wheels are off the ground, then start the engine. Increase the engine speed to about 1500 rpm.

5. Turn the wheels to the left and right, checking the fluid level and refilling as necessary.

9 · Brakes

1969

All Firebirds are equipped with two separate and independent brake systems, a front brake system and a rear brake system. This independence originates at the master cylinder. The master cylinder, mounted on the firewall, consists of two separate fluid reservoirs. They are independent of one another; fluid cannot pass from one to the other although they are contained within the same housing. The front reservoir supplies fluid to the front brakes only while the rear reservoir and outlet connects to the rear brakes. If a leak developed in either system, front or rear, the fluid level in the good system would provide enough pressure to stop the car. Situated below the reservoirs is a cylinder housing a primary and a secondary piston and springs. Fluid from the reservoirs drains down into this cylinder and the pistons—mechanically activated by the brake pedal—exert pressure on the fluid transmitting it through the brake lines to the wheel cylinders at each wheel. The fluid pressure then enters each wheel cylinder or caliper (disc brakes) and forces the pistons outward. These pistons are linked to the brake shoes or, as with disc brakes, contact the brake pads. When the pistons move, so do the shoes or pads. The pads contact a round flat disc and the shoes move outward to contact a round metal drum sur-

rounding them. The disc or drum is attached to the revolving wheel and the friction of the lining or pads against it slows the revolving wheel to a stop. With use, brake linings and pads gradually wear down and, if not replaced in time, their metal support plates (shoes) are exposed to contact and damage the drum or disc. The pad or lining surface attached to the metal shoe wears away and, eventually, braking ability decreases to a point requiring shoe and lining or pad replacement.

Self-adjusting drum brakes were standard equipment on all 1967–69 Firebirds. Front disc brakes were optional during these three years but became standard equipment on 1970 and later models. The drum brakes are the Duo-Servo, single-anchor (the brake shoes pivot on one anchor pin) type having bonded brake linings; that is, the linings are bonded rather than riveted to the metal shoes. The wheel cylinders each contain two pistons. Dirt and moisture are kept out of the cylinder by a rubber boot positioned over each end. The wheel cylinders are nonadjustable.

Beginning 1967, all cars were equipped with a brake pipe distribution and switch assembly mounted below the master cylinder. This assembly is approximately rectangular; attached to the top are two brake lines (one for the front system and one for the rear) coming from the master cylinder. Fluid comes from the master cylinder, passes through this assembly, and exits to the wheels through two outlet lines mounted at each end of the assembly. An electrical switch is situated at top center on the assembly. At the top of the switch is a wire going to the parking brake light on the instrument panel and at the bottom of the switch (within the assembly) is a retractable pin which, when contacted, activates the light on the dash. Directly below the switch pin and running the length of the assembly is a passageway or cylinder housing a piston. Connected to each end of this cylinder is the fluid outlet line going to the wheels. Fluid exits the master cylinder through its two outlet lines and then passes through the distribution assembly and out the outlet lines to the wheels. As long as no leaks exist within the system, fluid passes through the inlet ports and flows into the passageway containing the piston. This fluid exerts an equal pressure at each end of the piston thereby keeping the piston centered in one location. The piston is flat along its top except for a depression or dip in the center. When no leaks exist, this dip is directly beneath the electrical switch activator pin. If a leak develops within one of the systems (front or rear), fluid pressure at one end of the piston drops and the piston is forced to one end of its cylinder. The piston moves off center and the elevated area of the piston now contacts the switch pin and activates the light on the dash warning the driver that a leak has occurred. Brake pedal free-play will increase but the remaining system (front or rear) will stop the car. When the leaking system is repaired and the lines are bled of any air, then the piston will return to its central position and the switch will be reset to the off position causing the light to go out. This light will continue to go on but only when the parking brake is applied.

From 1967 to 1970, all Firebirds equipped with air conditioning, an 8⅞ in. rear axle ring gear (1969), or disc brakes, have a pressure regulator valve (called a metering valve on later disc brake cars) mounted on the left frame side rail (drum brake cars) or beneath the master cylin-

der (disc brake cars). On drum brake cars, this valve operates off the rear brake line but on disc brake cars, it is connected to the front brake line. This valve controls the hydraulic pressure to the rear brakes (drum brake cars) or to the front brakes (disc brake cars) so that front and rear brakes apply at the same time. It guards against early lock-up of the front or rear wheels during brake application. On disc brake cars, a pin on the end of this valve (underneath rubber boot) must be held down (this allows the valve to remain open) during bleeding operations. To depress the pin, press in on the rubber boot.

Beginning 1970, front disc brakes became standard equipment on the Firebird. Valving included the brake pipe distribution and switch assembly and the metering valve described above. Beginning 1971, all cars were equipped with a combination valve mounted below the master cylinder. This valve is the combination of the brake failure warning switch, metering valve, and the proportioning valve, all in one assembly. This valve is nonadjustable and non-serviceable; it must be replaced when defective. The proportioning valve (new in 1971) prevents early rear wheel lockup during quick, "panic" stops. Brake line fluid pressure is permitted to increase up to a certain point. When this point is reached, the valve begins to limit the amount of pressure going to the rear brakes. This prevents the rear brakes from locking up before the front disc brakes. If a leak occurs in the front system, a by-pass within this valve sends full pressure to the rear brakes. This is especially effective during a quick, "panic" stop in a light car. A sudden stop in a light car causes the front end to dip, resulting in weight transfer to the front, making the rear end even lighter and more susceptible to sliding. The proportioning valve does not work during normal stops. When bleeding the brakes, the combination valve must be held in the open position by pressing in on the pin at the end of the valve.

As mentioned earlier, front disc brakes were available only as an option from 1967 to 1969. The 1967 and 1968 brakes were of the four-piston, fixed-caliper type; in 1969 a change was made to a new single-piston, sliding-caliper type. In 1970, the sliding-caliper type became standard front wheel equipment and remains unchanged to date. The fixed-caliper type consists of the caliper, a rotating disc, a splash shield, and a mounting bracket. The caliper contains four pistons and two brake shoes (pads) with riveted linings. Behind each piston is a spring; assembled with each piston is a rubber seal and dust boot so that fluid can be kept in while keeping dirt and moisture out. A retaining pin, secured by a cotter pin, passes through each caliper half and both shoes to hold everything together. One caliper half with brake shoe is mounted to the inside of the disc while the other half is mounted to the outside of the disc. As the brakes are applied, fluid pressure behind each piston forces the pistons outward against each pad (shoe); each pad then contacts a side of the rotating disc and the friction created stops the car. The sliding-caliper type consists of a one-piece housing, bored on the inboard side for a single piston. A rubber seal within this bore retains fluid and prevents it from seeping between the piston and the cylinder. Stepping on the brake pedal causes fluid pressure to force the piston and shoe outward to contact the inboard surface of the disc. This causes the caliper to slide inward on four bushings and two bolts, thereby forcing the outboard pad (shoe and lining) against the outer surface of the disc.

The Duo-Servo drum brakes are used on all cars with front disc brakes. Rear brake design has remained unchanged since 1967. Power brakes have been available as an option on all Firebirds. This type of brake reduces pedal effort through the use of engine vacuum.

Hydraulic System

MASTER CYLINDER

Removal and Installation

1. Disconnect the hydraulic line(s) at the master cylinder.
2. Remove the two retaining nuts and lockwashers which hold the cylinder to the firewall.

NOTE: *Disconnect the pushrod at the brake pedal.*
3. Remove the master cylinder, gasket, and rubber boot.
4. Position the master cylinder on the firewall, making sure that the pushrod goes through the rubber boot into the piston.
NOTE: *Reconnect the pushrod clevis to the brake pedal.*
5. Install the nuts and lockwashers.
6. Install the hydraulic line(s), then check brake pedal free-play.
7. Bleed the brakes as described later in this chapter.
NOTE: *Cars having disc brakes do not have a check valve in the front outlet port of the master cylinder. If one is installed, front discs will immediately wear out due to residual hydraulic pressure holding the pads against the rotor.*

Overhaul

1. Remove the master cylinder from the car.
2. Remove the mounting gasket and boot, and the main cover. Empty the cylinder of all fluid.
3. Place the cylinder in a vise and remove the pushrod retainer and the secondary piston stop bolt that are found inside the front reservoir.
4. Remove the retaining ring and primary piston assembly.
5. Direct compressed air into the piston stop screw hole to force the secondary piston, spring, and retainer from the cylinder bore. If compressed air isn't available, use a hooked wire to pull out the secondary piston.
6. Check the brass tube fitting inserts and, if damaged, remove them; if not, leave them in place.
7. If insert replacement is necessary, thread a no. 6—32 x ⅝ in. self-tapping screw into the insert. Hook the end of the screw with a claw hammer and pull out the insert.
8. An alternative (but more troublesome) way to remove the inserts is to drill out the outlet holes with a ¹³/₆₄ in. drill and then thread them with a ¼ in.—20 tap. Position a thick washer over the hole to serve as a spacer and then thread a ¼ in.—20 x ¾ in. hex-head bolt into the in-

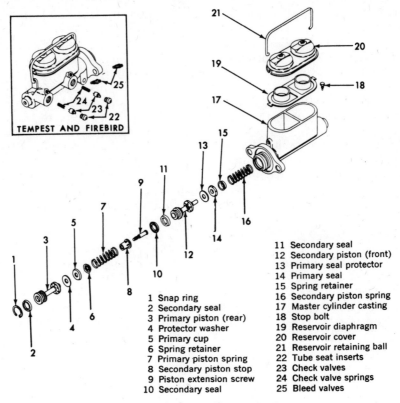

1 Snap ring
2 Secondary seal
3 Primary piston (rear)
4 Protector washer
5 Primary cup
6 Spring retainer
7 Primary piston spring
8 Secondary piston stop
9 Piston extension screw
10 Secondary seal

11 Secondary seal
12 Secondary piston (front)
13 Primary seal protector
14 Primary seal
15 Spring retainer
16 Secondary piston spring
17 Master cylinder casting
18 Stop bolt
19 Reservoir diaphragm
20 Reservoir cover
21 Reservoir retaining ball
22 Tube seat inserts
23 Check valves
24 Check valve springs
25 Bleed valves

TEMPEST AND FIREBIRD

Exploded view of master cylinder

sert and tighten the bolt until the insert is free.

9. Use only *denatured alcohol* or brake fluid and compressed air to clean the parts. Slight rust may be removed with crocus cloth.

CAUTION: *Never use any mineral-based solvents (gasoline, kerosene, etc.) for cleaning. It will quickly deteriorate rubber parts.*

10. Replace the brass tube inserts by positioning them in their holes and threading a brake line tube nut into the outlet hole. Turn down the nut until the insert is seated.

11. Check the piston assemblies for correct identification and, when satisfied, position the replacement secondary seals in the twin grooves of the secondary piston.

12. The outside seal is correctly placed when its lips face the flat end of the piston.

13. Slip the primary seal and its protector over the end of the secondary piston opposite the secondary seals. The flat side of this seal should face the piston's compensating hole flange.

14. Replace the primary piston assembly with the assembled piece in the overhaul kit.

15. Coat the cylinder bore and the secondary piston's inner and outer seals with brake fluid. Assemble the secondary piston spring to its retainer and place them over the end of the primary seal.

16. Insert the combined spring and piston assembly into the cylinder and, using a pencil, seat the spring against the end of the bore.

17. Coat the primary piston seals with brake fluid and push it (pushrod receptacle end out) into the cylinder.

18. Hold the piston in and snap the retaining ring into place.

10. Continue to hold the piston down to make sure that all components are seated and insert the secondary piston stop screw in its hole in the bottom of the front reservoir. Torque the screw to 25–40 in. lbs.

20. Install the reservoir diaphragm and cover.

21. It will save time to bleed the cylinder before installing it in the car. Do so in the following manner:

a. Install plugs in the outlet ports.

b. Place the unit in a vise with the front end tilted slightly downward. *DO NOT OVERTIGHTEN* the vise.

c. Fill both reservoirs with clean fluid.

d. Using a smooth, round rod (try the eraser end of a pencil), push in on the primary piston.

e. Release the pressure on the rod and watch for air bubbles in the fluid. Keep repeating this until the bubbles disappear.

f. Loosen the vise and position the cylinder so that the front end is tilted slightly upward. Repeat Steps "d" and "e."

g. Place the diaphragm and cover on the reservoir.

NOTE: *Master cylinder overhaul on cars with power brakes is the same as above.*

WHEEL CYLINDERS

Overhaul

As is the case with master cylinders, overhaul kits for wheel cylinders are readily available. When rebuilding and installing wheel cylinders, avoid getting any contaminants into the system. Always install clean, new high-quality brake fluid. If dirty or improper fluid has been used, it will be necessary to drain the entire system, flsuh the system with proper brake fluid, replace all rubber components, refill, and bleed the system.

1. Remove the rubber boots from the cylinder ends with pliers. Discard the boots.

2. Remove and discard the pistons and cups.

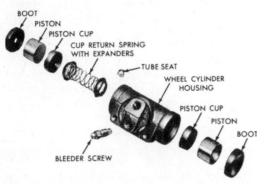

Exploded view of wheel cylinder

3. Wash the cylinder and metal parts in denatured alcohol or clean brake fluid.

CAUTION: *Never use a mineral-based solvent such as gasoline, kerosene, or paint thinner for cleaning purposes. These solvents will swell rubber components and quickly deteriorate them.*

4. Allow the parts to air dry or use compressed air. Do not use rags for cleaning since lint will remain in the cylinder bore.

5. Inspect the piston and replace it if it shows scratches.

6. Lubricate the cylinder bore and counterbore with clean brake fluid.

7. Install the rubber cups (flat side out) and then the pistons (flat side in).

8. Insert new boots into the counterbores by hand. Do not lubricate the boots.

9. Install the wheel cylinder to the backing plate and connect all pushrods and springs. Connect the brake line, install the brake drum, and bleed the brakes.

BRAKE BLEEDING

The hydraulic brake system must be bled any time one of the lines is disconnected or any time air enters the system. If the brake pedal feels spongy upon application, and goes almost to the floor but regains height when pumped, air has entered the system. It must be bled out. Check for leaks that would have allowed the entry of air and repair them before bleeding the system. Bleeding can be done manually or by the pressure method. The correct bleeding sequence is: left rear wheel cylinder, right rear, right front, and left front. If the master cylinder is equipped with bleeder valves, bleed them first then go to the wheel cylinder nearest the master cylinder (left front) followed by the right front, left rear, and right rear.

Pressure Bleeding

1. Clean the top of the master cylinder, remove the cover, and attach the pressure bleeding adaptor. Reduce fluid level in the master cylinder until it is only half-full.

2. Check the pressure bleeder reservoir for correct pressure and fluid level and then open the release valve.

NOTE: *On cars with front disc brakes,*

it is necessary, during bleeding, to hold in the metering valve pin (use tape). The valve is found beneath the master cylinder.

3. Fasten a bleeder hose to the wheel cylinder bleeder screw and submerge the other end of the hose in a glass jar partially filled with fluid.

4. Open the wheel cylinder bleeder screw and allow the fluid to flow until all air bubbles disappear and a free flow exists.

5. Close the bleeder screw, remove the hose, and repeat the procedure at each of the other wheel cylinders, according to the sequence listed above under "Brake Bleeding."

NOTE: *Disc brake calipers often trap air. To release these air bubbles, tap the caliper with a rubber mallet while bleeding it.*

Manual Bleeding

This method of bleeding requires two people; one to depress the brake pedal and the other to open the bleeder screws.

1. Clean the top of the master cylinder, remove the cover and fill the reservoirs with clean fluid. To prevent squirting fluid, replace the cover.

NOTE: *On cars with front disc brakes, it will be necessary to hold in the metering valve pin during the bleeding procedure. The metering valve is located beneath the master cylinder and the pin is situated under the rubber boot on the end of the valve housing. This may be taped in or held by an assistant.*

2. Attach a bleeder hose to the end of the bleeder screw and submerge the other end in a jar partially filled with brake fluid. Brake bleeding should follow a sequence; that is, start with the left rear wheel cylinder and then go to the right rear, followed by the right front and left front. If the master cylinder is equipped with bleeder valves, bleed them first and then go to the wheel nearest the master cylinder (left front) followed by the right front, left rear, and right rear.

3. Place the wrench on the bleeder screw and have an assistant pump the brake pedal several times. Instruct him to stop pumping and merely rest his foot on the pedal. Open the bleeder screw (counterclockwise) and have the assistant slowly press down on the pedal. Just before the pedal reaches the floor, close the bleeder screw. If the pedal is allowed to reach the floor, outside air will be sucked back into the system. Your assistant should let you know when to close the screw.

NOTE: *After bleeding each wheel cylinder, check the fluid level in the master cylinder. Do not allow the level to drop too low or else air will enter the master cylinder and return to the system.*

4. Allow the pedal to return from the floor and repeat this procedure until brake fluid flows into the jar without making any air bubbles.

5. Tighten the bleeder screw and go to the other wheels (in sequence) and repeat this procedure.

NOTE: *Disc brake calipers often trap air. To release these air bubbles, tap each caliper with a rubber mallet while bleeding it.*

6. When the job is completed, discard the brake fluid in the jar.

CAUTION: *Reusing brake fluid drained from the system during bleeding will return air to the system. This fluid in the jar has been completely aerated and is no longer any good.*

Brake Components

DISC BRAKES

Brake Pad Replacement

1967–68

1. Siphon off about two-thirds of the brake fluid from a full master cylinder.

CAUTION: *The insertion of the thicker replacement pads will push the caliper pistons back into their bores and will cause a full master cylinder to overflow causing paint damage. In addition to siphoning fluid, it would be wise to keep the cylinder cover on during pad replacement.*

2. Raise the car and support it with jackstands. Remove the wheels.

NOTE: *Replacing the pads on just one wheel will result in uneven braking.*

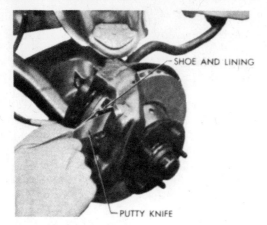

Replacing 1967–68 pads

Always replace the pads on both wheels.

3. Extract and discard the pad retaining pin cotter key.

4. Remove the retaining pin and, while removing one pad, insert its replacement before the piston has time to move outward. If you were too slow and the pistons were too fast, it will be necessary to use a wide-bladed putty knife to hold in the pistons while inserting the new pads. If this gives you difficulty, open the bleeder screw on that caliper and release some of the fluid, but do not allow the fluid to drain from the master cylinder. This may reduce the pressure and make it easier to push in on the pistons. After removing the outboard pad, inspect it and compare it with the inboard pad. They may be slightly different; if so, make sure that the replacement pads are installed correctly.

5. After installing the new pads, install the retaining pin and insert a new cotter pin.

6. Refill the master cylinder and bleed the system as necessary

1969–74

1. Siphon off about two-thirds of the brake fluid from a full master cylinder.

CAUTION: *The insertion of the thicker replacement pads will push the*

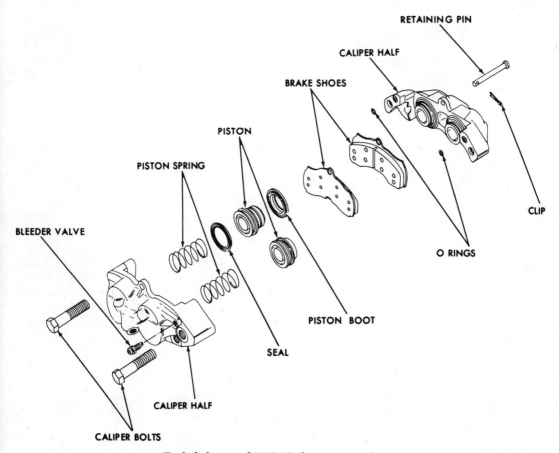

Exploded view of 1967–68 (four-piston) caliper

piston back into its bore and will cause a full master cylinder to overflow causing paint damage. In addition to siphoning off fluid it would be wise to keep the cylinder cover on during pad replacement.

2. Raise the car and support it with jackstands. Remove the wheels.

NOTE: *Replacing the pads on just one wheel will result in uneven braking. Always replace the pads on both wheels.*

3. Install a C-clamp on the caliper so that the solid side of the clamp rests against the back of the caliper and so that the screw end rests against the metal part of the outboard part.

4. Tighten the clamp until the caliper moves enough to bottom the piston in its bore. Remove the clamp.

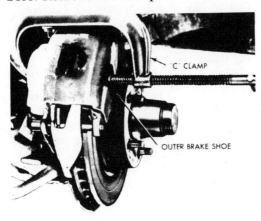

1969–74 pad removal

5. Remove the two allen-head caliper mounting bolts enough to allow the caliper to be pulled off the disc.

6. Remove the inboard pad and loosen the outboard pad. Place the caliper where it won't strain the brake hose. It would be best to wire it out of the way.

7. Remove the pad support spring clip from the piston.

8. Remove the two bolt ear sleeves and the 4 rubber bushings from the ears.

9. Brake pads should be replaced when they are worn to within 1/32 in. of the rivet heads.

10. Check the inside of the caliper for leakage and the condition of the piston dust boot.

11. Lubricate the two new sleeves and 4 bushings with a silicone spray.

12. Install the bushings in each caliper ear. Install the two sleeves in the two inboard ears.

13. Install the pad support spring clip and the old pad into the center of the piston. Push the pad down until it is flat against the caliper.

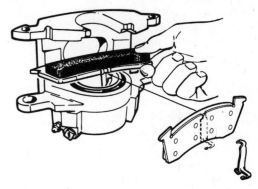

Installing pad support spring clip

14. Place the outboard pad in the caliper with its top ears over the caliper ears and the bottom tab engaged in the caliper cutout.

15. After both pads are installed, lift the caliper and place the bottom edge of the outboard pad on the outer edge of the disc to make sure that there is no clearance between the tab on the bottom of the shoes and the caliper abutment.

16. Clamp a 1/4 x 1 x 2½ in. metal plate across the bottom of the pad. Make sure that the clamp and plate are clean to avoid contaminating the pads. Tighten the clamp moderately.

17. Bend the upper ears of the out-

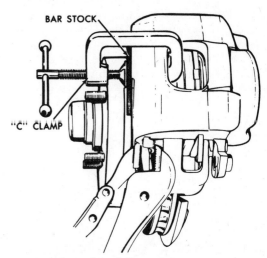

Bending the outboard shoe ears

board shoe over the caliper with arc joint pliers. Bend the ears until the clearance between the pad ear and the caliper is 0.005 in. or less.

18. Remove the C-clamp and install the new inboard pad in place of the old pad used for installation purposes.

19. Place the caliper over the disc and line up the mounting holes.

20. Insert the mounting bolts through the inboard caliper ear sleeves and mounting bracket. Make sure that the bolts go under the inboard pad retaining ears.

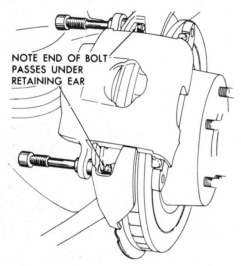

NOTE END OF BOLT PASSES UNDER RETAINING EAR

Be sure that the bolts go under the inboard pad retaining ears

21. Push the bolts through the outboard pads and caliper ears. Hand-tighten the bolts into the mounting bracket and then tighten them to 35 ft lbs.

22. Install the wheels, lower the car, and refill the master cylinder with new fluid. Pump the brake pedal to make sure that there are no air bubbles in the system.

Caliper Replacement and Overhaul

1967–68

1. Raise the car and support it on jackstands.

2. Remove the tire and wheel assembly from the side on which the caliper is being removed.

3. Disconnect the brake hose at the support bracket. Tape the end of the line to prevent contamination.

4. Remove the cotter pin from the brake pad retaining pin and remove the pin.

5. Remove the brake pads and identify them as inboard or outboard if they are being reused.

6. Remove the U-shaped retainer from the hose fitting and pull the hose from the bracket.

7. Remove the two caliper retaining bolts and also the caliper from its mounting bracket.

8. Separate the caliper halves. Remove the two O-rings from the fluid transfer holes in the caliper.

9. Push the piston all the way down into the caliper. Using the piston as a fulcrum, place a screwdriver under the steel ring in the boot and pry the boot from the caliper half.

10. Remove the pistons and springs, being careful not to damage the seal.

11. Remove the boot and seal from the piston.

12. Clean all metal components with clean brake fluid or denatured alcohol.

CAUTION: *Do not use gasoline, kerosene, or any other mineral-based solvent for cleaning. These solvents form an oily film on the parts which leads to fluid contamination and the deterioration of rubber parts.*

13. Blow out all fluid passages with an air hose.

14. Discard and replace all rubber parts.

15. Inspect all bores for scoring and pitting and replace as necessary. Minor flaws can be removed with very fine crocus cloth but do so with a circular motion.

16. Using a feeler gauge, check the clearance of the piston in its bore. If the bore is not damaged and the clearance exceeds the maximum limit below, then the piston must be replaced.

Bore Diameter	Clearance
$2\frac{1}{16}$ in.	0.0045–0.010 in.
$1\frac{7}{8}$ in.	0.0045–0.010 in.
$1\frac{3}{8}$ in.	0.0035–0.009 in.

17. Insert the seal in the piston groove nearest the flat end of the piston. The seal lip must face the large end of the piston.

The lips must be in the groove and may not extend beyond.

18. Place the spring in the piston bore.

19. Coat the seal with clean brake fluid.

20. Install the piston assembly into the bore, being careful not to damage the seal lip on the edge of the bore.

21. Install the boot into the piston groove closest to the concave end of the piston.

22. The fold in the boot must face the seal end of the piston.

23. Push the pistons to the bottom of the bore and check for smooth piston movement. The end of the piston must be flush with the end of the bore. If it is not, check the installation of the seal.

24. Seat the piston boot so that its metal ring is even in the counterbore. The ring must be flush or below the machined face of the caliper. If the ring is seated unevenly dirt and moisture could get into the bore.

25. Insert the O-rings around the fluid transfer holes at both ends of the caliper halves.

26. Lubricate the bolts with brake fluid, connect the caliper halves, and torque the bolts to 130 ft lbs.

27. While holding in the brake pistons with a putty knife, mount the caliper over the disc. Be careful not to damage the piston boots on the edge of the disc.

28. Install the two mounting bolts and torque them to 130 ft lbs.

29. Install the brake pads. If the same pads are being reused, return them to their original places (outboard or inboard) as marked during removal. New pads will usually have an arrow on the back indicating the direction of disc rotation. See "Brake Pad Replacement" for details.

30. Install the brake hose into the caliper, passing the female end through the support bracket.

31. Make sure that the tube line is clean and connect the brake line nut to the caliper.

32. Install the hose fitting into the support bracket and install the U-shaped retainer. Turn the steering wheel from side to side to make sure that the hose doesn't interfere with the tire. If it does, turn the hose end one or two points in the bracket until the interference is eliminated.

33. After performing the above check, install the steel tube connector and tighten it.

34. Bleed the brakes as instructed earlier in this Chapter.

35. Install the wheels and lower the car.

1969–74

1. Perform the removal Steps for pad replacement.

2. Disconnect the brake hose and plug the line.

3. Remove the U-shaped retainer from the fitting.

4. Pull the hose from the frame bracket and remove the caliper with the hose attached.

5. Clean the outside of the caliper with denatured alcohol.

6. Remove the brake hose and discard the copper gasket.

7. Remove the brake fluid from the caliper.

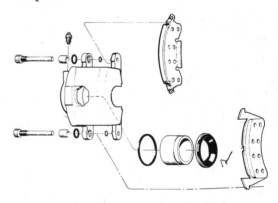

Exploded view of 1969–74 (single-piston) caliper

8. Place clean rags inside the caliper opening to catch the piston when it is released.

9. Apply compressed air to the caliper fluid inlet hole and force the piston out of its bore. Do not blow the piston out; use just enough pressure to ease it out.

10. Use a screwdriver to pry the boot out of the caliper. Avoid scratching the bore.

11. Remove the piston seal from its groove in the caliper bore. *Do not use a metal tool of any type for this operation.*

12. Blow out all passages in the caliper and bleeder valve. Clean the piston and piston bore with fresh brake fluid.

13. Examine the piston for scoring, scratches, or corrosion. If any of these conditions exist, the piston must be replaced because it is plated and cannot be refinished.

14. Examine the bore for the same defects. Light rough spots may be removed by rotating crocus cloth, using finger pressure, in the bore. Do not polish with an in-and-out motion or use any other abrasive.

15. Lubricate the piston bore and the new rubber parts with fresh brake fluid. Position the seal in the piston bore groove.

16. Lubricate the piston with brake fluid and assemble the boot into the piston groove so that the fold faces the open end of the piston.

17. Insert the piston into the bore, taking care not to unseat the seal.

18. Force the piston to the bottom of the bore. (This will require a force of 50–100 lbs). Seat the boot lip around the caliper counterbore. Proper seating of the boot is very important for sealing out contaminants.

19. Install the brake hose into the caliper with a new copper gasket.

20. Lubricate the new sleeves and rubber bushings. Install the bushings in the caliper ears. Install the sleeves so that the end toward the disc pad is flush with the machined surface.

NOTE: *Lubrication of the sleeves and bushings is essential to insure the proper operation of the sliding caliper design.*

21. Install the shoe support spring in the piston.

22. Install the disc pads in the caliper and remount the caliper on the hub (see "Disc Pad Replacement").

23. Reconnect the brake hose to the steel brake line. Install the retainer clip. Bleed the brakes (see "Brake Bleeding").

24. Replace the wheels, check the brake fluid level, check the brake pedal travel, and road-test the vehicle.

Disc Inspection

1. Tighten the spindle nut to remove all wheel bearing play.

2. Install a dial indicator on the caliper so that its feeler will contact the disc about 1 in. below its outer edge.

3. Turn the disc and observe the run-out reading. If the reading exceeds 0.002 in., the disc should be replaced.

4. Minimum thickness dimensions are cast into the caliper for reference.

Disc Replacement

1. Raise the car, support it with jackstands, and remove the wheel and tire assembly.

2. Remove the brake caliper as previously outlined.

3. Drill out the 5 rivets holding the disc to the hub.

4. Remove the disc.

5. Remove the rivet stubs from the hub.

6. Install the disc on the hub, aligning the lug bolts with the holes in the disc.

7. Install the brake caliper and shoes as previously outlined.

8. Bleed the brakes, install the wheel, and lower the car.

DRUM BRAKES

Brake Drum Replacement

1. Raise and support the car.

2. Remove the wheel or wheels.

3. Pull the brake drum off. It may be necessary to gently tap the rear edges of the drum to start it off the studs.

4. If extreme resistance to removal is encountered, it will be necessary to retract the adjusting screw. Knock out the access hole in the brake drum and turn the adjuster to retract the linings away from the drum.

5. Install brake drums after adjusting the linings.

6. Install the drums in the same position on the hub as removed.

Drum Inspection

1. Check the drums for any cracks, scores, grooves, or an out-of-round condition. Replace if cracked. Slight scores can be removed with fine emery cloth while extensive scoring requires turning the drum on a lathe.

2. Never have a drum turned more than 0.060 in.

Brake Shoe Adjustment

Rotate the starwheel adjuster until a slight drag is felt between the shoes and drum, then back off 1¼ turns on the adjusting wheel. Put the car in reverse and, while backing up, firmly apply the brakes. This will allow the self-adjusters to complete the adjustment.

Brake Shoe Replacement

1. Raise the car and support it on jackstands.

2. Slacken the parking brake cable.

3. Remove the rear wheel and brake drum. The front wheel and drum may be removed as a unit by removing the spindle nut and cotter pin.

4. Free the brake shoe return springs, actuator pull-back spring, hold-down pins and springs, and actuator assembly.

NOTE: *Special tools available from auto supply stores will ease removal of the spring and anchor pin, but the job may still be done with common hand tools.*

5. On the rear wheels, disconnect the adjusting mechanism and spring, and remove the primary shoe. The primary shoe has a shorter lining than the secondary and is mounted at the front of the wheel.

6. Disconnect the parking brake lever from the secondary shoe and remove the shoe. Front wheel shoes may be removed together.

7. Clean and inspect all brake parts.

8. Check the wheel cylinders for seal condition and leaking.

9. Repack wheel bearings and replace the seals.

10. Inspect the replacement shoes for nicks or burrs, lubricate the backing plate contact points, brake cable and levers, and adjusting screws and then assemble.

11. Make sure that the right and left-hand adjusting screws are not mixed. You can prevent this by working on one side at a time. This will also provide you with a reference for reassembly. The star-wheel should be nearest to the secondary shoe when correctly installed.

12. To install, reverse the removal procedure. When completed, make an initial adjustment as previously described.

NOTE: *Maintenance procedures for the metallic lining option are the same as those for standard linings. Do not substitute these linings in standard drums, unless they have been honed to a 20 micro-inch finish and equipped with special, heat-resistant springs.*

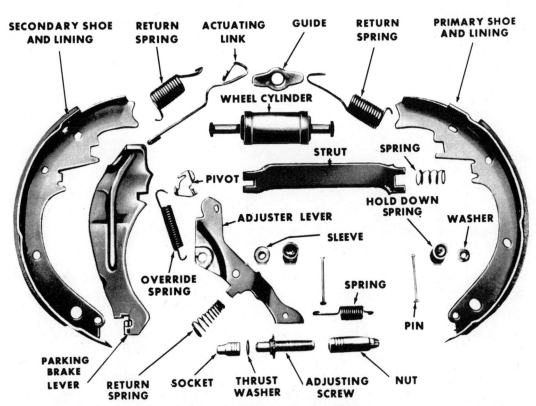

Exploded view of rear drum brake components

PARKING BRAKE

All Firebirds are equipped with a foot-operated ratchet type parking brake. A cable assembly connects this pedal to an intermediate cable by means of an equalizer. Adjustment is made at the equalizer. The intermediate cable connects with two rear cables and each of these cables enters a rear wheel.

Adjustment

1. Raise the rear of the car and support it with jackstands.

2. Push down on the parking brake pedal so that it is two notches (clicks) from the fully released position.

3. Loosen the forward equalizer check nut and adjust the rear nut as necessary to obtain a light drag when the rear wheel is turned forward.

4. Tighten both check nuts.

5. Fully release the parking brake lever and check to see that there is no drag present when the rear wheel is turned forward.

6. Lower the car.

7. If the parking brake has to be forcibly released, clean and lubricate the cables and equalizer, and also the parking brake assembly, then check the cables for straightness and kinks.

Wheel Bearings

Properly adjusted bearings have a slightly loose feeling. Wheel bearings must never be preloaded. Preloading will damage bearings and eventually spindles. If bearings are too loose, they should be cleaned and inspected and then adjusted. Hold the tire at the top and bottom and move the wheel in and out on the spindle. If the movement is greater than 0.008 in., the bearings are too loose.

Adjustment

1. Raise and support the car by the lower control arm.

2. Remove the hub cap, then remove the dust cap from the hub.

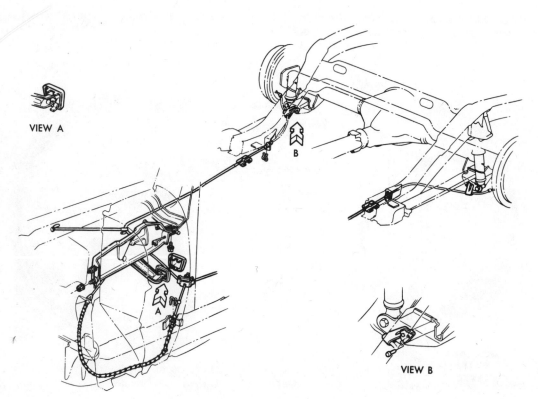

VIEW A

B

A

VIEW B

1967–69 parking brake linkage

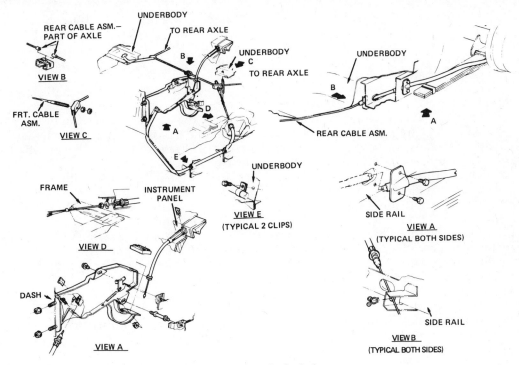

1970–74 parking brake linkage

3. Remove the cotter pin and spindle nut.

4. Spin the wheel forward by hand and tighten the spindle nut to 12 ft lbs. This 12 ft lbs seats the bearing.

5. Back off on the nut until it is just loose, then tighten it finger-tight.

6. Loosen the nut until either hole in the spindle lines up with a slot in the nut and then insert the cotter pin. This may appear to be too loose but it is the correct adjustment. The spindle nut should not even be finger-tight.

7. Proper adjustment creates 0.001–0.008 in. of end-play.

Removal and Installation

1967–69

1. Remove the wheel and tire assembly, and the brake drum or brake caliper.

2. On those cars with disc brakes, remove the hub and disc as an assembly. Remove the caliper mounting bolts and insert a block between the brake pads as the caliper is removed. Remove the caliper and wire it out of the way.

3. Pry out the grease cap, cotter pin, spindle nut, and washer, then remove the hub. Do not drop the wheel bearings.

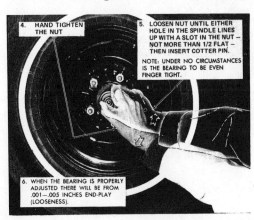

Wheel bearing adjustment

4. Remove the outer roller bearing assembly from the hub. The inner bearing assembly will remain in the hub and may be removed after prying out the inner seal. Discard the seal.

5. Clean all parts in solvent (air dry) and check for excessive wear or damage.

6. Using a hammer and drift, remove the bearing cups from the hub. When installing new cups, make sure that they are not cocked and that they are fully seated against the hub shoulder.

7. Using a high melting-point bearing lubricant, pack both inner and outer bearings.

8. Place the inner bearing in the hub and install a new inner seal, making sure that the seal flange faces the bearing cup.

9. Carefully install the wheel hub over the spindle.

10. Using your hands, firmly press the outer bearing into the hub. Install the spindle washer and nut, and adjust as instructed above.

1970–74

1. Remove the hub and disc assembly as described in Steps 1–3 above.

2. Remove the outer roller bearing assembly from the hub. The inner bearing assembly can be removed after prying out the inner seal. Discard the seal.

3. Wash all parts in solvent and check for excessive wear or damage.

4. To replace the outer or inner race, knock out the old race with a hammer and brass drift. New races must be installed squarely and evenly to avoid damage.

5. Pack the bearings with a high melting-point bearing lubricant.

6. Lightly grease the spindle and the inside of the hub.

7. Place the inner bearing in hub race and install a new grease seal.

8. Carefully install the hub and disc assembly.

9. Install the outer wheel bearing.

10. Install the washer and nut and adjust the bearings according to the procedure outlined above.

11. Install the caliper and torque the mounting bolts to 35 ft lbs.

12. Install the dust cap and the wheel and tire assembly, then lower the car to the ground.

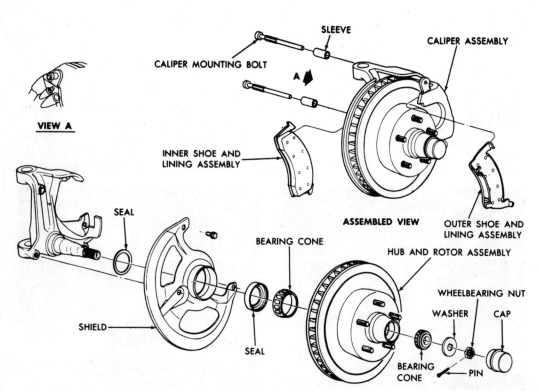

Exploded view of 1969–74 disc and caliper assembly

Brake Specifications

| Year | MASTER CYLINDER | | WHEEL CYLINDER | | | BRAKE DISC OR DRUM DIAMETER | | |
| | Disc | Drum | Front | | Rear | Front | | Rear |
			Disc	Drum		Disc	Drum	
'67–'68	1.125	1.0	2.062	1.125	.875	11.0	9.5	9.5
'69	1.125	1.0	2.938	1.125	.875	11.0	9.5	9.5
'70–'74	1.0①	——	2.938	——	.875	11.0	——	9.5

① 1.125—with power brakes
—— Not applicable

10 · Body

Doors

Removal and Installation

When removing the door, it is best to remove it from the hinges since the door hinge bolts are easier to get to than the bolts on the body.

1. Mark the position of the hinge on the door to facilitate adjustment after installation.

2. If the door has power windows or power door locks, remove the panel and disconnect the wiring harness.

3. Have an assistant hold the door open and remove the bolts attaching the upper and lower hinges to the door.

4. Remove the door. Reverse the removal procedure for installation

5. Door alignment is made by adjusting the floating anchor plates located behind the hinge in the door and body. When making adjustments, remove the door lock striker from the body so that the door can hang freely. It may be necessary to loosen the front fender to prevent interference during adjustments.

DOOR PANELS

A one-piece vinyl trim panel is attached to the inside of each door. The panel is secured to the door at the top by a metal trim support, by clips or nails down the sides, and by screws along the bottom.

Removal and Installation

1. Remove all door and window handles. These handles may be secured by either screws or a retaining clip. The retainer clip should be removed with a special clip removing tool (available at a low price at most auto supply stores). A screwdriver can be used but removal becomes more difficult and tearing the panel material becomes more possible.

2. Remove the lock knob—if so equipped.

3. Remove the door pull handle from those models so equipped.

4. On those cars having remote control mirrors, disconnect the control cable.

5. Remove the armrest screws.

6. If the panel contains any electrical switches, disconnect the wiring harness from the switch.

7. Remove the screws from the side and bottom of the panel. Insert a putty knife between the panel and door to disengage nails or clips from the door.

CAUTION: *Be careful not to damage the inner water deflector or the plastic cups securing the panel clips. These components act as seals to keep out water.*

8. Lift the panel up and slide it slightly to the rear to disengage it from the inner panel of the door. Remove this panel from the door.

9. To install, reverse the removal procedure.

Hood

Adjustments

Hood adjustment can be divided into three separate areas of adjustment: hood hinge, hood bumpers, and hood catch and lock mechanism. Hinge and bumper adjustment must be made before any adjustments to the catch and lock.

HOOD HINGE ADJUSTMENT

The hinge mounting holes are slotted to provide either horizontal or vertical adjustments.

1. Make a line around the hinge plate to be adjusted.

HOOD ASSEMBLY
SCREW
COWL TOP
1"
HINGE ASSEMBLY

1970–74 hood hinge mounting

2. Loosen the mounting screws and move the hood in the desired direction using the scribed line to check the amount of movement from the original position. Tighten the screws, *carefully* close the hood, and check the alignment. Repeating this procedure several times may be necessary before proper alignment is achieved.

NOTE: *On 1970–74 Firebirds there is an adjustable screw and nut at each rear corner of the hood. Each screw should be kept at a height of 1 in. to*

prevent the hood from going through the windshield during a collison.

HOOD BUMPER ADJUSTMENT

Each of the two hood bumpers is located at the top of the radiator support. The bumpers should be adjusted so that the top surface of the hood is flush with the top surfaces of the fenders and header (panel located just in front of hood) panel.

IMPORTANT: *On 1970–72 models, make sure that the rear of the hood is adjusted properly and sealed evenly just beneath the windshield. This will restrict the entrance of engine fumes into the cowl vent.*

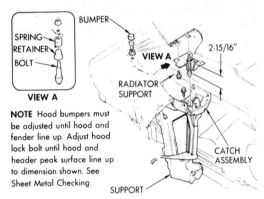

SPRING RETAINER
BOLT
BUMPER
VIEW A
2-15/16"
RADIATOR SUPPORT
CATCH ASSEMBLY
VIEW A
SUPPORT

NOTE Hood bumpers must be adjusted until hood and fender line up. Adjust hood lock bolt until hood and header peak surface line up to dimension shown. See Sheet Metal Checking.

1970–74 hood catch lock and bumpers

HOOD CATCH AND LOCK ADJUSTMENT

Adjust the height of the lockbolt so that the top surface of the hood is flush with the header panel surface. If adjusted properly, the hood bumpers will slightly compress under the fully closed hood and releasing the catch will not be difficult.

Trunk Lid

Alignment

When removing and installing the trunk lid, painted areas adjacent to the trunk lid should be protected against accidental chipping by tape or cloth. The location of the hinge straps should be marked prior to removal.

1. Side-to-side and fore-and-aft lid adjustment is controlled by the hinge strap-

to-lid bolts. Loosen the bolts, move the lid in desired direction, and tighten the bolts.

2. Vertical adjustment of the lid is made by placing shims between the hinge strap and the lid and by raising or lowering the lid lock striker.

3. To raise the sides of the lid, place a shim between the strap and the lid at the forward bolt. To lower the lid, install the shim at the rear bolt.

Fuel Tank

Removal and Installation

1. Disconnect the battery ground cable.

2. Disconnect the meter wire at the rear wiring harness connector.

3. Push out the grommet and pull the wire through the hole in the trunk floor pan.

4. Raise the car and drain the tank. There are no drain plugs so siphoning is necessary. On 1970–74 cars, the filler neck is too long for siphoning so fuel will have to be siphoned or pumped out through the fuel feed line.

5. Disconnect the fuel line hose from the gauge unit pick-up line. Disconnect all vent hoses from the tank.

6. Remove the gauge ground wire screw from the floor pan.

7. Remove the tank strap bolts and carefully lower the tank.

8. To install, reverse this removal procedure.

Appendix

General Conversion Table

Multiply by	To convert	To	
2.54	Inches	Centimeters	.3937
30.48	Feet	Centimeters	.0328
.914	Yards	Meters	1.094
1.609	Miles	Kilometers	.621
.645	Square inches	Square cm.	.155
.836	Square yards	Square meters	1.196
16.39	Cubic inches	Cubic cm.	.061
28.3	Cubic feet	Liters	.0353
.4536	Pounds	Kilograms	2.2045
4.546	Gallons	Liters	.22
.068	Lbs./sq. in. (psi)	Atmospheres	14.7
.138	Foot pounds	Kg. m.	7.23
1.014	H.P. (DIN)	H.P. (SAE)	.9861
——	To obtain	From	Multiply by

Note: 1 cm. equals 10 mm.; 1 mm. equals .0394".

Conversion—Common Fractions to Decimals and Millimeters

INCHES			INCHES			INCHES		
Common Fractions	Decimal Fractions	Millimeters (approx.)	Common Fractions	Decimal Fractions	Millimeters (approx.)	Common Fractions	Decimal Fractions	Millimeters (approx.)
1/128	.008	0.20	11/32	.344	8.73	43/64	.672	17.07
1/64	.016	0.40	23/64	.359	9.13	11/16	.688	17.46
1/32	.031	0.79	3/8	.375	9.53	45/64	.703	17.86
3/64	.047	1.19	25/64	.391	9.92	23/32	.719	18.26
1/16	.063	1.59	13/32	.406	10.32	47/64	.734	18.65
5/64	.078	1.98	27/64	.422	10.72	3/4	.750	19.05
3/32	.094	2.38	7/16	.438	11.11	49/64	.766	19.45
7/64	.109	2.78	29/64	.453	11.51	25/32	.781	19.84
1/8	.125	3.18	15/32	.469	11.91	51/64	.797	20.24
9/64	.141	3.57	31/64	.484	12.30	13/16	.813	20.64
5/32	.156	3.97	1/2	.500	12.70	53/64	.828	21.03
11/64	.172	4.37	33/64	.516	13.10	27/32	.844	21.43
3/16	.188	4.76	17/32	.531	13.49	55/64	.859	21.83
13/64	.203	5.16	35/64	.547	13.89	7/8	.875	22.23
7/32	.219	5.56	9/16	.563	14.29	57/64	.891	22.62
15/64	.234	5.95	37/64	.578	14.68	29/32	.906	23.02
1/4	.250	6.35	19/32	.594	15.08	59/64	.922	23.42
17/64	.266	6.75	39/64	.609	15.48	15/16	.938	23.81
9/32	.281	7.14	5/8	.625	15.88	61/64	.953	24.21
19/64	.297	7.54	41/64	.641	16.27	31/32	.969	24.61
5/16	.313	7.94	21/32	.656	16.67	63/64	.984	25.00
21/64	.328	8.33						

Conversion—Millimeters to Decimal Inches

mm	inches	mm	inches	mm	inches	mm	inches	mm	inches
1	.039 370	31	1.220 470	61	2.401 570	91	3.582 670	210	8.267 700
2	.078 740	32	1.259 840	62	2.440 940	92	3.622 040	220	8.661 400
3	.118 110	33	1.299 210	63	2.480 310	93	3.661 410	230	9.055 100
4	.157 480	34	1.338 580	64	2.519 680	94	3.700 780	240	9.448 800
5	.196 850	35	1.377 949	65	2.559 050	95	3.740 150	250	9.842 500
6	.236 220	36	1.417 319	66	2.598 420	96	3.779 520	260	10.236 200
7	.275 590	37	1.456 689	67	2.637 790	97	3.818 890	270	10.629 900
8	.314 960	38	1.496 050	68	2.677 160	98	3.858 260	280	11.032 600
9	.354 330	39	1.535 430	69	2.716 530	99	3.897 630	290	11.417 300
10	.393 700	40	1.574 800	70	2.755 900	100	3.937 000	300	11.811 000
11	.433 070	41	1.614 170	71	2.795 270	105	4.133 848	310	12.204 700
12	.472 440	42	1.653 540	72	2.834 640	110	4.330 700	320	12.598 400
13	.511 810	43	1.692 910	73	2.874 010	115	4.527 550	330	12.992 100
14	.551 180	44	1.732 280	74	2.913 380	120	4.724 400	340	13.385 800
15	.590 550	45	1.771 650	75	2.952 750	125	4.921 250	350	13.779 500
16	.629 920	46	1.811 020	76	2.992 120	130	5.118 100	360	14.173 200
17	.669 290	47	1.850 390	77	3.031 490	135	5.314 950	370	14.566 900
18	.708 660	48	1.889 760	78	3.070 860	140	5.511 800	380	14.960 600
19	.748 030	49	1.929 130	79	3.110 230	145	5.708 650	390	15.354 300
20	.787 400	50	1.968 500	80	3.149 600	150	5.905 500	400	15.748 000
21	.826 770	51	2.007 870	81	3.188 970	155	6.102 350	500	19.685 000
22	.866 140	52	2.047 240	82	3.228 340	160	6.299 200	600	23.622 000
23	.905 510	53	2.086 610	83	3.267 710	165	6.496 050	700	27.559 000
24	.944 880	54	2.125 980	84	3.307 080	170	6.692 900	800	31.496 000
25	.984 250	55	2.165 350	85	3.346 450	175	6.889 750	900	35.433 000
26	1.023 620	56	2.204 720	86	3.385 820	180	7.086 600	1000	39.370 000
27	1.062 990	57	2.244 090	87	3.425 190	185	7.283 450	2000	78.740 000
28	1.102 360	58	2.283 460	88	3.464 560	190	7.480 300	3000	118.110 000
29	1.141 730	59	2.322 830	89	3.503 903	195	7.677 150	4000	157.480 000
30	1.181 100	60	2.362 200	90	3.543 300	200	7.874 000	5000	196.850 000

To change decimal millimeters to decimal inches, position the decimal point where desired on either side of the millimeter measurement shown and reset the inches decimal by the same number of digits in the same direction. For example, to convert .001 mm into decimal inches, reset the decimal behind the 1 mm (shown on the chart) to .001; change the decimal inch equivalent (.039″ shown) to .00039″).

Tap Drill Sizes

National Fine or S.A.E.				National Coarse or U.S.S.		
Screw & Tap Size	Threads Per Inch	Use Drill Number		Screw & Tap Size	Threads Per Inch	Use Drill Number
No. 5	44	37		No. 5	40	39
No. 6	40	33		No. 6	32	36
No. 8	36	29		No. 8	32	29
No. 10	32	21		No. 10	24	25
No. 12	28	15		No. 12	24	17
1/4	28	3		1/4	20	8
5/16	24	1		5/16	18	F
3/8	24	Q		3/8	16	5/16
7/16	20	W		7/16	14	U
1/2	20	29/64		1/2	13	27/64
9/16	18	33/64		9/16	12	31/64
5/8	18	37/64		5/8	11	17/32
3/4	16	11/16		3/4	10	21/32
7/8	14	13/16		7/8	9	49/64
1 1/8	12	1 3/64		1	8	7/8
1 1/4	12	1 11/64		1 1/8	7	63/64
1 1/2	12	1 27/64		1 1/4	7	1 7/64
				1 1/2	6	1 11/32

Decimal Equivalent Size of the Number Drills

Drill No.	Decimal Equivalent	Drill No.	Decimal Equivalent	Drill No.	Decimal Equivalent
80	.0135	53	.0595	26	.1470
79	.0145	52	.0635	25	.1495
78	.0160	51	.0670	24	.1520
77	.0180	50	.0700	23	.1540
76	.0200	49	.0730	22	.1570
75	.0210	48	.0760	21	.1590
74	.0225	47	.0785	20	.1610
73	.0240	46	.0810	19	.1660
72	.0250	45	.0820	18	.1695
71	.0260	44	.0860	17	.1730
70	.0280	43	.0890	16	.1770
69	.0292	42	.0935	15	.1800
68	.0310	41	.0960	14	.1820
67	.0320	40	.0980	13	.1850
66	.0330	39	.0995	12	.1890
65	.0350	38	.1015	11	.1910
64	.0360	37	.1040	10	.1935
63	.0370	36	.1065	9	.1960
62	.0380	35	.1100	8	.1990
61	.0390	34	.1110	7	.2010
60	.0400	33	.1130	6	.2040
59	.0410	32	.1160	5	.2055
58	.0420	31	.1200	4	.2090
57	.0430	30	.1285	3	.2130
56	.0465	29	.1360	2	.2210
55	.0520	28	.1405	1	.2280
54	.0550	27	.1440		

Decimal Equivalent Size of the Letter Drills

Letter Drill	Decimal Equivalent	Letter Drill	Decimal Equivalent	Letter Drill	Decimal Equivalent
A	.234	J	.277	S	.348
B	.238	K	.281	T	.358
C	.242	L	.290	U	.368
D	.246	M	.295	V	.377
E	.250	N	.302	W	.386
F	.257	O	.316	X	.397
G	.261	P	.323	Y	.404
H	.266	Q	.332	Z	.413
I	.272	R	.339		

ANTI-FREEZE INFORMATION

Freezing and Boiling Points of Solutions
According to Percentage of Alcohol or Ethylene Glycol

Freezing Point of Solution	Alcohol Volume %	Alcohol Solution Boils at	Ethylene Glycol Volume %	Ethylene Glycol Solution Boils at
20°F.	12	196°F.	16	216°F.
10°F.	20	189°F.	25	218°F.
0°F.	27	184°F.	33	220°F.
−10°F.	32	181°F.	39	222°F.
−20°F.	38	178°F.	44	224°F.
−30°F.	42	176°F.	48	225°F.

Note: above boiling points are at sea level. For every 1,000 feet of altitude, boiling points are approximately 2°F. lower than those shown. For every pound of pressure exerted by the pressure cap, the boiling points are approximately 3°F. higher than those shown.

To Increase the Freezing Protection of Anti-Freeze Solutions Already Installed

Cooling System Capacity Quarts	Number of Quarts of ALCOHOL Anti-Freeze Required to Increase Protection													
	From +20°F. to					From +10°F. to					From 0°F. to			
	0°	−10°	−20°	−30°	−40°	0°	−10°	−20°	−30°	−40°	−10°	−20°	−30°	−40°
10	2	2 3/4	3 1/2	4	4 1/2	1	2	2 2/3	3 1/4	3 3/4	1	1 3/4	2 1/2	3
12	2 1/2	3 1/4	4	4 3/4	5 1/4	1 1/4	2 1/4	3	3 3/4	4 1/2	1 1/4	2	2 3/4	3 1/2
14	3	4	4 3/4	5 1/2	6	1 1/2	2 1/2	3 1/2	4 1/2	5	1 1/4	2 1/2	3 1/4	4
16	3 1/4	4 1/2	5 1/2	6 1/4	7	1 3/4	3	4	5	5 3/4	1 1/2	2 3/4	3 3/4	4 3/4
18	3 3/4	5	6	7	7 3/4	2	3 1/4	4 1/2	5 3/4	6 1/2	1 3/4	3	4 1/4	5 1/4
20	4	5 1/2	6 3/4	7 3/4	8 3/4	2	3 1/4	5	6 1/4	7 1/4	1 3/4	3 1/2	4 3/4	5 3/4
22	4 1/2	6	7 1/2	8 1/2	9 1/2	2 1/4	4	5 1/2	6 3/4	8	2	3 3/4	5 1/4	6 1/2
24	5	6 3/4	8	9 1/4	10 1/2	2 1/2	4 1/2	6	7 1/2	8 3/4	2 1/4	4	5 1/2	7
26	5 1/4	7 1/4	8 3/4	10	11 1/4	2 3/4	4 3/4	6 1/2	8	9 1/2	2 1/2	4 1/2	6	7 1/2
28	5 3/4	7 3/4	9 1/2	11	12	3	5 1/4	7	8 3/4	10 1/4	2 1/2	4 3/4	6 1/2	8
30	6	8 1/4	10	11 3/4	13	3	5 1/2	7 1/2	9 1/4	10 3/4	2 3/4	5	7	8 3/4

Test radiator solution with proper tester. Determine from the table the number of quarts of solution to be drawn off from a full cooling system and replace with concentrated anti-freeze, to give the desired increased protection. For example, to increase protection of a 22-quart cooling system containing Alcohol anti-freeze, from +10°F. to −20°F. will require the replacement of 5 1/2 quarts of solution with concentrated anti-freeze.

Cooling System Capacity Quarts	Number of Quarts of ETHYLENE GLYCOL Anti-Freeze Required to Increase Protection													
	From +20°F. to					From +10°F. to					From 0°F. to			
	0°	−10°	−20°	−30°	−40°	0°	−10°	−20°	−30°	−40°	−10°	−20°	−30°	−40°
10	1 3/4	2 1/4	3	3 1/2	3 3/4	3/4	1 1/2	2 1/4	2 3/4	3 1/4	3/4	1 1/2	2	2 1/2
12	2	2 3/4	3 1/2	4	4 1/2	1	1 3/4	2 1/2	3 1/4	3 3/4	1	1 3/4	2 1/2	3 1/4
14	2 1/4	3 1/4	4	4 3/4	5 1/2	1 1/4	2	3	3 3/4	4 1/2	1	2	3	3 1/2
16	2 1/2	3 1/2	4 1/2	5 1/4	6	1 1/4	2 1/2	3 1/2	4 1/4	5 1/4	1 1/4	2 1/4	3 1/4	4
18	3	4	5	6	7	1 1/2	2 3/4	4	5	5 3/4	1 1/2	2 1/2	3 3/4	4 3/4
20	3 1/4	4 1/2	5 3/4	6 3/4	7 1/2	1 3/4	3	4 1/4	5 1/2	6 1/2	1 1/2	2 3/4	4 1/4	5 1/4
22	3 1/2	5	6 1/4	7 1/4	8 1/4	1 3/4	3 1/4	4 3/4	6	7 1/4	1 3/4	3 1/4	4 1/2	5 1/2
24	4	5 1/2	7	8	9	2	3 1/2	5	6 1/2	7 1/2	1 3/4	3 1/2	5	6
26	4 1/4	6	7 1/2	8 3/4	10	2	4	5 1/2	7	8 1/4	2	3 3/4	5 1/2	6 3/4
28	4 1/2	6 1/4	8	9 1/2	10 1/2	2 1/4	4 1/4	6	7 1/2	9	2	4	5 3/4	7 1/4
30	5	6 3/4	8 1/2	10	11 1/2	2 1/2	4 1/2	6 1/2	8	9 1/2	2 1/4	4 1/4	6 1/4	7 3/4

Test radiator solution with proper hydrometer. Determine from the table the number of quarts of solution to be drawn off from a full cooling system and replace with undiluted anti-freeze, to give the desired increased protection. For example, to increase protection of a 22-quart cooling system containing Ethylene Glycol (permanent type) anti-freeze, from +20°F. to −20°F. will require the replacement of 6 1/4 quarts of solution with undiluted anti-freeze.

ANTI-FREEZE CHART

Temperatures Shown in Degrees Fahrenheit
+32 is Freezing

Quarts of **ALCOHOL** Needed for Protection to Temperatures Shown Below

Cooling System Capacity Quarts	1	2	3	4	5	6	7	8	9	10	11	12	13
10	+23°	+11°	−5°	−27°									
11	+25	+13	0	−18	−40°								
12		+15	+3	−12	−31								
13		+17	+7	−7	−23								
14		+19	+9	−3	−17	−34°							
15		+20	+11	+1	−12	−27							
16		+21	+13	+3	−8	−21	−36°						
17		+22	+16	+6	−4	−16	−29						
18		+23	+17	+8	−1	−12	−25	−38°					
19		+24	+17	+9	+2	−8	−21	−32					
20			+18	+11	+4	−5	−16	−27	−39°				
21			+19	+12	+5	−3	−12	−22	−34				
22			+20	+14	+7	0	−9	−18	−29	−40°			
23			+21	+15	+8	+2	−7	−15	−25	−36°			
24			+21	+16	+10	+4	−4	−12	−21	−31			
25			+22	+17	+11	+6	−2	−9	−18	−27	−37°		
26			+22	+17	+12	+7	+1	−7	−14	−23	−32		
27			+23	+18	+13	+8	+3	−5	−12	−20	−28	−39°	
28			+23	+19	+14	+9	+4	−3	−9	−17	−25	−34	
29			+24	+19	+15	+10	+6	−1	−7	−15	−22	−30	−39°
30			+24	+20	+16	+11	+7	+1	−5	−12	−19	−27	−35

+ Figures are above Zero, but below Freezing.

− Figures are below Zero. Also below Freezing.

Quarts of **ETHYLENE GLYCOL** Needed for Protection to Temperatures Shown Below

Cooling System Capacity Quarts	1	2	3	4	5	6	7	8	9	10	11	12	13	14
10	+24°	+16°	+4°	−12°	−34°	−62°								
11	+25	+18	+8	−6	−23	−47								
12	+26	+19	+10	0	−15	−34	−57°							
13	+27	+21	+13	+3	−9	−25	−45							
14			+15	+6	−5	−18	−34							
15			+16	+8	0	−12	−26							
16			+17	+10	+2	−8	−19	−34	−52°					
17			+18	+12	+5	−4	−14	−27	−42					
18			+19	+14	+7	0	−10	−21	−34	−50°				
19			+20	+15	+9	+2	−7	−16	−28	−42				
20				+16	+10	+4	−3	−12	−22	−34	−48°			
21				+17	+12	+6	0	−9	−17	−28	−41			
22				+18	+13	+8	+2	−6	−14	−23	−34	−47°		
23				+19	+14	+9	+4	−3	−10	−19	−29	−40		
24				+19	+15	+10	+5	0	−8	−15	−23	−34	−46°	
25				+20	+16	+12	+7	+1	−5	−12	−20	−29	−40	−50°
26					+17	+13	+8	+3	−3	−9	−16	−25	−34	−44
27					+18	+14	+9	+5	−1	−7	−13	−21	−29	−39
28					+18	+15	+10	+6	+1	−5	−11	−18	−25	−34
29					+19	+16	+12	+7	+2	−3	−8	−15	−22	−29
30					+20	+17	+13	+8	+4	−1	−6	−12	−18	−25

For capacities over 30 quarts divide true capacity by 3. Find quarts Anti-Freeze for the $\frac{1}{3}$ and multiply by 3 for quarts to add.

For capacities under 10 quarts multiply true capacity by 3. Find quarts Anti-Freeze for the tripled volume and divide by 3 for quarts to add.

WHEN WOULD YOU RATHER DEAL WITH A PROBLEM DRINKER?

AT THE PARTY.

AFTER THE PARTY.

There is only one answer, of course. But there is another question.

Will you deal with a problem drinker?

It won't be easy. He's your friend. You don't want to hurt him or insult him. You don't want to lose a friend. But that is just what may happen.

After the party, your friend is potentially a killer. He's speeding and weaving, endangering his life and the lives of others.

Problem drinkers were responsible for 19,000 highway deaths last year. They killed themselves. They killed innocent people.

And they didn't only kill. They crippled and maimed and destroyed lives without actually taking them.

If your friend has a drinking problem, there are many ways you can help him. But first you must help him stay alive.

If you are really his friend, don't help him drink. If he has been drinking, don't let him drive.

Drive him yourself. Call a cab. Take his car keys.

Everything you think you can't do, you must do. At the party.

Write Drunk Driver, Box 2345, Rockville, Maryland 20852.

WHEN A PROBLEM DRINKER DRIVES, IT'S YOUR PROBLEM.

U.S. DEPARTMENT OF TRANSPORTATION • NATIONAL HIGHWAY TRAFFIC SAFETY ADMINISTRATION

Space for this public service message contributed by CHILTON BOOK COMPANY